A HUNDRED AND ONE NIGHTS

LETTER FROM THE GENERAL EDITOR

The Library of Arabic Literature series offers
Arabic editions and English translations of
significant works of Arabic literature, with an
emphasis on the seventh to nineteenth centuries. The Library of Arabic Literature thus
includes texts from the pre-Islamic era to the
cusp of the modern period, and encompasses a wide range of genres,
including poetry, poetics, fiction, religion, philosophy, law, science, history,
and historiography.

Books in the series are edited and translated by internationally recognized scholars and are published in parallel-text format with Arabic
and English on facing pages, and are also made available as English-only
paperbacks.

The Library encourages scholars to produce authoritative, though not
necessarily critical, Arabic editions, accompanied by modern, lucid English
translations. Its ultimate goal is to introduce the rich, largely untapped
Arabic literary heritage to both a general audience of readers as well as to
scholars and students.

The Library of Arabic Literature is supported by a grant from the New
York University Abu Dhabi Institute and is published by NYU Press.

Philip F. Kennedy
General Editor, Library of Arabic Literature

About this Paperback

This paperback edition differs in a few respects from its dual-language hardcover predecessor. Because of the compact trim size the pagination has changed, but paragraph numbering has been retained to facilitate cross-referencing with the hardcover. Material that referred to the Arabic edition has been updated to reflect the English-only format, and other material has been corrected and updated where appropriate. For information about the Arabic edition on which this English translation is based and about how the LAL Arabic text was established, readers are referred to the hardcover.

A Hundred and One Nights

TRANSLATED BY
BRUCE FUDGE

FOREWORD BY
ROBERT IRWIN

VOLUME EDITORS
PHILIP F. KENNEDY
MAURICE POMERANTZ

NEW YORK UNIVERSITY PRESS
New York

NEW YORK UNIVERSITY PRESS
New York

Copyright © 2017 by New York University

Library of Congress Cataloging-in-Publication Data

Names: Fudge, Bruce, 1967– translator.
Title: A hundred and one nights / translated by Bruce Fudge ; foreword by
    Robert Irwin.
Other titles: Mi'at laylah wa-laylah. English.
Description: New York : New York University Press, 2017. | Series: Library of
    Arabic literature | Includes bibliographical references and indexes.
Identifiers: LCCN 2017026047 (print) | LCCN 2017024579 (ebook) |
    ISBN 9781479873234 (pbk.) | ISBN 9781479894963 (Ebook) |
    ISBN 9781479808526 (Ebook)
Classification: LCC PJ7760.M53 A35 2017 (ebook) | LCC PJ7760.M53 (print) |
    DDC 892.7/34—dc23
LC record available at https://lccn.loc.gov/2017026047

New York University Press books are printed on acid-free paper,
and their binding materials are chosen for strength and durability.

Series design and composition by Nicole Hayward
Typeset in Adobe Text

Manufactured in the United States of America

10 9 8 7 6 5 4 3 2 1

Contents

Foreword

This collection of wonder tales is known to us via a number of North African manuscripts, whose origins can be traced to the tenth century and earlier. In its opening frame story, Shaykh Fihrās the Philosopher tells a tale which begins with a beautiful youth called Zahr al-Basātīn (Flower of the Gardens) being fetched by an Indian at great expense from the Eastern land of Babel. For the inhabitants of the medieval Maghreb, Asia was a place of romance and India was preeminent as a territory of mysteries and marvels. India was also the setting for strange adventures in several stories in the *Thousand and One Nights*. The compiler of *A Hundred and One Nights* was not very familiar with oriental geography and thus, for example, the Indian finds the beautiful youth after disembarking at "the port near the city of Khorasan." But Khorasan did not in fact have a port, but was an inland province without a shoreline.

Be that as it may, the storyteller's shaky grip on oriental geography was padded out in the tales that follow with a beguilingly imaginative toponymy. Adventures were to be had in the Land of Flowers, the Palace of the Eagle, the Valley of Jinn, the Valley of Strangers, the Palace of Lights, the Valley of Blood, and the Amalekite Palace. Some adventurers set sail on the Sea of Darkness, while others disembarked on the Camphor Island. In the *Thousand and One Nights* stories are often set in identifiable locations within Baghdad, Cairo, and Damascus, but *A Hundred and One Nights* shows little interest in actual North African locales: cities like Fez, Tunis, and Algiers are nowhere to be found here. Wastelands are the preferred settings for adventures in which men roam "as ostriches do." "The land kills those who don't know it well," and it is almost always dangerous to go to sleep in this sort of territory. It is "a land of mirage where melancholy dwells." However, Cairo is the setting of "The Story of the Young Egyptian and his Wife," while Baghdad and the harem of the Abbasid Caliph al-Muʿtaṣim feature in "The Story of Gharībat al-Ḥusn and the Young Egyptian," and the city also features in "The Story of the Four Companions."

Not only did marvels occur in distant lands, but they also happened long ago.

As the fourteenth-century philosopher-historian Ibn Khaldūn noted, North Africa was a region that abounded in ruins. In the stories of *A Hundred and One Nights* there are repeated references to the buildings of the Amalekites, a people borrowed from the Old Testament and added to the Arab pseudo-history of pre-Islamic Egypt, in which they featured as its fabulous conquerors and its pharaohs. The treasure of Camphor Island was guarded by a sword-wielding automaton whose mechanism was set in motion centuries ago. Ruins and tombs in the stories bear moralizing messages that warn of the perishability of material wealth and the inevitability of death. So it is that the treasure hunters discover a royally robed corpse and beside it a tablet on which is written, "I am ʿImlāq the Younger. I have ruled and I have vanquished; I have given gifts and I have withheld them; I have lived a noble and comfortable life; I have freed slaves and deflowered virgins. All this I did until the Almighty God decreed that my time had come, and look at me now. Let this be a lesson to all who would take heed: Do not be seduced by the world. It will only dupe and deceive you." And in another tale Najm al-Ḍiyāʾ ibn Mudīr al-Mulk enters a mysterious dome in which there is tomb on which is written:

> Death has ousted me from my palace.
> I had been honored then Death showed me malice.

> Take heed, God's servant, when you see this tomb of mine
> and fear what fate will bring further down the line.

Alas for the past! And the reader is reminded at the end of every story of the inevitability of death for its rejoicing and feasting heroes and heroines.

Though it is tempting to think of *A Hundred and One Nights* as the little brother of the *Thousand and One Nights*, all the indications are that *A Hundred and One Nights* is the older sibling, for it was put together centuries before the version of the Thousand and One Nights which was translated by Antoine Galland. Both story collections owe a lot to earlier Sanskrit stories which Arab authors adapted and reworked but, in cases where the collections draw on the same Indian story elements, the versions contained in *A Hundred and One Nights* are closer to the to the original Sanskrit stories. It is curious to think of Indian stories making their way in ghostly form as far west as Tunisia.

Hārūn al-Rashīd, who has a walk-on part in so many of the stories in the *Thousand and One Nights*, features briefly in two of the stories of *A Hundred and One Nights*. But in several other stories much greater prominence is given to the Umayyad Caliphs who ruled over the Islamic lands from 41/661 to 132/750. It would seem then that, though the stories were compiled in Abbasid times, memories of the Umayyads were still treasured in North Africa. (It is perhaps noteworthy, however, that these Umayyads are referred to not as "caliphs," but as "kings," perhaps by analogy with the *mulūk al-ṭawā'if*, or "party kings" of Muslim Spain.) Islam does not feature very prominently in these tales, but when, in "The Story of King Sulaymān ibn 'Abd al-Malik," King Namāriq accepts Islam, there is a big celebration and "the wine flowed freely."

Young men have adventures. Old men guide the young men or narrate those adventures when they are over. The wisdom of the old validates the excellence of the tale, and it is noteworthy that even Shahrazād's storytelling has to be framed or mediated by that of Fihrās the Philosopher. The adventurous young men are usually princes or merchants. It is likely that many of the readers of these tales were merchants or shopkeepers (but not princes). The readership seems to have had a mysterious obsession with warrior women, for these women, armored and disguised as knights, turn up in story after story. Their long black hair usually betrays them; none of them seem to be blondes. In general, there is an earthy stress on sensual pleasures and opulence. Sex is brisk, if it happens at all, and there is more emphasis on food and drink: "They ate and drank together, and he lived with her in the palace for a long time, eating and drinking to his heart's content."

In the paratactic style of storytelling adopted in *A Hundred and One Nights* multiple storylines and parallel developments are eschewed: for example, the second danger will only manifest itself after the first one has been surmounted and so the cannibalistic demon woman, the sword-wielding automaton, the dragon, and the warrior riding on a lion, form a disorderly queue in successive adventures. Wish-fulfilment and dangerous curiosity give these narratives their pell-mell pace. So peril follows peril and wonder succeeds to wonder. This is the first time that these stories have been translated into English. Read and marvel.

Robert Irwin

Acknowledgments

All students and scholars of Arabic literature owe a debt to Philip Kennedy for his initiative in establishing the Library of Arabic Literature. My own debt to him extends further. I am grateful for his invitation to be a part of this endeavor from the start and, since he served as Project Editor for the present work, for his wise counsel and gentle criticisms.

Another major debt is owed to Maḥmūd Ṭarshūnah, whom I do not know but who was responsible for the previous Arabic edition of *Kitāb Miʾat laylah wa-laylah*. I have seen fit to create a new edition that differs from his in many respects, but I fully admit that his pioneering efforts made mine much easier than they otherwise would have been.

I would like to thank David Bond and Kyle Liston for their help in obtaining digital copies of the Tunisian manuscripts, and the Faculty of Arts and Sciences at Ohio State University for financing the acquisition of manuscript copies. Ryan Schaffner, graduate student at Ohio State, provided a concordance of stories, nights and folio numbers that allowed me many a shortcut. Hala Abdel Maguid, graduate student at the University of Geneva, gave generously of her time in checking the discrepancies between the base manuscript and the previous edition.

A number of colleagues kindly provided me with sources, references, and answers to my questions. I thank Dionisius Agius, Ibrahim Akel, Aboubakr Chraïbi, Dick Davis, Paulo Horta, Ulrich Marzolph, Claudia Ott, Dwight Reynolds, Paula Sanders, and Akiko

Sumi. The executive editors of the Library of Arabic Literature, James Montgomery and Shawkat Toorawa, provided much support, encouragement, and valuable counsel for which I am very grateful. I have also appreciated the efficiency and cheerfulness of Chip Rossetti and Gemma Juan-Simó at LAL.

Several individuals deserve special thanks. Zina Maleh's assistance in proofreading and standardizing the Arabic text was invaluable, and the fidelity of the edition to the manuscript owes a great deal to her careful work. Maurice Pomerantz, Project Co-Editor, is responsible for countless improvements to translation and edition. While I am happy to have completed this work, I will miss the Skype sessions with my editors Phil and Mo; mulling over text and translation with them has been a rare combination of the instructive and the entertaining. Last but never least, I thank the most important reader, my wife Louisa Shea.

INTRODUCTION

The story of Shahrazād is well known. The heroine of the *Thousand and One Nights* (*Kitāb Alf laylah wa-laylah*) is married to a king who, convinced of the perfidy of women, marries a virgin each night and has her killed in the morning. Shahrazād stays her execution by telling him stories and delaying the conclusions until the following night. Both the king and the reader are captivated by her tales, which prove a testament to the power of narrative and storytelling.[1]

But the *Thousand and One Nights* was not Shahrazād's only literary appearance. She is also the heroine of the present work, the *A Hundred and One Nights* (*Kitāb Mi'at laylah wa-laylah*). At first glance the two works are similar: they share essentially the same frame story and the tales Shahrazād recounts are drawn from the same well of medieval Arabic narratives, stories of various genres generally intended for entertainment and excluded from the canon of "classical" or learned literature of the court and the scholars.

There exist vast quantities of this type of Arabic literature. Libraries in Europe and the Middle East contain untold numbers of neglected manuscripts, often not even catalogued let alone edited or published. The *Thousand and One Nights* itself, in its most common form (the nineteenth-century editions), is composed of tales that existed independently of that great collection; we can say the same for much of *A Hundred and One Nights*. It is common to hear or read that the Arab literati considered the *Nights* aesthetically inferior and unworthy of serious attention, and certainly there is little trace of it in the "high" literary tradition. But as is often the case, that which is frowned upon by the literati enjoys great popularity with others (and, one suspects, more than a few of the literati themselves). The quantity of these manuscripts is such that, clearly, many people must have been reading them, and little wonder, given that even today the *Nights* remain a literary classic. But there are many other delightful tales out there, and the present work is an effort to bring more of this kind of Arabic literature to a wider audience. Other than the *Thousand and One Nights*, the only other example of this kind of story collection to have received scholarly attention is that known as *Kitāb al-Ḥikāyāt al-ʿajībah wal-akhbār al-gharībah*, only recently translated into English in its entirety as *Tales of the Marvelous and News of the Strange*.[2] Despite its exclusion from the classical canon, this genre of semi-popular storytelling should be recognized as part of the larger corpus of Arabic literature. It deserves a much wider readership, whether in the original or in translation.[3]

On the face of it, *A Hundred and One Nights* may appear merely a condensed version of the *Thousand and One Nights*. Beyond the shared form and genre, though, the two works are quite distinct. *A Hundred and One Nights* is a short work with a very pronounced character. While it is unfortunate that it must always reside in the considerable shadow of the *Thousand and One Nights*, it is nonetheless true that for the purpose of introduction, the qualities of the former are best brought out by comparison with the latter. The larger work is a rattle bag of tales of wildly different lengths, styles, and genres. Its diversity is one of its defining qualities: warrior epics of hundreds of pages are found alongside moralizing or amusing anecdotes extending only a few lines; there are travelers' tales and poetic romances and stories of Indian kings and Muslim caliphs. In some stories a somber morality sets the tone; elsewhere a manic humor dominates. But the collection has a thematic unity that is particularly evident in the early sections. Shahrazād's story, the "frame-tale," raises moral questions, not just about the fidelity or treachery of women but also of power and its abuse, of punishment and justice, of the consequences of impetuous decisions. It is hard not to believe that Shahrazād's tales contain lessons for the murderous king.[4] These tales' explorations of power, justice, and fidelity (not to mention the importance of narration, as storytelling frequently saves lives in these tales) add a degree of complexity to the suspense, romance, and humor of the stories themselves.

A Hundred and One Nights has a different type of unity. If the original core of the Thousand and One Nights has a thematic unity, the smaller work is characterized by a formal unity. With just over three months (as opposed to three years) to spin her yarns, Shahrazād tells fewer tales: seventeen, in the version here edited and translated, as opposed to about 260 in the Būlāq and Calcutta II editions of the Thousand and One Nights. Her selection has also an appropriate variety: tales of warriors and buried treasure, romances, and stories of clever ruses and spectacular good fortune are all present. But in the frame story of A Hundred and One Nights, Shahrazād has no pretentions of saving her community or reforming the king, and the implicit invitation to reflect on moral issues is absent. She tells her tales merely to save her own life (and that of her sister).

Instead, the primary quality of A Hundred and One Nights is its efficiency. In some respects this is conventional narrative economy. Nothing is wasted; nothing is superficial. All we have here are the absolutely essential elements of the tale. Moreover, the raw materials of the stories are also recycled. The reader cannot fail to notice the repetition of motifs, both within individual tales and throughout the collection itself. To a degree, this is simply part of the repertoire of motifs found in medieval Arabic narratives. Any reader of the Thousand and One Nights (or other similar collections) will soon enough ask: How many brass horsemen, desert palaces, rebellious demons, childless kings, forbidden doors, etc. can there be?

Nowhere is this limited repertoire more conspicuous than in A Hundred and One Nights. Caves, disappearing brides or beloveds, secret nocturnal visits to the palace: these and many more appear and reappear. And it is not only motifs that repeat themselves: we have repetition on the lexical level as well. Some of this consists of well-worn phrases describing beautiful girls or lush gardens or heroic warriors. Sometimes it is even smaller units, as in the phrase "a steed of noble stock," employed repeatedly to describe a horse. In this relatively short work, such repetition conveys the sense of an author or compiler with limited resources reworking the same material to fashion new and different narratives. But the result is a consistency—the sense of a unified work with its own character despite the variety of the tales being told. Indices of recurrent motifs and stock phrases at the back of this edition demonstrate how frequently the same material reoccurs.

So in addition to the fast pace and colorful, exotic components (and they were exotic to the original audiences as well), we have the pleasure of recognition. The repetition of motifs allows for the pleasure of recognizing the patterns of narrative combinations, and the skillful combination of recurrence and variation allows us to enjoy something familiar and something new at the same time.

The vast majority of our knowledge of premodern Arabic literary culture comes from those who belonged to the scholarly tradition: well-educated judges and jurists, courtiers and poets, and so on. These people were largely silent on the matter of semi-popular storytelling and as a result there are huge gaps in our understanding of the history of these texts' transmission, circulation, and consumption.

There is, however, one aspect of the transmission of the *Nights* (whether the *Hundred and One* or the *Thousand and One*) that is beyond dispute and worth stressing here. It consists of a *written* transmission. These collections and the tales they contain were not part of an oral tradition. *A Hundred and One Nights* exist in seven known manuscripts, and despite a number of differences, sometimes quite significant, between the different versions of a given tale or in the overall contents, much of the material is identical, virtually word for word. Such consistency does not occur with orally transmitted folktales. In fact, recognized folklore motifs are not as prominent in the *Nights* as might be expected.[5]

The features that distinguish *Nights*-style narrative from the classical and canonical are not to be confused with oral tradition. Abdelfattah Kilito has noted some of the qualities required for a book to attain "classical" status: it must be written down; it should have an author, preferably one whose *vita* is public knowledge; it should ideally have been composed for a patron; it should contain references to earlier books; one should need a commentary in order to fully understand and unlock its complexities.[6] To which one might add: it should have a title. Obviously the *Nights* falls far short here. Their authors remain anonymous (though some manuscripts ascribe the entirety to one "Fihrās the philosopher"), they are often not copied carefully, and they never formed part of any curriculum of study. The language of these texts is usually very simple in syntax and vocabulary; basic rules of Arabic grammar are treated with often breathtaking insouciance. (The manuscript on which this edition is based is especially egregious in this regard.) But despite all this, the tales were read and reread, recopied and rewritten, and this type of literature was widespread. One should also add that its linguistic simplicity is one of several reasons why it is more accessible in translation than many of the "classics."

THE ORIGINS OF THE FRAME STORY

One of the reasons that *Mi'at laylah wa-laylah* (*A Hundred and One Nights*) is of particular interest to scholars is because its frame story is believed to be older than that of its larger counterpart, and it should hold clues to the history of Shahrazād and her tales.

The origins of the *Thousand and One Nights* (*Alf laylah wa-laylah*) are murky. Two tenth-century Arabic works refer to a Persian book called *A Thousand Nights* that was translated into Arabic, and give brief descriptions of the story of Shahrazād. There is even a manuscript fragment dated to the ninth (third Islamic) century, and scattered references, usually disapproving, in subsequent centuries. But all these tell us virtually nothing of the stories she recounted; for that we have to wait until the fifteenth century, the likely date of the oldest manuscript of *Alf laylah wa-laylah*, and even then the subsequent chronology of the collection and the relationship of the extant manuscripts to each other are far from clear.[7]

Yet the origins of *A Hundred and One Nights* are even more obscure. The extant manuscripts all date to the eighteenth or nineteenth centuries AD, with one likely slightly older. Each is written in Maghrebi (North African) script. It is mentioned only once in the Arabic bibliographical literature (one should add that Arab-Muslim scholars were assiduous bibliographers), and that mention comes not from the Maghreb but from Istanbul. The seventeenth-century scholar Ḥājjī Khalīfah in his bibliographical work, *Kashf al-ẓunūn*, records the following:

> *The Book of One Hundred Nights*, by Shaykh Fihrās (or: Firdās) the Philosopher (*al-faylāsūf*). It consists of one hundred stories.[8]

This is a precious piece of information, but his entry does not accord with any of our extant manuscripts. The title is missing a night. Also, in the manuscripts, each tale is spread out over several nights, so the number of nights in the title does not correspond to the number of stories. Finally, the author's name differs from manuscript to manuscript.

Despite the late date of the manuscripts, there are a number of clues within the tales suggesting far earlier origins. The most important of these concerns the frame story itself. In 1909 Emmanuel Cosquin published an important article on the *Thousand and One Nights'* frame tale, in which he suggested that the frame story of Shahrazād and the murderous king was composed of three sections, each originally independent and traceable to South Asian tales of relative antiquity. In the first section of the frame story as it appears in the *Thousand and One Nights*, the king Shahriyār invites his brother, whom he has not seen for many years, to visit him. The brother, Shahzamān, sets out to make the journey, but turns back almost immediately because he has forgotten something at home. Entering his house he finds his wife in bed with another man. He kills them in a rage and resumes his journey. However, he is so distraught at his wife's betrayal that his health and physical appearance decline drastically. His brother asks the cause of his malady, but he refuses to speak of it. Then Shahzamān sees his brother's wife cavorting with a black slave in circumstances even more outrageous than his own wife's infidelity. Seeing that even a great and powerful king like his brother is not exempt from female treachery, Shahzamān takes heart and regains his strength and his healthy countenance. His brother, in turn, demands to know what has prompted his recovery, and thereby learns the truth about his own wife. The brothers conclude that women, by their very nature, are never to be trusted.

Cosquin pointed out the similarity of this tale to one in a Chinese Buddhist work held to have been been translated from Sanskrit in the third century AH. The Sanskrit version, long lost, was supposedly of much greater antiquity; Cosquin knew the Chinese version via a French translation, *Cinq cents contes et apologues: Extrait du Tripitaka chinois* (trans. Chavannes, Paris 1910).[9] This story begins quite differently. Instead of two brothers who had not seen each other for some time, there is a king who holds an annual beauty contest of sorts in which he demands to know if there is anyone in the world more beautiful than he. Informed that, yes, there was an extraordinarily handsome youth living far away, the king has him summoned. It is this youth who, returning to fetch something he has forgotten at home, finds his wife *in flagrante delicto*, and whose anxiety and distress cause his beauty to fade. When he reaches the court, the king demands to know the reason for his changed appearance, and the youth eventually informs the king of his own wife's debaucheries and how he had come to realize that if even a great king could be cuckolded, then his own position was not so bad. The two men head to the mountains to live as ascetics.[10]

Excluding the final scene in which the two men depart for a life of renunciation, this is the same version of the story we find in *A*

Hundred and One Nights. Cosquin was also aware of three manuscripts in Paris containing a version of this story. Two were Arabic collections entitled *Les cent nuits* and the other a Berber version of this same work.[11]

Cosquin argued that the "beauty-contest" motif provides a more convincing motivation for bringing the two cuckolds together than what happens in the *Thousand and One Nights,* where a king suddenly desires to see his brother. The similarity between the Chinese-Sanskrit version and the frame story of *A Hundred and One Nights* led Cosquin to believe that the latter's version must be more ancient than that of the *Thousand and One Nights.*

Another intriguing piece of the puzzle is the fact that the beauty-contest version of the story is found in Ariosto's *Orlando Furioso,* an Italian epic of the early sixteenth century.[12] However, to date there is no plausible explanation of how the story might have reached Italy.

The second section of the *Alf laylah* frame has the two brothers Shahriyār and Shahzamān encountering a woman held captive by a demon. As the demon sleeps, she forces the two men to have sex with her, and, taking Shahriyār's signet ring, shows them her collection of rings, each taken from a man with whom she has cuckolded the demon. The brothers are somewhat consoled by the fact that even a powerful demon is no match for the deviousness of the gentler sex. This passage too has its Asian precursors. This narrative does not appear in *A Hundred and One Nights,* though, which passes directly from the first section to the third.[13]

In the third and final section of the *Alf laylah* frame, the two men return home. The King Shahriyār eventually adopts a policy of taking a virgin each night and having her killed in the morning, which he continues until, suitable virgins in increasingly short supply, his vizier's daughter offers herself, and thus the king meets the formidable. Cosquin asserted that the "fabric" of this motif was Indian, and he gave various instances in which a young woman delays a dreaded event by telling a succession of stories.[14]

Subsequent research over the past century has found no reason to challenge this conclusion. What subsequent research has revealed, though, is the great difficulty in saying anything more specific as to how these motifs traveled and how the frame stories of the Arabic *Nights* developed over time. The earliest extant manuscript of *Alf laylah* dates to the fifteenth century; it contains only 282 nights. This was the manuscript acquired by Antoine Galland and the basis for the first European translation. The "complete" versions we know today were compiled in the late eighteenth or early nineteenth centuries, and appear to be reworked and bulked-up versions of that of the Galland manuscript.

An interesting aspect of the South and East Asian variants is that the young storyteller almost always has an accomplice, a servant or a sister who plays some part in the ruse. In the *Thousand and One Nights*, it is the sister, usually named Dīnārzād. Shahrazād contrives to have the sister join her and the king, so that she can request a story from Shahrazād and thus set in motion the plan to distract the king from his deadly routine. Here the variant versions of the frame of *A Hundred and One Nights* add to the puzzle. In two of the manuscripts, it is Shahrazād's sister who sleeps with the king. In the remaining five (as in the *Thousand and One Nights*), Shahrazād serves as both the king's wife and storyteller. The latter versions are much clumsier, and it does look like the figure of Dīnārzād has been deprived of her original role and left with little to do.[15] Did Shahrazād's sister originally have a greater role? It seems likely in the case of *A Hundred and One Nights*. Whether this applies to the *Thousand and One Nights* as well is less clear but in the state of current research remains a distinct possibility.[16]

There are, then, two arguments indicating that the frame tale of *A Hundred and One Nights* represents an older version of the tale. First of all, it bears closer resemblance to the supposed Chinese/Sanskrit original. Secondly, the beauty-contest motif provides a much stronger motivation for setting the story in motion than that of a brother who suddenly wishes to see his sibling. But some precisions are necessary. One should not confuse the frame tale with the contents of the collections themselves. As is the case with *Alf laylah*, it is likely that the framing motif is much more ancient than both the stories themselves and this particular configuration of frame and stories as we know it today. As mentioned above, there exists a fragment of *Alf laylah* dating to the ninth century. What little can be gleaned about the stories it contains suggests something quite different from the collection as we have it, which took its definitive form several centuries later. A similar situation likely obtained in the case of *Mi'at laylah*. [17]

The two *Nights* collections (*Thousand and One* and *Hundred and One* as presented here) have two stories in common: "The Ebony Horse" and "The Prince and the Seven Viziers." "The Story of the Ebony Horse" is one of the most widespread of this sort of popular Arabic fiction, appearing in many versions of the *Nights* and countless other unpublished manuscripts. Probably of Indian origin, we know that from an early date it was in circulation in this type of story collection.[18] The version presented here is more refined than in the Būlāq and Calcutta II versions of the *Thousand and One Nights*, and no doubt reflects an earlier stage of Islamization, in that the specifically Islamic references are fewer, and the geographical indications are less clearly Middle Eastern. "The Tale of the Prince and the Seven Viziers" is likewise a tale of Iranian or Indian origin, widely diffused in both Middle Eastern and European versions. With its tales embedded in a frame story in which characters recount anecdotes to save a life, the structure of the "Seven Viziers" shares much with that of *Alf laylah*. "Seven Viziers" too contains fewer clear instances of Islamization; and although it contains fewer embedded stories than *Alf laylah*, the frame story itself is lengthier and richer.[19]

At least two other tales in *Mi'at laylah* are rudimentary versions of those in *Alf laylah*, suggesting an earlier phase of development: the first part of "The Story of the Young Merchant and His Wife" is clearly based on the same tale as "The Story of the Three Apples," one of the most carefully crafted episodes of the *Thousand and One*

Nights. Similarly, "Gharībat al-Ḥusn" is a skeletal version of the story of "Nuʻm and Niʻmah" in the *Thousand and One Nights*.[20]

However, all of the manuscripts of *Miʼat laylah* date to the late eighteenth or nineteenth centuries. One (that of the Agha Khan Museum) is older, but almost certainly not dating to the seventh/ thirteenth century, as has been suggested (see the following "Note on the Text"). Moreover, all are in Maghribi script, and some have posited a North African or Andalusian "origin" for the collection.[21]

It is surely significant that all of the known manuscripts are in Maghribi (or possibly Andalusian) script. Further, the manuscripts contain, in varying degrees, traces of Maghribi dialect and vocabulary. It is also curious that in all manuscripts the hero of Shahrazād's first story is named Muḥammad ibn ʻAbdallāh al-Qayrawānī, i.e., "of Qayrawān," or Kairouan in present-day Tunisia. This would be an unusual, though by no means implausible, choice of name for a story originating in the eastern part of the Arab-Islamic world. Such regional and dialectal features can creep into a tradition over time, but they are not definitive indications of the collection's regional origins.

The other reason for the claim that *Miʼat laylah* has North African or Andalusian origins is the predominance of figures from the Umayyad caliphate (661–750). The Umayyads were overthrown by the Abbasids (750–1258), who founded Baghdad and presided over one of the most glorious periods in Islamic history. A scion of the Umayyads managed to escape and founded a counter-caliphate in the Iberian Peninsula, based in Cordoba (756–1031). In al-Andalus, a nostalgia developed for the glories of Umayyad power and for memories of Damascus. In most of the Abbasid lands, however, the Umayyads were viewed less favorably overall. Thus the fact that *A Hundred and One Nights* features a number of Umayyad caliphs and notables as heros might be seen a sign of an Andalusian attitude. This is possible. But this interpretation neglects the fact that *A Hundred and One Nights* also contains stories featuring the Abbasids in contexts that are not unfavorable. One might note as well that most of the tales here involving the Umayyads are set in the lands of jihād, along the Byzantine frontier, or at least stem from that milieu, and that stories of Arab heroics in the Umayyad period are known also in Eastern sources. This is the case even in the *Thousand and One Nights*. In the present work, for instance, "Story of Maslamah ibn 'Abd al-Malik" (d. 121/738) is set on the Byzantine frontier, and the historical Maslamah was renowned for leading an assault on Constantinople in 98–99/716–18. Thus it is possible, but far from assured, that the presence of these figures indicates Andalusian or Maghribi origins.[22]

The mention by Ḥajjī Khalīfah of a book entitled *Hundred Nights* demonstrates that some version of the work was known in the East, but since the reference says nothing about the content of the collection, it is difficult to say more. There is one bit of evidence of a transfer from east to west. In all the extant versions of "The Young Egyptian and His Wife," the merchant throws his wife into the Nile. This first part of this tale is a rudimentary version of "The Three Apples" from the *Thousand and One Nights*, in which the merchant lives in Baghdad and dumps the unfortunate spouse in the Tigris. In a now-lost manuscript of *A Hundred and One Nights*, also written in Maghribi script, the story is set in Baghdad. This suggests that this story at least existed first in a Baghdad version, but the setting was later changed to the only city in the North of Africa with a large river running through it.[23]

None of this evidence is conclusive about where the collection was first written. In the absence of any Eastern manuscripts of *A Hundred and One Nights*, one should refrain from any categorical statement. What we can say is the following: The first part of its frame tale is almost certainly of great antiquity, as Cosquin claimed. However, the versions that we possess to date are probably not so ancient: they share a suspicious number of motifs with later recensions of the *Alf laylah* frame.[24] There is a good, though not definitive, case to be made that the version where Dīnārzād sleeps with the king is the older one. A collection known as the *Hundred/*

Hundred and One Nights was known in the East.[25] The contents of this collection may or may not have been similar to the versions known today from the North African manuscripts. The stories have no specific geographical ties, but it is possible that the version as we know it was compiled in the Islamic West, even if the materials were of Eastern origin.

THE TALES TOLD BY SHAHRAZĀD

What of Shahrazād's stories themselves? Some, as noted already, are well known and have their origins farther East; others are more clearly the product of an Arab-Islamic milieu. Most escape strict generic classification, although romance is certainly prominent. The most easily identified genre or style is that of the Arabic popular epic (in condensed versions, of course) in which warriors fight a series of battles against a variety of foes (such as "Najm al-Ḍiyā'," "Ẓāfir ibn Lāḥiq," and "Sulaymān ibn 'Abd al-Malik").[26]

But for all the variety, we can still identify three main components shared in varying degrees by all of the stories. First is the romance element, in which the conclusion sees the hero united with the beloved (or, in some cases, the beloveds). Second is what I will call "adventure," in which the hero faces and overcomes threats and dangers to his life, be they in the form of enemy soldiers, malevolent demons, odd monsters, stormy seas, or the beloved's overly protective male relatives. Third is an element of cleverness, in which some trick or ruse is employed in order to achieve the hero's goals.

Whether the dominant element be romance or adventure, there is one common link: all the stories end well, with the hero wealthy and happily united with a suitable partner. There is an essential optimism, that however grim or hopeless the situation, all will end well. In premodern Arabic narratives, especially of this semi-popular variety, tragic endings are uncommon. A small but significant genre of "deliverance after distress" stories exists, known in Arabic as *al-faraj ba'da l-shiddah*.[27] In this genre, it is ostensibly the hand of God that steers the protagonist towards salvation of various kinds, be it through sheer luck or coincidence or via his own wits and skills; though when God Himself was less obtrusive it usually made for a better story.[28] This narrative paradigm appears to be at work in *A Hundred and One Nights*.

The world of the tales is a simple one. It is ostensibly a Muslim world, although in some tales, Islamic references have been added to more ancient tales (the case with the frame story, "The Seven Viziers," and "The Ebony Horse"). Most of the remainder have some referent to Umayyad or Abbasid figures, even if they were likely composed well after those periods. Geography is hopelessly confused but generally reliant on well-known referents such as Cairo, Damascus, Basra, Khurāsān, and Baghdad. (And there seems to be a certain disdain for Persia and the Persians.) Heads of state are "kings," even though in some cases they are historical caliphs ('Abd al-Malik, Hārūn al-Rashīd, al-Muʿtaṣim); on occasion these caliphs are referred to more accurately as "Commander of the Faithful" (*amīr al-muʾminīn*).

The heroes tend to be princes or merchants. The heroines may be princesses or faithful wives (or both). Though not especially misogynistic by medieval standards, *A Hundred and One Nights* has a view of women epitomized by a sentence from "The King and the Serpent": "He satisfied his every desire, while she lay there sound asleep." (§15.22)

Medieval standards notwithstanding, the treatment of women in these tales does deserve comment. The Shahrazād frame and "The Seven Viziers" are premised on the assumption that women are possessed of an insatiable heterosexual desire that will cause them to betray their menfolk at any opportunity. The latter story cycle, known as "The Seven Sages" in its European versions, is one of the best-known examples of the "Wiles of Women" literature. Much of the humor here has not aged well, and it may be difficult to appreciate the tales of tricks and clever ruses against the backdrop of cruelty and casual rape. It is a misogynist world, and this cannot be excused or explained away. It is true that the frame tale and the

"Seven Viziers" do invite reflection on the justice of such a negative portrayal of women, but that is certainly not the case for the rest of the tales in this collection.

Religion is less in evidence in *A Hundred and One Nights* than in the *Thousand and One Nights* or in the collection *al-Ḥikāyāt al-ʿajībah*, whether in terms of references to explicitly Islamic practices or to implicit moral codes. In one area, though, one finds an explicitly religious message, and that is in references, usually via poetic inscriptions, to mortality and the futility of worldly gain. These verses often put the greed of the treasure-hunters into perspective. The juxtaposition of vast ancient treasures with renunciatory verses has its apotheosis the *Thousand and One Nights'* version of "The City of Brass," whose constituent parts are drawn from the same pool as our stories. Some manuscripts of *A Hundred and One Nights* include a "City of Brass," but not that used for the present edition.[29]

If the world portrayed in *A Hundred and One Nights* is a simple one, it is also the case that the portrayal itself is exceedingly simple. The various versions of *A Hundred and One Nights'* manuscripts seldom give polished or refined versions of their stories. The modern reader might be slightly surprised to see, for example, the way in which the narrator dispenses with the opportunities to create suspense or tension. Take the story of Shahrazād herself: she is telling stories to save her and her sister's life, and their lives depend on her ability to keep the king entertained night after night. Admittedly this is more of a narrative conceit than a real occasion for suspense, but it is nonetheless surprising to find that in two of our manuscripts (T, B1) the end is given at the beginning: before Shahrazād utters a word of her tales, the narrator tells us that she successfully kept the king's attention until he, seeing that one of the sisters was pregnant, decided to spare them both.[30] Many such examples occur throughout the individual tales, in which the reader is presented with information that might have been better withheld.

Elsewhere, the action follows the pattern of a "stock scene"—whose outcome is already well known—which does little to create suspense. The most notable example is the recurrent scene in which the mighty warrior turns out to be . . . well, you will find out soon enough. In any case what this might tell us is that our storytellers had other goals in mind. For them, the pleasures of the tale lay elsewhere: exoticism, fear, happy endings, and fast-paced action.

Another curious feature is that some tales seem to be composed of two originally distinct stories. For example, "The Young Merchant," Muḥammad ibn ʿAbd Allāh al-Qayrawānī, consists of two separate and distinct narratives, the first involving a merchant's ruse, the second more of a fairy tale or adventure with a demoness jinn and princesses. More than once does a tale start out in one direction and then depart in another with no attempt to provide explanation or tie up loose ends (notably, to my mind, in the case of "The King and the Serpent," where there is no explanation or follow-up to the curious sequence involving the deranged camel; it serves only to introduce the next episode).

The reader may also puzzle over inconsistent naming, confused geography, unexpected changes in narrative voice, and various passages that need to be clarified by consulting another manuscript. Along with this, the language is very basic in terms of both syntax and vocabulary. A too-literal translation would be exceedingly monotonous, for two main reasons. First, there are very few subordinate clauses, and if this parataxis is not modified in some way, it quickly becomes tedious. Second, Arabic tends to use a single verb for "to say" where English would supply one of countless others that indicate something of the emotional or physical state of the speaker.

Virtually all translators of the *Thousand and One Nights* have faced this problem and dealt with it in several ways. In the recent French version published by the Bibliothèque de la Pléiade, co-translator André Miquel describes how the minimalist Arabic prose needs to be "bulked up" in order to satisfy the needs of the contemporary reader and to maintain the pleasure of reading. In the Penguin translation of 2008, Malcolm C. Lyons takes a different tack. He sees this type of literature as meant primarily to be read aloud (he is not saying that this is oral tradition—an important distinction). In a brief but very perceptive passage, he outlines some of the Arabic text's qualities that make it suitable for the ear: rhymed prose and poetry; repetition of names, details, and phrases (as the audience cannot flip back a few pages to check); and parataxis. Lyons' translation, then, attempts "to speed up the pace of the narrative to what is hoped to be more nearly adapted to the eye rather than the ear of the modern reader."[31]

Lyons also put his finger on one of the essential aspects of the *Nights* and its siblings. Despite the repetitive and simple language, despite the occasional clumsiness of the storytelling, the stories remain a pleasure to read. In Arabic, this is due in part to what Lyons refers to as "the decorative elaboration of the original, as well as the extra dimension of allusiveness it provides." He continues:

> In the latter case, it is not merely that one incident will recall another, either within the *Nights* themselves or, more widely, in the huge corpus of Arabic popular literature, but a single phrase, one description or one line of poetry must have served to call other contexts to the mind of the original audience.[32]

The Arabic of *A Hundred and One Nights*, with its repetition of phrases and motifs, illustrates these features clearly; how well they can be rendered in translation is another matter.

The other feature mentioned by Lyons is what he calls "the fundamental patterns of the genre of storytelling." What he intends here are the motifs and plot structures common to narratives everywhere, be they international folktales or more learned collections such as the Sanskrit *Panchatantra*, the Florentine *Decameron* or the Icelandic *Saga of Gunnlaug Serpent-Tongue*. *A Hundred and One Nights* shares motifs and narrative elements with European folktales as well as medieval Indian legends; it is part of the vast circulation of narratives and their components. But at the same time it is equally rooted in the Islamic tradition, with references, poetry, and motifs common to that world. It therefore comprises the global and the regional in ways that much of the canonical "classical" Arabic literature does not.

As mentioned at the outset, the Arabic literary establishment has always professed to disdain or censure the reading of books like *A Hundred and One Nights*. There are a number of reasons to believe that this negative attitude has been exaggerated, for even while condemning these works the critics seem to be familiar with their contents, and there is good evidence that learned scholars played a crucial role in the creation of the *Alf laylah* as it is known today. But there is no denying that there is a long tradition of criticizing fictional stories.[33] Critics cited the plain language and style, the fact that the books were composed of lies, and in modern times, the obscene or pornographic elements. All good selling points, one would think. The fourth/tenth century author al-Tawḥīdī speaks disparagingly of stories such as the *Nights* that merely "provoke wonder and laughter without leading to any benefit or knowledge."[34] The present work certainly falls into this category. But there have always been those who felt that wonder and laughter were worthwhile goals in themselves. *A Hundred and One Nights* has much historical, linguistic, and literary value, but its main virtue is its pursuit of pleasure through the telling of stories.

A Note on the Text

The format of the Library of Arabic Literature hardcover editions does not permit the full apparatus required for a critical edition of the Arabic text. This is just as well, as works such as *Miʾat laylah wa-laylah* are not amenable to critical editions for two reasons. First, with their obscure and diverse origins, the possibility of reconstructing an archetype or original is extremely limited. Second, the variations that do occur in the stories may consist of entire episodes, so keeping track of them while maintaining a consistent narrative thread would be very difficult for both the editor and the eventual reader. The present work is thus an edition of a single version or recension of *Miʾat laylah wa-laylah*.

A core corpus of stories is easily identified. Five of the seven manuscripts contain the same sixteen tales in identical order:

1. Frame Story
2. The Young Merchant Muḥammad ibn ʿAbd Allāh al-Qayrawānī
3. Najm al-ḍiyāʾ
4. The Camphor Island
5. Ẓāfir ibn Lāḥiq
6. The Vizier and His Son
7. Sulaymān ibn ʿAbd al-Malik
8. Maslamah ibn ʿAbd al-Malik
9. Gharībat al-ḥusn
10. The Young Egyptian and His Wife
11. The King and His Three Sons
12. The Young Man with the Necklaces

One should note that while this "core corpus" of the same stories in a particular order predominates in the known manuscripts, it is not necessarily more ancient or authentic than the other arrangements. Each of these contains the version of the frame tale in which Shahrazād acts as both wife and storyteller. As suggested in the Introduction, it is likely that the version of the frame given in the remaining two manuscripts (with Dīnārzād as wife) represents an anterior version. I have included a translation of this alternative version in the Appendix.

Mi'āt laylah wa-laylah has been published previously, once in Arabic and four times in translation. To take these volumes in the order of their appearance:[40]

1. French: *Les Cent et une nuits* trans. Maurice Gaudefroy-Demombynes (Paris: Sindbad/Actes Sud, 1982). Gaudefroy-Demombynes' translation appeared in 1911.

2. Arabic: *Kitāb Mi'at laylah wa-laylah*, ed. Maḥmūd Ṭarshūnah (Tunis and Libya: al-Dār al-ʿArabiyyah lil-Kitāb, 1979).

3. Portuguese: *Cento e uma Noites: Histórias Árabes da Tunísia*, trans. Mamade Mustafa Jarouche, 2nd ed. (São Paulo: Martins Fontes, 2005). The first edition appeared in 2001.

4. Japanese: *Hyakuichiya Monogatari: Mōhitotsu no Arabian Naito* [*"The Hundred and One Nights": Another "Arabian Nights"*], trans. Akiko Sumi (Tokyo: Kawade Shobō Shinsha, 2011).

5. German: *101 Nacht*, trans. Claudia Ott (Zurich: Manesse, 2012).

For further information on the manuscripts on which I relied to create my Arabic edition, please consult the full "Note on the Text" in the bilingual hardcover edition of *A Hundred and One Nights*.

Notes to the Introduction

1   There are two excellent introductions to the *Thousand and One Nights*: Irwin, *The Arabian Nights: A Companion*; Marzolph and van Leeuwen, eds., *Arabian Nights Encyclopedia*.

2   Wehr, ed., *Al-Ḥikāyāt al-ʿajībah*; *Tales of the Marvelous and News of the Strange*, trans. Lyons. David Pinault, in *Story-telling Techniques in the Arabian Nights*, makes good use of a variety of untitled and anonymous manuscripts containing analogues to tales of the *Thousand and One Nights*.

3   Interestingly enough, most often one finds the tales gathered apparently randomly in untitled manuscripts. One of the reasons the *Nights* collections are known is precisely because they have titles. The same is true for *Tales of the Marvelous and News of the Strange*, a title now associated with that particular collection. However, the title is in fact a generic one, bestowed by the editor, based on the book's own introduction: "This is a book containing marvelous tales and strange accounts, and it is the known book [sic] containing forty-two stories." Wehr, *Ḥikāyāt*, 2.

4   On this line of argument, see for example, Jerome W. Clinton, "Madness and Cure in the *1001 Nights*." The thematic unity is especially clear in the initial sections, or in the tales contained in the earliest known manuscript (*Kitāb Alf laylah wa-laylah*, ed. Muḥsin Mahdī); the case for the unity of the later printed editions is less clear. A recent argument for coherent editorial intent (if not exactly thematic unity) of the 1835 Būlāq edition is Jean-Claude Garcin, *Pour une lecture historique des* Mille et Une Nuits.

5   *See Chraïbi, Les Mille et une nuits*, 15–19, and Marzolph, "The *Arabian Nights* in Comparative Folk Narrative Research."

6   Kilito, *Les arabes et l'art du récit*, 131–4.

7   An excellent introduction to this complex history is Irwin, *Arabian Nights: A Companion*, 42–62. For what is known about the early history of the *Nights*, one may consult Chraïbi, *Mille et une nuits*, 23–49. On the manuscript tradition and the genesis of the later printed editions: Muḥsin Mahdī, *Kitāb Alf laylah wa-laylah* I: 12–36 (in Arabic); III: 1–126 (in English).

8   Ḥājjī Khalīfah, *Kashf al-ẓunūn*, 2: 1676.

9   The Sanskrit provenance may not be as straightforward as Cosquin seemed to think; see Perry, "Origins of the Book of Sindbad," 26n53.

10 Cosquin, "Le prologue-cadre des *Mille et une nuits*," 13–14.

11 Cosquin, "Le prologue-cadre des *Mille et une nuits*," 12. These collections were previously noted by René Basset in *"Les Cent Nuits* et le *Kitab ech chelha"* 449–65. The two Arabic manuscripts are BN Arabe 3660 and 3661 (B1 and B2—see "A Note on the Text").

12 Ariosto, *Orlando Furioso*, Canto XXVIII, 931–58. To make matters more complicated, a century earlier Giovanni Sercambi published his *Novella d'Astolfo*, which employs the first two elements (the two cuckolds and ring collector) of the *Nights'* frame tale. The "beauty-contest" motif is absent, but "Astolfo" is also the name used by Ariosto. *Arabian Nights Encyclopedia*, 2: 483–84, 698. A Hungarian folktale combines the two: see Cosquin, "Le prologue-cadre des *Milles et une nuits*," 29.

13 In the *Thousand and One Nights* as well as the supposed oriental precursors of the "Two Cuckolds," the first scene concludes with the two men setting out on a journey. This moves easily into the second section, in which they encounter the demon and his woman. In *A Hundred and One Nights*, there is no journey; the story passes to the third stage, and thus the conclusion of the first section (departure on a journey) is not present. One might add that the story reoccurs in the *Thousand and One Nights* as one of the tales told by the

"Seven Viziers" in order to persuade the king of the perfidy of women (Lyons, trans., *Arabian Nights*, 2:601–2).

14 Cosquin, "Le prologue-cadre des *Mille et une nuits*," 31–43.

15 The narrative superiority of the Dīnārzād-as-wife version is well demonstrated in Marzolph and Chraïbi, "A Newly Discovered Manuscript," 312–13.

16 I will treat the question of Shahrazād's sister and the twin frame stories more generally in a separate article.

17 On the fragment, see Abbot, "A Ninth-Century Fragment"; on historical indications within the tales, see Garcin, *Pour une lecture historique des* Mille et Une Nuits.

18 On the "Ebony Horse," see Chauvin, *Bibliographie*, 5:221–31; *Arabian Nights Encyclopedia*, 1:172–74; Garcin, 164–71. The tale is listed in the contents of *Al-Ḥikāyāt al-ʿajībah*, but that section of the manuscript is unfortunately lost (*Al-Ḥikāyāt al-ʿajībah*, 5).

19 On the "Seven Viziers," see Chauvin, *Bibliographie*, 8:33ff; *Arabian Nights Encyclopedia*, 1:160–61, 2:703–4; Chraïbi, *Mille et une nuits*, 171–90, and the notes to Gaudefroy-Demombynes' French translation, 287–98. Ṭarshūnah notes how the *Miʾat laylah* version contains fewer overtly Islamic references, 23.

20 For a comparison of these latter two: Gaudefroy-Demombynes, 281–82n10. Note that in the case of Indo-Iranian tales, *Miʾat laylah* gives overall more sophisticated versions while those of Arab-Islamic origins ("Gharībah," "Young Egyptian and Wife") are more rudimentary. Also, analogues of those two stories occur in the oldest manuscript of *Alf laylah*, while "Ebony Horse" and "Seven Viziers" do not.

21 Marzolph and Chraïbi, "A Newly Discovered Manuscript," 303; Ott, *101 Nacht*, 242–45, 276–77. In the introduction to his edition, Ṭarshūnah claims that the work's final form is uniquely Tunisian, 28–32; Pinault summarizes Ṭarshūnah's views in *Story-telling Techniques in the Arabian Nights*, 152–54. Houdas thought that the language of at least one manuscript indicated "very probably" a Tunisian scribe (*Chrestomathie maghrébine*, i).

22 Gaudefroy-Demombynes' remarks are more prudent. On "The Story of Sulaymān ibn 'Abd al-Malik," he notes: This tale is one of the Arabic adventure epics, of which there are several in *Hundred and One Nights*; it belongs with the 'Antar cycle and the conquest stories of Pseudo-Wāqidī. Like "The City of Brass," it is situated historically in the Umayyad age, which is the time of the conquests of the Maghreb and the period when the Eastern caliphate held the greatest authority in Africa. This is a tradition known to the *Thousand and One Nights* and it is natural that one would find it in a more specifically Maghrebi collection like *A Hundred and One Nights*. Why would the storyteller have chosen as hero the Caliph Sulaymān ibn 'Abd al-Malik, whose ephemeral reign was marked above all by war with Byzantium? Is it supposed to recall the legends of Mūsā ibn Nuṣayr at the court of al-Walīd or Sulaymān? In this tale, which is not historical in the least, the names are nonetheless those of historical figures. *Cent et une nuits*, 285n1.

23 Chauvin, *Bibliographie*, 4:144–46.

24 To be discussed in a future article, see n16.

25 It is interesting that Ḥājjī Khalīfah identifies the book with its purported author, "Fihrās the Philosopher." The earliest references to *Alf laylah* identified it by its frame tale. We cannot be entirely certain that the book Ḥājjī Khalīfah saw contained the Shahrazād frame; the two may have existed independently.

26 Gaudefroy-Demombynes points out that the first two of these bear similarities to *Sayf al-tījān*, another epic found in manuscript form in the Bibliothèque Nationale and translated into French in 1862. Perron, trans., *Glaive des couronnes*, (Paris: B. Duprat).

27 The most famous of these is al-Tanūkhī (d. 384/994), *Al-Faraj ba'd al-shiddah*.

28 In other collections, one sometimes finds stories prefaced with "a tale of deliverance after distress." Such is the case with a number of the *Tales of the Marvelous and News of the Strange* (*Al-Ḥikāyāt al-'ajībah*) as well as a section of anecdotes in the memoirs of Usāmah ibn Munqidh (d. 584/1188), *Kitāb al-I'tibār*.

29 "The City of Brass" is in B1 and T; it appears in A as well, but as one of the additional tales outside the frame of *A Hundred and One Nights*.

30 Obviously, over the course of a hundred (or a thousand) nights, the reader will tend to forget about Shahrazād herself. However, some versions of the *Thousand and One Nights* do preserve the tension surrounding her fate, as the king remains ready to kill her until the final night.

31 *The Arabian Nights: Tales of 1001 Nights*, 1:xx. On the recent English and French renditions of the *Thousand and One Nights* as well as the difficulties of translating this type of literature, see Fudge, "More Translators of the *Thousand and One Nights*."

32 *The Arabian Nights: Tales of 1001 Nights*, 1:xxi. See also Fudge, "More Translators."

33 It appears that well-respected Egyptian scholars were involved in the redaction and publication of *Alf laylah* in the eighteenth and nineteenth centuries. Mahdi, *Alf laylah*, 3:98–99 and Garcin, *Pour une lecture historique*, 16–24.

34 Al-Tawḥīdī, *Al-Imtāʿ wa-l-muʾānasah*, 1:23. The reference to the *Nights* is in fact to the Persian title, *Hizār afsānah*. Further, the mention of *Hizār afsānah* is supplied by the editors; the manuscript in fact reads حسبان (1:23, n6).

35 It is quite possible that the wide-ranging research into manuscript collections led by Aboubakr Chraïbi will reveal more manuscripts of the *101 Nights*, but as of this writing their results have not been published.

36 The section of tales preceding *Miʾat laylah* (up to 153r) says the copying was completed in Ṣafar 1190/March–April 1776 by Aḥmad al-Badāwī bin Masʿūd bin Mūsā al-Bījāʾ al-Ṭabīb (a tentative reading of the name). The text of *Miʾat laylah* is written in an identical hand, with the exception of a small number of pages. One of those exceptions is the final page and colophon, which gives only the year 1190 and no name.

37 Ibrahim Akel informs me that attempts to procure a copy of the manuscript itself have proven fruitless.

38   A judgement based on O. Houdas, "Essai sur l'écriture maghrébines,"
      85–112.

39   See Chauvin, *Bibliographie*, 4:218, and D. B. MacDonald, "The Earlier
      History of the *Arabian Nights*," *Journal of the Royal Asiatic Society* 56,
      no. 3 (1924): 355–57.

40   Two stories ("Muḥammad ibn ʿAbdallāh al-Qayrawānī" and "al-Malik
      wa-awlāduh") were printed in 1891 in O. Houdas, *Chrestomathie
      maghrébine*, 1–9 (apparently on the basis of B1).

41   See the brief description in Marzolph and Chraïbi, "A Recently Dis-
      covered Old Manuscript," 307–10. The case for the thirteenth-cen-
      tury dating is in Ott, 252–56. It is not even clear that the colophon
      dating al-Zuhrī's work to 1235 should be accepted. To give one indica-
      tion, the text itself on the same page states that it was composed in
      699/1299, sixty-four years *after* the date on the colophon.

42   At least six names in all, if one counts the variant *Q-m-r-mās* in Sh,
      199.

43   Such a procedure is more feasible if one concentrates on a single tale
      and its variants.

44   Comprehensive introductions are those of Jérôme Lentin, "Middle
      Arabic," and Kees Versteegh, *The Arabic Language*, 114–29. A differ-
      ent style of Middle Arabic may be seen in James Montgomery's alter-
      nate Web edition to *Kitāb Aḥmad Ibn Faḍlān* (*Mission to the Volga*)
      on the Library of Arabic Literature website: http://www.libraryo-
      farabicliterature.org/assets/Mission-to-the-Volga-Alternate-Web-
      Edition-corrected-2014-03-17.pdf).

45   Lentin, "Variétés d'arabe dans des manuscrits syriens du *Roman de
      Baybars*," 108 and n48; Gavillet Matar, *La Geste du Zīr Sālim*, 1:72,
      91–92; Bellino, "Stylistic and Linguistic Features of the theme of the
      Duel in the *Ġazwat raʾs al-ġūl*," 46–47, 60–61.

46   See Lentin, "La langue des manuscrits de Galland," and "Variétés
      d'arabe dans des manuscrits syriens du *Roman de Baybars*."

47   Lentin, "Unité et diversité du moyen arabe au machreq et au
      magheb," 316.

48 The other manuscripts are all in forms of Middle Arabic, running a range from relatively few divergences from Classical Arabic (B2) to a very high degree of divergence (A, AKM).

49 In Classical Arabic the *yā'* seat of the *hamzah* would be undotted; in manuscript A the dots are frequently maintained, but this orthographic peculiarity has not been retained for this edition.

50 *Fīsān* ("axes") is an attested North African feature (Lentin, "Unité et diversité du moyen arabe au machreq et au maghreb," 313); *aṭyār* ("birds") is also found in Syrian Middle Arabic (Lentin, "La langue des manuscrits de Galland," 446).

51 Harrell, *A Short Reference Grammar of Moroccan Arabic*, 98.

52 Some scholars have speculated as to whether certain types of errors indicate whether a copyist was working with another printed version or transcribing an oral recitation. For example, dittography would likely point to written transmission, errors in formulaic passages to oral transmission, as the reciter would repeat stock phrases more quickly. See Gavillet Matar, *La Geste du Zīr Sālim*, 1:68–72. This is speculative, of course, but as Gavillet Matar shows, the manuscripts can provide us with much to speculate on.

53 In one case (§12.3) I have "restored" a *hamzah* in order to clarify what seems to be the most likely reading (*baka'at* for the text's *bakat*).

54 In contrast, *qālā ṣāḥib al-ḥadīth* appears twice in A, each time "correctly." A possible explanation for the unusual "incorrect" form, *qāla al-rāwī al-ḥadīth*, is that it is an amalgam of two phrases that occur more frequently, here and elsewhere: *qāla l-rāwī* (which does occur in A at §3.7) and the most common form, *qālā ṣāḥib al-ḥadīth*.

55 Lentin notes that "normalization" is perhaps the major characteristic of Middle Arabic: that regardless of what kind of Middle Arabic we are dealing with, a set of norms is readily perceived. ("Variétés d'arabe dans des manuscrits syriens du *Roman de Baybars*," 96–97; "La langue des manuscrits de Galland," 436).

56 Lyons for the most part lets them stand; Miquel corrects them or painstakingly points them out in his notes.

57 Heinrichs, "Modes of Existence of the Poetry in the *Arabian Nights*."

58 See, for example, the two verses in §9.12 in the present edition and that of Ṭarshūnah. The latter does not always give variants for the verses, but here he does. Cf. Gaudefroy-Demombynes, *Cent et une nuits*, 89.

59 I refer to the Web-only version; see n. 44 above.

60 See, e.g., Gavillet Matar, *La Geste du Zīr Sālim*, 1:73.

A Hundred and One Nights

In the name of God, the Merciful and Compassionate,
God bless our lord Muḥammad and his family.

The Story of a Hundred and One Nights

1.1

Shaykh Fihrās the Philosopher spoke:
A king named Dārim once heard about this book and sent for me. I came to his palace and enjoyed his hospitality. A month later he ordered me to appear before him.

"I want to ask you something," he said to me.

"Ask whatever you wish," I replied.

"Tell me about the *Hundred and One Nights*. Put the whole story, from beginning to end, in a book."

"Of course," I said.

I hear, Your Majesty—and God is Wise and All-Knowing of the unknown—that in India a just king would hold a magnificent annual festival which he would attend with his companions and men of state. He would command them to don their best garments and would provide them with food and drink. During the feasting and the drinking, the king would disappear briefly into his palace, and then appear before them in the finest raiment. He would sit on his throne and call for a great Indian mirror, mounted on an iron wheel. He would then contemplate his face in the mirror and ask the assembled company, "Do you know anyone more handsome than me?"

And they would say, "No, Your Majesty, we do not."

This would please him greatly.

1.3 One time, he did as he was wont to do every year, when an elderly man of state came up to him and said, "Your Majesty, beware of being too self-satisfied, for I have traveled to the great cities and wandered through many countries, and, in the land of Babel, in the city of Khorasan,[1] I saw a youth, a merchant's son, who was more handsome than you. His beauty is ravishing, his allure astonishing."

"How can we bring him here?" the king asked, "If he is as you say, I'll reward you handsomely, but if he is not, then by God I'll make you pay!"

"Money and gifts are the only way to get him here," said the old man.

"Then you shall have them," the king replied.

1.4 So the old man took the goods and the gifts he required and had a great ship prepared, on which he and his companions set sail. The winds blew favorably for two whole months. They entered the port near the city of Khorasan, where the old man disembarked and unloaded all the treasures and money he had brought. He left one of his companions in charge of the ship, purchased animals to carry the goods and gifts from India, and headed for the city of Khorasan. Once there, he sought out the best merchant inn in the city and rented a charming, exquisite apartment. Here he unloaded all his goods and treasures and then he rested.

1.5 Three days later, he left the hotel and went to the shop of the Khorasanian merchant, the father of the handsome youth, in the market of the druggists and perfumers. He greeted him and took a seat.[2] The merchant's son sat on a mattress of silk brocade, with a white turban on his head. He was just as the poet said:

> Between his turban and his cheek there shines a light
> As t'were a full moon in the red of early night.
> When he comes and looks and smiles and mutters,
> The limbs go weak and the heart, it flutters.

In the shop, the Indian showed the Khorasanian merchant some of the treasures he had brought.

The perfume merchant was astonished, for he had never seen anything like it in his own country. The Indian said, "Do you know, Abū Muḥammad, that the only reason I left India was to seek you out, because I had heard of your virtue, your friendship, and the excellence of your company?"

"May God bless you and may He assist us in treating you as you deserve," said the Khorasanian. "I will look after everything for you; I will spare no effort in trading your goods, God willing."

"May God reward you," replied the Indian.

The perfume merchant summoned one of his slaves, and spoke to him in a language the old man did not understand, then he turned to the Indian and said, "My lord, perhaps you will oblige me and favor me by dining at my house. I think we are going to work well together and enjoy a long-lasting friendship!" The Indian agreed, and they left, accompanied by the youth.

When they arrived at the house, the youth knocked on the door and it was answered by a slave girl, slender as a willow branch[3] or bamboo stalk. When she saw who it was, she kissed the ground, and her master said to her, "Have the women retire so that we may come in." She went away briefly and then gave the all clear for them to enter. The house was beautiful and spacious inside. The salon they entered was furnished in brocade and expensive mats, fine felt carpets, and Persian pillows. A fresh breeze blew and the fabrics fluttered. There was a chair on the right and another on the left, both raised on legs of gold. They each took a seat.

The perfume merchant gave his son a silent signal, a wink with his eyes. He called for the slave girls, who laid before them all manner of delicious dishes to satisfy their every wish: bread, the flesh of beasts and birds, and other delicacies of Khorasan. The Indian enjoyed the charity and generosity of the Khorasanian merchant for three days. Then the merchant lodged him in a house directly across from his own, and provided him with the furnishings and utensils he required. He made the Indian his friend, swearing to eat and drink with him every day until they became like two souls in one body.

It was then that the Indian turned to the Khorasanian and said, "I want to show you all the treasures I've brought with me from India and beyond!"

1.9 The Khorasanian saw things the likes of which he had never seen before. When he had taken it all in, the Indian said to him, "Abū Muḥammad, why don't you send your son to India with me so that I can introduce him to our kings and leaders and merchants. That way they can get to know him and they'll honor and protect him. He should learn the business of trade—I can see he's suited to it. He's clearly a shrewd, intelligent, and astute young man."

1.10 "Well, he's just recently married," answered the Khorasanian, "and so he cannot travel until the year is up. But as you are my best friend, I'll agree, out of honor for your friendship. But you must stay with us until his time is done."

So the Indian stayed to the end of the year, and then the Khorasanian went to his son and said to him:

"Zahr al-basāṭīn,⁴ get ready to travel to India with this gentleman so you can see their cities and get to know their kings and merchants."

"Father, I hear and obey God first, and then you."

1.11 The merchant got everything his son needed for the trip and, when the time came, the young man left by the city gate and camped nearby. But then, having bid his father and his wife farewell, he realized that he had left behind something he needed. "Sir," he said to the Indian, "I have forgotten something at home! Please wait until I get back."

1.12 Upon his return, he found the door open. He entered and called for his wife. She did not answer. He pulled back the curtain at his bed and saw his wife lying asleep next to a black man.

1.13 Seeing her like this, he lost his mind. His hand went straight to the hilt of his sword and he killed them both. He placed the girl's head on the black man's chest, and the black man's head on the girl's chest. Then he returned to the Indian. The old man looked at him and noticed a change in his color. Something was different. But the youth would not answer his questions about what was wrong, and stayed like this until they reached the ship.

They were at sea for many days, and each day the youth's appearance changed for the worse. At the city of the king, the capital of India, ships from every land were at anchor. The news of the ship's arrival at the port was conveyed to the king, and skiffs came out to meet it. The people turned out in all their finery. The king rode a mighty elephant. On his right you could see ten banners of different silks and spearheads fitted with precious stones so brilliant they nearly blinded the eyes. 1.14

The Indian went ashore by skiff with Zahr al-basātīn. He went to the king and greeted him. The king looked at the youth and, in the Indian tongue, said to the old man, "O Royal Aide!" (for that was what he called him) "Is this the handsome youth of which you spoke?" 1.15

"He fell seriously ill on the journey, Sire, and this has changed his color and his whole appearance. I swear it, Majesty."

The king ordered that the youth be lodged in the guest house opposite his palace and that no expense be spared to help him rest and recover from his travels. The old man, the Royal Aide, would check on the youth every day, bringing him electuaries and medicines and potions and anything he thought might help, but the youth just got worse and worse. 1.16

One day the youth was thinking about how he had found his wife with the black man, and could take it no more—the grief was killing him. He began to wander through the house from room to room. Noticing a small door, he pushed it open. It revealed a flight of stairs made of veined marble. He climbed the stairs to the upper stories of the house, where he discovered a dome with four doors and where he could feel the four winds blow. The doors were made of red sandalwood, ivory, and ebony, fastened with gold and silver studs. He opened them and saw that he looked out over the king's palace, where he espied a garden of lofty fruit trees, where birds chirped and water spouted from the mouths of statues onto 1.17

pools of veined marble. In the middle of the garden stood a tall tree with lush branches that hung down on all sides, like a huge pitched tent.

1.18   He was feasting his eyes on the scene, taking in the scent of the flowers and enjoying the singing of the birds, when he heard a sound coming from the garden. Suddenly, a door opened and forty slave girls, each as beautiful as the moon, bejeweled and clad in fine raiment, entered the garden. One of them was as stunning as the rising sun; her body seemed to be made of light or have the clarity of crystal. It was as if roses took their color from her cheeks and gazelles borrowed their looks from her face and eyes. She wore a garment woven with gold. She wore a crown wreathed with various jewels and studded with precious stones on her head and a diadem on her brow. She was adorned most beautifully. The slave girls held long- and short-necked lutes, drums, timpani, and flutes[5] in their hands and they began to move and dance and wave their arms about.

1.19   When they reached the raised area at the center of the garden, the music of passion burst out everywhere, from all sides. You could hear voices singing in time to the plucking of double and triple chords; you could see feet beating on the ground and arms waving all around. Thus did they carry on for a good part of the day.

        Then the woman shouted and the slave girls, each and every one of them, quickly took cover. She walked through the garden to the lofty tree just described and went under its branches. As she beat the ground with her foot, up rose a trapdoor and a black man came out. He was very tall, as big as a date palm or the heavy bough of a tree, and had lips that drooped and eyes that glowed.

1.20   "You leave me here," he said, "you daughter of a whore, to suffer the agonies of death while you are busy eating and drinking?"

        She apologized, saying, "My lord, I swear on your head, I was busy with the king. My only goal is to kill and destroy him so that I can be with you! But I haven't been able to do it—I just haven't found a way. But I am determined to kill him and be done with him."

        The black man smiled and laughed loudly.

"Excellent! Then your love for me is still strong!"

Then he struck the woman with his hand and laid her out on the ground and did to her what man does to woman.

When he saw this, the youth from Khorasan said to himself, "My God! How can I be sad about my wife when this is the king's wife? She has slave girls and all kinds of jewelry and finery and wealth and all the fine food and drink she could want, and yet she betrays the king, despite all that he has given her! Why should I be sad, when I don't have a tenth of his wealth or position?" 1.21

Then he recited:

> Woman, even if described as chaste—
>   who tested by life's affairs does not understand?—
> Is meat that hungry dogs circle round,
>   so guard her, or she will go from hand to hand.
> Today her secret and her story belong to you,
>   tomorrow another will have her mouth and bond.
> She is like a house you live in; you never know
>   who'll live there next, when empty it's left to stand.

At the end the youth said, "By God, my heart will never be stricken like this again!" He closed the door, went back downstairs and started eating and drinking again. Barely ten days later, his beauty and good looks had returned.

The old man was overjoyed to see this. He kissed the youth on the brow, then went to tell the king the news. The king commanded that the festival be held as usual, and it was proclaimed throughout the realm that all should attend the festival on the appointed day, dressed in their finest clothing. 1.22

On that day, the people came, both from the city and the countryside, clad in their finest raiment. The king too adorned himself in his fashion and ordered his companions to don their best clothes. They took their seats. The king had ordered his eunuchs to wear clothes of silk brocade and purple belts adorned with pearls and coral. In their hands they held fly-whisks and fans. The king had also 1.23

ordered the youth to put on a beautiful cloak and to dress in the finest Khorasanian attire. Thus did he come before the king.

1.24   Everyone in the assembly stood up to gaze on his consummate beauty.

The king took his hand and seated him on his throne and ordered that a crown be placed on his head, and a diadem on his brow. Then the king called for the Indian mirror which was wheeled out before him. The king looked at his own face in the mirror and then at the face of the youth from Khorasan and its reflection in the mirror. He addressed everyone in his audience chamber and said to them, "Speak truthfully and speak only the truth: Who is more beautiful, this youth or I?"

1.25   They said to him, "Your Majesty, in our time we have never seen anyone more beautiful than he."

The king said, "True. You have spoken truthfully." Then he ordered that the mirror be returned to its place, and that the people from the city and the countryside be fed. At the end of the feast, he sent them away and only the youth remained with the king.

1.26   The king stood up, put his hand on the hilt of his sword and pulled it from its scabbard. The youth could see that he was about to be cut in two, and cried out, "Why, Your Majesty? What have I done?"

"I am going to have to kill you," the king said, "if you don't tell me why your looks and your color have changed since you arrived in my country."

1.27   "Your Majesty, my story is this . . ." And he related how he had found his wife with the black slave and had killed them. "And it was all the grief and anxiety that changed my looks and ruined my health."[6]

1.28   He then told the king of what he had seen in the garden, how the black man had come out from the chamber, what had passed between him and the woman, and their plans to destroy him. "And after seeing this, Your Majesty, I was consoled. My anxiety disappeared, I got rid of my distress and I began to eat and drink again and so my health returned and I regained my beauty and good looks."

When the king heard this he leaned menacingly towards him. 1.29

"What proof do you have for what you are saying about my wife and the black man?"

"Come with me to the house you lodged me in, and we will go up to the dome so you can see for yourself."

The king stood up and said, "This is a day of rest and leisure." Then he took the youth's hand and said, "Lead the way."

Off they went to the house and up to the dome, where the youth 1.30 opened the window that overlooked the garden. He began to converse with the king and tell stories, and while they were talking they heard a great uproar. The king looked and saw the slave girls and the woman come into the garden as usual, where they began to move about and dance and to play their instruments.

The king suddenly became indignant and jealous, and said to the 1.31 youth, "This isn't what you described to me! You just wanted to get a look at my women! You should know that there are three things that kings will not tolerate: the slandering of other kings, the exposure of their women, and the divulging of their secrets."

The youth replied, "Please, Your Majesty, don't be hasty. Be patient just a little while longer and you'll see something astonishing."

The two of them waited, then all of a sudden the young woman 1.32 shouted and the slave girls fled and hid. She approached the very same tree and stamped her foot on the ground. The trapdoor to the underground chamber was raised and out came the black slave. He grabbed her by the hand and rebuked her violently for her absence. She apologized as she had done the first time, then he had his way with her as the king looked on.

"What do you think, Your Majesty?" 1.33

"You are not to blame," said the king.

1.34   Then the king went back down to his palace. He had the woman and the slave girls that were with her seized and beheaded. Then he summoned the black slave and killed him. He put the heads of the slave and the young woman in a bowl and sent them to the youth. When the youth came in and saw the two heads he exclaimed, "Your Majesty! What is this?"

"Those are the heads of the black slave and the woman," he said.

Then the king forswore marrying women.

1.35   When the youth began to long for his own people, he told this to the king, who prepared a ship loaded with all sorts of treasures and Indian goods. Then he bade him farewell, and the youth returned to his father.

1.36   For a long time the king did not remarry again, but eventually he wedded a beautiful girl, spent the night with her and killed her the next day. From then on he began to sleep with a different girl each night and have her killed in the morning. He had gone through the whole country and only two girls, the daughters of the vizier, were left. So the king asked to marry one of them, whose name was Dīnārzād. The vizier had barely heard the question before he said, "Yes, she is yours."[7]

1.37   The vizier returned home anxious and worried. His other daughter, whose name was Shahrazād, asked him, "Why do you look so anxious and worried?"

"How could I not be upset?" he said. "The king has just asked for your sister, and he will spend the night with her, and then kill her. And he'll finish by doing the same to you the next day!"

"Don't worry." Shahrazād said to her father. "Go to him and tell him, 'The girls enjoy each other's company, so take both of them. Sleep tonight with Dīnārzād and tomorrow with Shahrazād. She can stay with her sister in another room and keep her company.'"

1.38   The king liked the idea and said, "Very good. I'll take them both."

"They are yours," replied the vizier.

So the king slept with Dīnārzād and when the time approached for the king to kill his wife, she said, "Shahrazād my sister! Come and tell the king one of your excellent stories."

"I'm coming," she answered.

And so she began to tell the story of Muḥammad ibn ʿAbdallāh al-Qayrawānī.

The king enjoyed listening to her, and when day began to break, Shahrazād said, "If you let my sister live another night I'll tell you an even more astonishing story."

The king agreed to this, and then he sealed the door with his seal and went to court to see to the running of his kingdom.

The king and the girl spent the next night together until the appointed time. When Dīnārzād sensed the king was awake she called out, "Shahrazād my sister! Come and tell our master one of your fine stories."

1.39

So she resumed the story from the point where she had left off at the end of the first night, and when the blessed morning came the king did as he had done the first day.

And thus every night, she told her stories, until a hundred and one nights had passed and Dīnārzād had become pregnant by the king. He assured both of them of their safety and security, and Shahrazād ceased to come to him.

The Story of the Young Merchant

2.1   They say—and God is Wise and All-Knowing of what is unseen— that there once lived a merchant, a man of great wealth who lived a very good life. This merchant had a son more handsome than any had ever seen. His father taught him literature, history, and all the topics that children of merchants should be taught.

When the father felt the end was near, he called for his son.

"My boy," he said, "I am dying, there is no doubt about it. But I am going to give you some counsel. I want you to accept it and never forget. If you do, you'll regret it."

"And what is it, father?" asked the youth.

"Do not trade on credit, be it yours or someone else's."

"Yes, father," he said.

2.2   The father passed away some few days later, may God show him mercy. The son gathered together his father's money and found that he had two thousand dinars. He said to himself, "I must return to my father's shop and stick to buying and selling, and just as he advised me, I will not sell or buy on credit."

So he went to his father's shop and conducted his business as his father ordered him. By the year's end, all the merchants knew it for a fact that he neither bought nor sold on credit.

2.3   One day some brokers paid him a visit in his shop.

"You have two thousand dinars," they said. "How would you like to see your shop full of twelve thousand dinars' worth of goods? We can make it happen."

"How is that possible?" he asked.

"We'll sell you goods worth twenty thousand dinars. These you sell. You give something to the owners and keep a similar amount for yourself. All you have to do is pay us a fee—nothing more."

They pressured him relentlessly until he gave in and forgot his father's advice. The brokers flooded to him from everywhere with their goods and provisions, which he took, giving each broker his fee. By the time of the call for the afternoon prayer, he had paid out the two thousand dinars and his shop was packed full of merchandise.

He remained there the rest of the day, but by nightfall he had not sold or bought a thing, so he went home. When the blessed morning came, the youth went to his shop and stayed there the whole day, again without buying or selling anything. He became very upset and worried about this. He returned home anxious and sad, thinking about his father's advice and regretting what he had done. He said to himself, "What I am going to do when the owners of the goods come asking for their merchandise? What do I say to them? I'll have to sell the merchandise of one in order to pay the other, but their money will soon be all gone and I'll be left with nothing!"[8]

He was sitting outside his house when suddenly he was joined by an elderly man, one of his father's former companions. They greeted each other, and the old man said, "What's wrong? What has possessed you and distressed you?"

"I disobeyed my father," said the youth. "I did not take his advice and now I've lost two thousand dinars in a single day."

"Go back inside your house and pretend to be ill," instructed the old man. "Do not let anyone in or out and be absolutely firm about it. If anyone asks about you, tell him you are sick."

2.4

2.5

2.6

Here the dawn reached Shahrazād so she ceased to speak. The king got up, astonished at her tale. He closed and sealed the door, then left for his court.

Fihrās the Philosopher spoke:

The next night the king returned and, as was his custom, broke the seal and spent the night with the woman until the appointed time. Then Dīnārzād called: "Sister, Shahrazād! Tell our lord the king one of your excellent stories!"

She said, "Very well . . ."

2.8   So the youth pretended to be ill and the old man spent the night there with him.

When the blessed morning came, the old man walked to the market and sat in the first of the merchants' shops. He was known for probity and propriety, and for being friendly with the young merchant. The other merchants asked about the youth and he informed them he was not well. The old man went from shop to shop, spreading the word that the youth was ill, until he had made the rounds of the market, from one end to the other and everyone had heard the news.

2.9   On the third day, the man gathered around him ten of his fellow elders and off they went to the market, where they proclaimed loud and clear, "O people, may God show you mercy! Those of you who are good and able, let them attend the funeral of the honorable, young merchant, Muḥammad ibn ʿAbdallāh al-Qayrawānī, who passed away yesterday, may God show him mercy." The people began to wail and lament the young man's death.

The old man went to the shop and cut a long piece of fabric into a shroud. He then gave a dirham to a man to buy the embalming materials and everything else that's needed to prepare the dead.

2.10   When the merchants who owned the goods in the youth's shop saw this, they came up to the old man.

"Sir," they said to him, "this young man owes us a great deal of money for merchandise that he took but never paid for."

"I don't know what you're talking about," he replied. "He traded only with capital—he never bought or sold on credit."

"But he has all our goods!"

At which the old man called out, "People of the market! Have you ever known this youth, ever since he has been among you in this shop, to do business on credit?"

"We have never, ever, seen him do business on credit," they all replied.

The merchants were confounded and did not know what to do.

But there was one among them, a man who had lived and learned, who approached the old man and whispered in his ear, "Excuse me, sir, have I really lost everything? Tell me what I need to do."

"You can buy it back with your own money. Give me two dinars, one for the fee and a dinar extra, and take what's yours."

"Very well."

The merchant gave him two dinars, took back his goods, and departed. Upon seeing this, the rest of the merchants hurried over to the old man.

"Who are you to give the boy's goods to that fellow?" they demanded.

"The fact is that before he died, he made me his executor," said the old man.

And here the dawn reached Shahrazād so she ceased to speak.

Shahrazād said: And at that, my master, another merchant approached the old man, asked him what was what, and was told the same thing. Thus it continued, each of the merchants giving two dinars and taking his merchandise until the old man had received all of the youth's money plus an extra thousand dinars. He put it in the youth's shop and locked everything up. Then he left with the other mourners and went to the young man's house. Everyone was weeping, and the elderly men shuffled along with the group, one of them carrying the shroud and embalming materials. As they drew near the house, they heard a great outcry and commotion arising

2.11

2.12
The Third Night

from within, of such volume and such intense joy that it echoed in the surrounding quarters.

2.13   The old man had given the people of the house an order.

"When I come to the door with the people and the elderly gentlemen," he had instructed, "I want you to begin to wail, all of you together, and come out to us and say, 'Our master lives! Whatever it was he suffered from is gone! He's awake!'"

When the servants came out to meet the crowd, the old man asked them, "What's going on?"

"Our master has revived!" they cried.

At this the old man was very pleased. He distributed money throughout the youth's household, gave the shroud and embalming materials as alms, nodded to the elderly gentlemen and thanked them for their kind deed. Then he went in to see the youth.

"So my son, what do you think? Did you see how I dealt with them?"

"God has made you an excellent man, Uncle."

2.14   "But be warned," said the old man, "don't do this again, and keep to the advice of your father." Then he added, "Stay at home. Don't show yourself to anyone for thirty days and don't let anyone in to see you."

"Very well."

He did as the old man had ordered him. When thirty days had passed, he thought about leaving the city and traveling, for his father had also given him another piece of advice: "My son, if you travel, do not walk with the caravan; stay ten miles ahead, or ten miles behind."

Then the youth bade farewell to his family and the old man and began to wander far and wide.

2.15   One day while traveling, having kept about ten miles ahead of his companions, he heard a voice calling him by name: "Muḥammad ibn ʿAbdallāh al-Qayrawānī!"

He turned towards the voice, which seemed to come from a rock by the side of the road. Upon approaching, he discovered a young woman behind the rock. She was stark naked, not wearing a thing.

"And who are you?" he asked.

"I am the daughter of So-and-So the merchant," she said, naming one of his father's friends, with whom the youth was acquainted.

And here the dawn reached Shahrazād so she ceased to speak.

Fihrās the Philosopher spoke:

She said, Master, the merchant's son asked the girl, "How on earth did you end up here?"

"I was traveling with my father when we were attacked by thieves," she replied. "They killed the people in the caravan and took my father prisoner. I fled here on my own. Then, my lord, I called for your help and protection."

The young man gave her some of his own clothes to wear, seated her behind him and rode on to the next encampment. He had just pitched a tent for her when his traveling companions caught up with them. He told them to dismount and gave some dirhams to a servant to purchase a ram. He slaughtered and prepared the animal, and fed all the people of the caravan. Taking some of the meat and the bread, he put it on a plate and brought it to the girl. He gazed at her—her face was as radiant as the half-moon or an ingot of silver.

The young man was smitten. "When night falls and everyone is asleep," he said to himself, "I'll go to her and get what I want from her."

When night fell and everyone was asleep the youth arose and went to the girl, but could find no trace of her. He was astonished.

"If only I knew what had happened and who she is! Is she human or is she one of the jinn?" he asked himself. He spent all night thinking about her, his heart blazing with a fire that not even the seven seas could extinguish.

When the blessed morning came, he bridled his she-camel and struck out ahead of his companions. Along the way, he suddenly heard his name being called: "Muḥammad ibn ʿAbdallāh al-Qayrawānī!"

2.18   He turned to look and there, behind a rock in the middle of the road, was the girl, looking just as she had the previous day. He greeted her, but now her response was different.

"You deceitful wretch! You wanted to betray the Almighty, the Omnipotent! Can you not control yourself until it is lawful for you to have your way? But your sin can be forgiven because you are young and don't have any experience in such things."

The youth gave her some clothing to wear and she put it on. He seated her behind him and made his way to the next encampment, where he set her down amid the caravan and pitched her tent as he had before.

He made no move during the day, but in the night he arose and went to her to do what he had wanted to do the previous night. But when he reached her tent he found neither hide not hair of her.

2.19   He looked for her amongst his companions but still could not find her. Astonished at this, he passed an anxious night.

When the blessed morning came, the caravan traveled on, and he struck out ahead as usual. As he was going along a stretch of open desert he heard a voice calling him: "Muḥammad ibn ʿAbdallāh al-Qayrawānī!"

He looked and there was the girl, naked. Again he greeted her and she replied, "You deceitful wretch! Yesterday you tried to go against the Almighty, the Omnipotent and do what you tried to do the first night. But your sins will be forgiven, since we were created as a temptation for men."

2.20   The youth covered her and seated her behind him as he had done previously. They went on their way until the midday sun overwhelmed them and they were half-dead from the heat.

"My lord, this heat is killing us," said the girl. "Let's turn off the path. I know a tree nearby, with a spring. We'll stay in the shade and drink from the spring, and we can rest until the caravan catches up with us and the temperature has cooled down."

"That's a good idea," he replied.

The girl led him to a spot where the caravan would not be able to find them.

As he arrived at the tree he was thinking to himself, "I'll get what I want from this girl. I am going to have my way with her."

He was still dreaming of what he was going to do with her when suddenly she jumped to her feet, seized him, and threw him down on the ground. Then she shackled him and tied him to the tree.

And here the dawn reached Shahrazād so she ceased to speak.

Fihrās the Philosopher spoke:

She said, Master, when the young man regained consciousness and found himself tied to the tree, he asked, "What is going on?"

"No one can save you now!" she said. "I've waited years for you to fall into my hands, and now I've finally got you!"

Then she mounted the youth behind her and rode across the open country to a palace in the desert. It was surrounded by fruit trees and flowing streams, but there was no other sign of civilization. She dismounted, tied the youth to a tree, and left him there.

As evening approached, ten knights came out from the palace. At their head, one knight rode a great elephant and another a lion.

"Who could this be?" said the lion rider as they drew near. "I know this place, and no one comes here!"

"He must be a stranger," said one of the companions, "far from home, attacked by thieves, robbed, and left here as he is."

"He'll be our guest tonight," said the leader.

They untied him and took him into the palace. What the youth saw cannot be described. In a salon where a fresh breeze blew and fabrics fluttered, the lion rider and his companions sat down and called for food and drink. They ate and drank long into the night. When it grew dark candles were set on a candelabra of gold, and they feasted until the whole group was drunk. Then their turbans were thrown from their heads and their hair tumbled out, in locks like camels' tails.

2.25   They were girls dressed as warriors, and the one who rode the lion was the girl who had tricked him!

She said to him, "What do you think, Muḥammad ibn ʿAbdallāh al-Qayrawānī? May you never leave this palace, by God. All the food and drink you could desire will be yours."

And so the youth spent ten days eating and drinking to his heart's content.

On the eleventh day the girl turned to him.

"Muḥammad ibn ʿAbdallāh," she said, "we wanted you all for ourselves, but you won't get what you're after until I return. I'll be away for seven days, and when I get back you'll get what you want, and I'll get what I want. But there is one condition."

"What's the condition?"

2.26   "You may go wherever you please in the palace except for that room," she said, gesturing. Then she said goodbye and set out with the rest of the girls.[9]

The youth passed five days in the palace, eating and drinking. On the sixth day he felt very, very lonely, and as he thought about his isolation, he began to recite:

> A lonely stranger recalls and remembers;
>   there's fire in his heart like the hottest of embers.
> If my Lord has decreed my isolation
>   then let me be patient in tribulation.

When he had finished reciting, he said to himself, "By God, now there's nothing left to do but die! I can't bear to live in this world! Why don't I open the door and see what's inside? God's will be done."

2.27   He got up, went to the door of the forbidden room and opened it. There was nothing there.

"By God, this is strange!"

As he stood there in his astonishment, he looked more closely and saw two tombs. They had marble tablets engraved with an incomprehensible Indian inscription. As he stared, about the room, he noticed an iron trapdoor with a ring of white silver.

He said to himself, "This must be the way out of the palace, and that's why she wouldn't let me in here, so I wouldn't escape!"

He took hold of the ring and turned it. The trapdoor opened onto 2.28 another chamber. Inside, he saw a series of steps leading down.

And here the dawn reached Shahrazād so she ceased to speak.

Fihrās the Philosopher spoke: 2.29

She said, Master, the young man walked down five steps. The door *The* shut behind him and he was plunged into darkness. He wanted to *Sixth* turn back but could not find his way. He tried to lift the door but it *Night* was closed and would not move. He had no doubt: this was the end.

"I will die here and this place will be my tomb!" he thought in despair.

He went down and at the last step he was in a great open space. 2.30 A light shone in the distance and he could hear the sound of running water. Going toward the sound, he discovered a stream flowing from a cave into a fragrant meadow. The banks of the verdant riverbed were infused with the smell of musk and crushed ambergris. The youth was contemplating the river, wondering at its lush beauty, when he spotted some skiffs made of Indian aloewood in the middle of the river. In these vessels were young women each as beautiful as the moon. They wore long, loose garments of red silk and in their hands were lutes, short-necked and long, and timpani and drums. They began to move about and dance.

A domed white tent, tied with cords of green silk and pegs of yellow brass, was pitched on the riverbank.

The canopy of the tent was raised high, and in its middle stood 2.31 a great bench, furnished with silks and brocade. On it sat the most beautiful girl ever to walk on two feet, be it Arab or non-Arab. Forty other girls, adorned with fine jewelry and clothing, moved around her. A golden crown decorated with all sorts of pearls, sapphires, and precious stones worth the whole of the world sat on her head. When the girls in the skiffs saw the youth emerge from the cave, there was a great hue and cry and they fled to the tent.

2.32   Next to this was a great domed city, built of carved stone[10] and engraved marble, and while the youth stood looking at the city, forty slaves appeared out of nowhere, wearing caftans and holding iron clubs in their hands. They surrounded him and asked, "Human or jinni?"

"I'm human," he replied.

"Then how did you get here? How could you get out of the cave? That's the cave of the demons!"

Then the youth heard them utter cries and wails and words he did not understand. "Look, I'm human" he told them. "I don't know what you're talking about."

2.33   With that they took him, carried him to the city, and brought him before the king.

"Who's this?" asked the king.

"Your Majesty," they said, "we found him coming out of the cave of the demons, so we brought him to you."

When the king heard this news he was overjoyed. He asked the youth his story, and he told the king everything that had happened with the jinni girl.

"Young man," said the king, "you are the one I saw in a dream. Only you can inherit my kingship."

"Your Majesty, do with me as God wills!" replied the youth.

2.34   With that the king summoned his ministers and men of state. He married the youth to his daughter at a great festival the likes of which had never been seen before. The youth lived with the king who died shortly thereafter and then he assumed the throne. He sent for his family, relatives and loved ones, who arrived in the utmost splendor. The youth lived in his kingdom, eating and drinking to his heart's content, until there came that from which there is no fleeing, and praise be to God, Lord of all being.

The Story of Najm al-Ḍiyā' ibn Mudīr al-Mulk

She said: They claim, Your Majesty, that there once lived a king named Mudīr al-Mulk ibn Tāj al-ʿUzz,[11] whose domains stretched far and wide. He had a son, Najm al-Ḍiyā,[12] who was handsome and practiced in the arts of the horse and the fight and the raid in the black of night, in spearmanship and swordsmanship, and in dueling with knights and warriors.

His father wanted to marry him to a princess, so he summoned his male relatives and men of state.

And here the dawn reached Shahrazād so she ceased to speak.

Fihrās the Philosopher spoke:
She said, Master, the king assembled his family and his people.

"I wish to marry my son, Najm al-Ḍiyā," he told them, "and I want you to find me the most beautiful princess ever created by God, and I'll marry him to her."

An old man who had traveled in many lands and was acquainted with all kinds of people stood to speak.

"O fortunate king," he said, "I will introduce you to the most beautiful girl there is. Her name is Nāyirat al-Ishrāq bint Jidār al-ʿUzz,[13] and her father is the master of the Land of White Blossoms and the Palaces of the Yellow Flowers."

3.3   So the king selected a suitably impressive gift, the likes of which had never been seen before, and sent one of his viziers and a number of his men with it to Jidār al-ʿUzz. He also wrote a letter expressing his desire to marry his son to the king's daughter.

Jidār al-ʿUzz came to greet the bearers of the gift. He accepted the gift and installed the vizier and his companions in a fine palace and treated them most generously. They enjoyed his hospitality for an entire month.

Then the king ordered that the marriage contract be drawn up, and held a great festival. He chose a grand gift for his daughter to bring and sent her off with the vizier.

3.4   When the princess arrived with the gift, an encampment was set up for her in a pleasant meadow. Fragrant musk wafted from all its corners, birds warbled, and sweet-smelling flowers were everywhere. You could not take your eyes off it. Cutting through the meadow was a wondrous, steep valley, like one of the verdant valleys of al-Ḥamād or al-Khaḍūrah.[14]

No one alive could resist the captivating beauty of the spot. This was the Meadow of al-Nawāwīr,[15] but people called it the Meadow of al-Azhār.[16] This is where they pitched a large domed tent of silk brocade, tied with ropes of red silk and pegs of brass, and topped with a ruby so dazzling that it almost blinded the eyes.

3.5   The king ordered his slave girls to dress in their choicest raiment and sent them to the meadow to show off their fine brocade. They carried lutes, short-necked and long, and timpani and drums. Tents and encampments were set up all around.

The king placed a crown on his son's head and all the people, from both city and countryside, feasted together at a magnificent banquet.

Then Mudīr al-Mulk, the king of the land of Nawāwīr, ordered his warriors to surround the meadow on all sides and guard against any night-time intruders. The young prince entered the great tent of Nāyirat al-Ishrāq.

They sat together, eating and drinking, but eventually drunkenness got the better of them and they fell asleep without having consummated the marriage.[17]

The prince did not rouse before the sun was well up. He looked
for the girl but she was not to be found. Stepping out of the tent, he
saw dead bodies everywhere. Each one of the slave girls had been
slaughtered. He let out an anguished cry and the warriors guarding
the meadow hurried to help him.

"Sir," they asked, "what is the matter?"

When he told them what had happened and asked if they had
seen anyone, they replied, "By God, we have seen no one and not
one of us has been out of the saddle."

When the news reached his father, he and his soldiers searched
high and low but they could find nothing. A few days later the king
returned home.

The loss of the girl was a painful blow for the prince. For a
long time, there was nothing he could do, but one day, he waited
patiently until he knew that no one, not even his father, was paying
attention. He took a steed of noble stock and as much food as he
needed, and set out from the city. He traveled for many days and
nights until he reached a spot overlooking a river whose banks were
lined with fruit trees. The prince crossed the river and climbed a hill
where a large tent was pitched.

"I give you the greeting of peace, people of this tent," he called out.

The tent flaps were pulled up, and an extraordinarily handsome
youth emerged.

He returned the greeting most politely, but wept as he did so.

Fihrās the Philosopher spoke:

She said, Master, then the prince asked, "Young man, why do you
weep and look so confused?"

"I am a son of the Arabs, and I had gone out for a walk to this
river with my cousin, my wife. I fell asleep and when I awoke I could

not find her anywhere. I don't know if she was taken up to heaven or down below the earth."

"I can't believe it," muttered the prince. "Just when you think that things can't get worse, they do."

3.9 He dismounted and entered the domed tent with the youth, where they spent the night. When the blessed morning came, the prince turned to his companion.

"Do you know of any new building or tall palace around here? Or do you imagine one of your people could have done this?"

"Yes," answered the young man. "I know a place near here where there is just such a palace. It was built by Amalekites, slaves, patriarchs, and brave warriors. Now a great warrior lives there, invincible and solitary."

"Take me there," said the prince.

They rode to the palace. It was an astonishing place—no description could do it justice. As they were dismounting, the palace gate opened and a black servant emerged.

"Who are you?" she asked.

3.10 "Strangers," they replied. "We've come to the palace in the hope that its lord might take us in for the night."

"You are welcome here," said the servant. She pitched a tent for them in the middle of a meadow just in front of the palace and brought food and drink and all they needed for the night.

When the blessed morning came, the prince looked about for the young man only to find him butchered by the entrance to the tent.

"Power and strength come from Almighty God alone!" he exclaimed when he saw the dead body.

3.11 He rose, put on his armor, and rode towards the palace gate. Suddenly the gate opened and a horseman on a steed of noble stock rode forth. He charged at the prince with a great cry, hurling his lance. The prince dodged the lance. Then he let loose another awful cry that signaled the beginning of a long battle. After a while the prince cried out again and attacked the horseman like a lion pouncing on its prey. He lifted him out of the saddle and held him upside down. He gave him such a yank that the horseman's turban came flying off. Eighteen locks of black hair shook loose. It was a girl!

He let her go.

"And who are you, young woman?" asked the prince.

"I am the mistress of this palace," she said, "and I am the one who   3.12 killed the young man who was with you and it was I who kidnapped your wife. You are the only warrior who has ever defeated me. And you, brave warrior, who are you?"

"I am an Arab, a vagabond," he replied. "I'm looking to earn something and make a living."

"By God," she said, "you are no vagabond. You are a prince."

She took him by the hand and led him into a palace the likes of which had never been seen before. She seated him on a great bench and ordered food to be brought. They ate and drank together, and he lived with her in the palace for a long time, eating and drinking to his heart's content.

And here the dawn reached Shahrazād so she ceased to speak.

Fihrās the Philosopher spoke: 3.13

She said, Master, then one day the prince asked for news of the girl   *The* but there was none. The thought of her troubled him greatly and he   *Ninth* was seized with desire.   *Night*

"Young lady," he said, "I would like to take a look around your country."

"As you like," she answered. "Go ahead."

So he rode out from the palace gate, clad in his cuirass, lance in hand. He rode until the heat of the sun was so fierce that he had to seek shade. He sat there, under a tree, thinking of how far he was from home and how he had been separated from his wife, and how he had not even been able to satisfy his desires with her.

He recited: 3.14

> A lonely stranger recalls and remembers;
>   there's fire in his heart like the hottest of embers.

If my lord has decreed my situation
then let me be patient in tribulation.[18]

Then he heard a voice but could not see the speaker. It said:

The star sets then rises high;
the sun goes down then climbs the sky.
Happiness may depart and disappear;
but it will always return and be near.
Trust in God and be patient with His decree,
then relief from despair will come swiftly.

3.15 The sound of the disembodied voice brought the prince great relief. The words made him feel much better. He stood up and decided to return to the castle he had left that morning. But he took the wrong path and lost his way. As they say, "the land kills those who don't know it well."

So he wandered like an ostrich through the open country for three days. On the fourth day he came to a spot that overlooked an attractive valley full of fruits and flowers and birds. Everything came in pairs: there were nightingales, partridges, turtledoves, and wood pigeons.[19] They warbled in the trees and sang their melodies. The valley itself was incomparable, like one of the valleys of paradise.

3.16 The prince was astonished at this verdant splendor, and stood there contemplating its beauty and bloom. But then he noticed something else: a dome on the side of the valley, supported by columns of dappled marble. It appeared to hang in the air above the columns, and in length and width it was more like a city. It was surrounded by gardens, parks, and rivers.

And here the dawn reached Shahrazād so she ceased to speak.

3.17 *Fihrās the Philosopher spoke:*

The Tenth Night She said, Master, the prince left his horse to graze and approached the dome. He saw that words were written all around it:

Are those fallen stars or blossoms
    or strings of pearls like a flower?
The singing of the nightingales
    sounds like music from the bower.
Welcome to the spring, they say,
    but the spring will soon lose its power.

When he had finished reading the verses, he entered the dome. A tomb of dappled marble stood in the center, and on the sides of the tomb he read these words:

Death has ousted me from my palace.
    I had been honored then Death showed me malice.
Take heed, God's servant, when you see this tomb of mine
    and fear what fate will bring further down the line.

When the prince had read these verses, tears fell from his eyes.   3.18
"Fate be damned!" he said, "How wickedly it seduces!"
Then he looked at the head of the tomb and read these verses:

When days are good, you think everything is alright;
    you don't fear what fate may bring in the night.
The nights are happy, but there's the delusion;
    the clear night is when comes confusion.

When the prince finished reading, he began to weep and recited:

Who knows if time flees
    as Fate misses a step? Time itself deceives.
Hopes are realized; desires are achieved,
    things to other things give way and cede.
The nights go on; they come together, they part,
    and at night the stars rise and downward dart.
You believe your joy will through time perdure?
    Impossible! Joy cannot endure.

When the prince had recited these lines, he went to look for his   3.19
horse, but could find no trace of it.

"Power and strength come from Almighty God alone," he exclaimed. "This is God's wish and there is no turning back for «none repels His judgment»."[20]

And he began to recite:

> I am like the hawk, its wings spread, light
> > that sees a bird take to the air in fright
> Fluttering, frozen at the sight,
> > and attacks it in its power and might.
> In the meadow, Fate was full of kindness, bright,
> > gave everything needed to lessen the bird's plight.
> Then one day Fate lets her arrow loose in flight
> > and clips both its wings, without a fight.

3.20   His mental and emotional state improved, he started up the valley to look around, when all of a sudden he came upon a lion crunching the bones of his horse. He dealt the lion a deadly blow with his sword, then continued down the valley, where he met a lone shepherd tending a large flock. He approached him with a greeting. The shepherd returned the greeting.

"And who are you, young man?" he asked.

"I am a stranger who has lost everything," he replied. "As you can see, I am merely looking for some way to get by."

And here the dawn reached Shahrazād so she ceased to speak.

3.21   *Fihrās the Philosopher spoke:*

The Eleventh Night   She said, Master, the shepherd spoke: "Did no one warn you not to enter this valley? Didn't anyone try to stop you? This is the Valley of the Jinn, where a sorcerer demon lives. He's just arrived with a girl, took her right from her very own palace. And I swear, if he lays eyes on a human, they won't live to tell of it."

"What is the name of the girl?" asked the youth.

"Her name is Nāyirat al-Ishrāq."

3.22   "How is it that you are human, but you are tending sheep in this valley? Why are you safe from him?" asked the prince.

"I was raised in his palace, and I look after his sheep."

"How about I help you look after the sheep, in return for some food?" asked the prince.

"May God give me recompense!" cried the shepherd. "I have advised you; I've given you every warning. Now think about the consequences! Take what food you need and go in peace, before the demon finds you. If he does, it will end really badly for you!"

"May God bless you!" said the prince. "But tell me this: does this demon have some place where he takes shelter or refuge?" 3.23

"Yes," said the shepherd. "There's a palace on the other side of this hill. You'll see it. It's enormous."

The prince said goodbye to the shepherd and headed for the palace. He had accepted a piece of barley bread from the shepherd and on the way he thought about how he had abased himself before the shepherd and how he had wanted to help him tend the sheep.

He recited: 3.24

> How many hands I've been forced to kiss
>   that I'd rather have seen chopped off at my behest.
> But fickle fate has many guises,
>   and people see only what seems best.[21]

On his way to the palace the shepherd caught up with the young prince.

"Stay where you are," he told the prince, "until I talk to the mistress of the palace and let her know your situation."

"Go, then, and don't dawdle!" said the prince.

The shepherd entered the palace, but not by his usual route, so the mistress got a fright when she saw him. 3.25

"What brings you here at this hour?" she demanded.

"Madame," he said, "a man came up to me. He is handsome, eloquent, and sweet-smelling as well. He said that he is a shepherd and knows how to look after the animals."

"Bring him here so I can have a look at him," she said.

The shepherd went back and brought the young man in. The woman took a good look and recognized her husband. She sent the shepherd back to his sheep, then threw herself into the prince's arms and they both wept.

3.26   "God be praised for allowing me to see you again," she said. "But who told you I was here?"

"It was God, may He be exalted, who guided me and brought me to you," he replied. "But tell me your story. How did you come to be in this palace?"

"I have no idea," she said. "I was sleeping next to you, and the next thing I knew I awoke and found myself here in this palace."

But as they were talking, the demon appeared, tearing up the earth, flames coming from his mouth.

And here the dawn reached Shahrazād so she ceased to speak.

3.27   *Shaykh Fihrās the Philosopher spoke:*

The   She said, Master, when the girl saw the demon approach she took
Twelfth   the prince by the hand and quickly hid him in a closet with some
Night   food and drink. And all the while she was thinking that there had to
be some way to kill the demon.

3.28   She noticed that the demon was covered in blood.

"May my soul be your ransom!" she exclaimed. "What has happened to you?"

"Today I fought a sorcerer from the jinn," said the demon. "I have never met a more powerful sorcerer. He gave me this wound that by God nearly did me in. I was afraid for my life. A wound there can kill me: I'm not quite sure I'll recover from this."

"Tell me. Do you need some medicine? What kind do you need?" asked the girl. "Perhaps I can help you, maybe ease the pain. I don't want you to die."

"Don't worry about it," he said. "There is nothing to fear. The only thing that can kill me is a knife made from a certain kind of cane, and it only grows around here, nowhere else. And anyway, nobody can get near this place."

"God be praised for what you say," she said.

When the blessed morning came the demon, wearing a snake-skin turban and armed with two swords, mounted a great lion and rode into the open country. The girl got up and went to the prince.

"Take this sword and go to the shepherd," she told him. "Ask him where such-and-such a cane grows. The only way to kill the demon is with a knife made from that kind of cane. He and the shepherd are the only ones who know about it. Once he tells you where it is, kill him. Then take the cane we need and come back here quickly."

The young man went to the shepherd about the cane. When the shepherd had told him where to find it, the prince killed him. He followed the directions, took as much cane as he needed, and returned to the palace, where he made knives from the cane. He hid them and then he and the girl plotted how they were going to kill the demon.

They waited and waited, but when night had fallen he still hadn't returned.

"The demon is really late in coming back," said the prince. "Is this normal?"

"I swear on your dear life," said the girl, "he has never stayed away for even one night. Something must have happened to him."

So the prince spent a night of comfort and joy with the girl.

When the blessed morning came, they waited for the demon until nightfall. But there was no sign of him for seven days.

On the eighth day the girl noticed clouds rise up in the air at a great distance away. She knew that it must be the accursed demon.

"It is time to get ready," she told the prince. "Watch out for yourself and be careful how you deal with him. For now just stay hidden here until I tell you to come out."

She hid him in a closet, and closed and locked it.

It was not long before the demon arrived and entered the palace. The girl greeted him warmly and smiled.

"Tell me," she said, "what kept you?"

"I'll tell you," he replied. "I have been wreaking destruction on lands that are far away, at the farthest reaches of human civilization.

I was looking for a king's daughter, because I wanted to bring back someone to keep you company. I have been away too much, and I'm afraid that something bad may have happened to you while I was away."

She thanked him, kissed his hands and prayed for his life.

Then he started to look around. He looked at her, then he looked to the left and the right, sometimes he looked at the ground and sometimes right at her face.

"What's the matter?" she asked. "Are you looking for something?"

3.33 "Has anyone been here while I was away?"

"By God, no," she replied.

"I smell a human," he said. "Here, in my palace! And I can smell it on you, a smell I'm not used to . . ."

And here the dawn reached Shahrazād so she ceased to speak.

3.34 *Shaykh Fihrās the Philosopher spoke:*

The
Thirteenth
Night

She said, Master, then the girl said to the demon:

"Does the rabbit enter a forest full of lions? Could anybody enter your domain, or set foot there? Could they even find it? How could anyone enter your palace? I am on the lookout every day for anyone who might turn up so that I can ask for news of my country and my own people. And I haven't seen a single soul."

3.35 "By God yes of course I know that." said the demon, "What a relief."

"I swear nobody has been here except for the shepherd who looks after your sheep, and that is because he comes at night to keep me company and tell me strange and wonderful stories and by God, he's a good companion!"

The demon fell silent when he heard her words, then told her to bring him something to eat and drink. She brought it to him, and together they ate.

Shortly after their meal, he fell into a deep sleep, exhausted from all his travels. The girl got up and rushed to the door of the closet where the prince was hiding.

"What happened?" he asked as she led him out. "What did you say?"

She told him what the demon had said, and how she had kept   him occupied until he fell asleep.

"Go to him now," she said, "and may Almighty God help you to kill him—it is His assistance we seek. May you rid the land of this evil!"

The prince repeated the name of God as he advanced, repeating the name of God as he went, until he stood over the demon, who was making noises in his sleep. He took one of the cane knives and plunged it hard into the demon's chest. The demon let out a terrible cry and died.

The prince took the girl and all the precious treasures in the palace and returned to his country. He shared a most comfortable life with her, eating and drinking to his heart's content, until there came to them that from which there is no fleeing, and praise be to God, Lord of all being.

The Story of Camphor Island

4.1 Then she said: They say, Your Majesty, that the King of Fars, Khus-raw Anūshīrwān, was seated one day with his viziers and men of state in the upper stories of his palace, when something caught his attention.[22] Clouds of dust and smoke were rising and swirling in the distance. A terrifying, ferocious, and grim horseman emerged from the dust and the smoke. He advanced quickly to the palace gate and called in a loud voice:

"Greetings to the people of the capital, home of generous souls and skilled horsemen! I have come with words of counsel for the king!"

4.2 The king ordered that the visitor be brought before him. When he entered the king saw that he was an elderly man.

"So, old man, what is your advice?" asked the king.

"I have traveled through many deserts, lands, and cities, through India and Sind and Yemen and China. My name is Saʿādah ibn ʿĀmir ibn ʿImlāq the Younger and I am three hundred years old. In all that time there is no island in the sea or province on land that I have not visited. I sailed all the way from Sarāb to India and did not stop. I kept going from ship to ship, country to country, until I came to the land of Yemen. There I came upon a great towering city, full of countless paths and alleyways, a city built by Amalekite craftsmen and Byzantine generals. And this, as I say, Your Majesty, was in the land of Yemen.

"As we hove into view, the inhabitants came out with clubs and spears. There was a great commotion within the city, and we stood there bewildered, with nowhere to run. Now the name of their king was Ḥamdān—he was a tyrant, an emperor of great lineage, strong, brave, and haughty."

And here the dawn reached Shahrazād so she ceased to speak.

Shaykh Fihrās the Philosopher spoke:

She said, Master, "Listen to what I have to say!" the old man admonished the king.

"You have my full attention, so go ahead: speak. I'm eager to hear your story," replied the king.

"We had stopped in front of the city, and were brought before its ruler, the king. His palace defied description.

"And I tell you, Your Majesty, my companion and I walked on and on and then came to a great gate that led to an inner enclosure, surrounded by high walls and sturdy pillars. There were rivers and trees and fruit there; there were cloves and peppers and lavender, saffron and bamboo, and canals of silver and gold ran through it all. We saw a marble dome with parapets of red gold and on each parapet stood a figure of pure gold; the figures each had tails in the shape of palm leaves, and when flies landed on them, the figures would speak. On the highest part of the dome stood a golden peacock, with eyes of ruby, legs of emerald and wings studded with jewels."

The old man continued:

"The chamberlain left us there and hurried to ask permission for us to enter. Permission was given, and we entered the chamber. Inside, the king sat in splendor on his regal throne; on his right were twenty slave girls holding fans of fine silk, with another twenty on his left. He wore a golden crown studded with pearls, precious stones, and rubies; his clothes were woven with gold. Servant girls, graceful as gazelles, stood before him.

"The chamberlain greeted the king and introduced us; the king returned the greeting in words I didn't understand.

4.7 "The chamberlain turned to us.

"'What has brought you to our city?' he asked.

"'I was on my way home,' I told him, 'and I wanted to see your kingdom for myself, for I have heard that you are a good and just ruler to your subjects. I've come to ask for your favor and your generosity.'

"'The king asks if you know about the kings of this world?' said the chamberlain.

4.8 "'Yes,' I said. 'The largest kingdom belongs to those who rule Iraq, for it is in the center of the world, and all the other kingdoms surround it.'

"'Yes,' said the chamberlain. 'This is what we find in our books.'

"'And after him comes this king of yours, known as the King of Mankind, and then the one known as the King of the Wild Beasts, and he is King of the Turks, since they are the beasts of the human race. After him comes the King of the Elephant, who rules India; then comes the King of Abyssinia, who is known as the King of Wisdom, since that country is the source of wisdom; and then the King of Byzantium, whom we call the king of Men, since there are none on earth more handsome and fine looking than they. These are the most important kings; all the rest are beneath them.' [23]

4.9 "'Yes,' he said. 'You've spoken the truth.'[24]

"Then the king ordered that I be given the finest hospitality. I followed the chamberlain to a palace that defied description, where I stayed as their guest for a whole month and when I wanted to return to my country the king gave me gifts of precious treasures and prepared a ship laden with every wonder. I bade him and the chamberlain farewell and set sail.

"The winds blew favorably across the dark and distant sea until we came to a rock in the middle of the ocean. It was a bright island, whiter than snow or camphor, and in the middle was a stone with the following inscription:

4.10 "'This is Camphor Island,[25] and here lived 'Imlāq the Elder. All his wealth and treasures are under this stone, but they are protected by a magic spell: only a descendant of 'Imlāq the Younger will be able to enter the place.'

"I tried to lift up the rock but it wouldn't budge."

And here the dawn reached Shahrazād so she ceased to speak.

Shaykh Fihrās the Philosopher spoke:

She said, Master, the old man carried on talking.

"I braved the waves of the sea to reach you, Your Majesty. I would like to ask your help in getting hold of those precious treasures."

"Very well," said the king. "You shall have it."

The king gave orders for everything he[26] needed: pickaxes, shovels, sacks, ropes, candles, and other provisions for the voyage. Then he chose one hundred of the bravest men of the kingdom and made them accompany the old man. The winds blew favorably across the dark and distant sea, as they headed for the island.

It was said that near the island lived a people who ate human flesh and who would put perfumes and camphor in skulls and hang them in their homes. They worshipped these heads instead of the One True God, bowing down to them and asking them all sorts of things. Demons would speak the answers to their questions through the skulls. These people lived on nothing but human flesh.[27]

So for ten days the old man Saʿādah traveled with the crew toward Camphor Island.

They stopped to replenish their supply from an island that had fresh water. When the men disembarked they heard a loud rustling sound. They looked up to see an enormous bird swooping down to attack them. The bird grabbed one of the men in its talons and carried him off into the air.

The remaining men were in an uproar.

"You are trying to get us all killed!" they shouted at the old man.

"If someone dies," he responded, "it is because his time has come."

They stayed there until nightfall, when once again they heard the loud noise, coming from the sea. They stood there in terror, dumbfounded, when a group of young women emerged from the water, each like a gazelle in flight, or the full moon at night, hair flowing down to their hips.

When the crew saw this, they rushed to the women, who made no attempt to flee. The men enjoyed the women; the women were pleased with the men. Each sailor[28] passed the night with a young woman, and when the dawn light appeared the women called to each other and disappeared beneath the waves. The men tried to grab them and hold them back, but they were not able to.

4.15   They sailed farther for several days across the dark and distant sea until they reached Camphor Island. Its whiteness shone like a glittering star. They dropped anchor and unloaded the tools, sacks, pickaxes, shovels, candles, and ropes.

Digging around the stone and prising it from its place, they found underneath it a white marble tablet. They lifted it out to reveal the mouth of a cave. Candles lit, they entered and came upon an iron door. The door was open, but a figure in the shape of a lion stood guard on the other side.[29]

4.16   "Which one of you will approach the lion?" the old man asked.

They cast lots, and the loser advanced. He moved closer and closer, and the lion pounced and crushed the man horribly. Then it dropped the corpse down into a large chamber and returned to its place.

"You're going to get us all killed!" they screamed at the old man. "We've had enough!"

4.17   But the old man managed to come up with a ruse to disable the lion and stop it moving. Then he laid planks across the opening of the chamber and the men crossed over in this way, one by one. [30]

Now they were confronted by a slab of black marble with a bolt of yellow brass in it. When they turned the bolt, the slab lifted to reveal a small door that led to a large open space. In the middle stood a spring, surrounded by trees and fruits and with all kinds of birds, everything fashioned from gold and silver. A gate so magnificent that it defied description stood before the spring, and in front of the gate stood a statue in the form of a man with an unsheathed sword in his hand, turning round like a millstone.

"What now?" they demanded of the old man. "How can you get us out of this?"

And here the dawn reached Shahrazād so she ceased to speak.

Shaykh Fihrās the Philosopher spoke:

She said, Master, the old man approached the gate, to look for a way to disable it. One of the men walked in front of him. As the man drew near the figure with the sword, he was stricken with fear and tried to turn back, but it was too late: he was already within reach of the sword, and the figure sliced him in two. His companions stood dumbfounded at what they had seen.

But the old man managed to find a way to stop the figure from moving, and he and his companions were able to enter. They found themselves in a great palace, replete with cups overflowing with red gold, gems, and precious stones. In the center stood a sandalwood door, covered in leaves of gold studded with sapphires; to the right there was a great salon with a throne of gold in the middle. A figure was seated on the throne, and to look at him you would swear he was asleep. His clothes were woven with gold thread, and by his head stood a tablet of red gold that read:

"I am 'Imlāq the Younger. I have ruled and I have vanquished; I   4.20
have given gifts and I have withheld them; I have lived a noble and comfortable life; I have freed slaves and deflowered virgins. All this I did until the Almighty God decreed that my time had come, and look at me now. Let this be a lesson to all who would take heed: Do not be seduced by the world. It will only dupe and deceive you."

Beneath the lines were the following verses: 4.21

> With my right hand I took what I pleased
> > when I saw the sun's colors burst in full glory,
> I took from it my desire, with my right hand.
> > But death is preferable to the ignominy of ignorance,
> living a wretched life, devoid of any certainty.

When the old man had read these lines he tried to take the tablet with him, but he was stopped by a loud cry that echoed through the palace. He collapsed to his knees as the others fled left and right. When the old man, terrified and distraught, came to, he gathered what treasures he could and headed back to the ship. They put all the jewels and precious stones they could manage on board, but the marble tablet could not be moved. They put the stone back as they had found it.

4.22   They were ready to depart when they heard many loud footsteps behind them. They turned around and saw a group of human-looking creatures with tails, covered only by their own hair, rushing toward them. They ran to the ship in terror, weighed anchor, and set sail. They could see the island swarming up with the creatures, who dived into the water and made for the boat.

On board, the old man gave the order to blow the horns, sound the trumpets, and beat the drums. At the sound, the creatures turned back and fled to the island.

The old man and his companions sailed on, across the dark and distant sea, for ten days.

And here the dawn reached Shahrazād so she ceased to speak.

4.23   *Shaykh Fihrās the Philosopher spoke:*

The Seventeenth Night   She said, Master, on the tenth day they reached the city of King Khusraw. The old man sent a messenger to announce their arrival, and the king, overjoyed at the news, rewarded the messenger with a gift of slaves and a steed of noble stock.

The king greeted the old man and congratulated him on a safe arrival. The king received all the treasures and was astonished to find himself so wealthy. He took the old man as a companion and made him a royal counselor. They lived a most comfortable life until there came to them that from which there is no fleeing, and praise be to God, Lord of all being.

The Story of Ẓāfir ibn Lāḥiq

Then she said: they say, Your Majesty, that in the land of India there   5.1
once lived a king who had a son named Ẓāfir ibn Lāḥiq, born to him
of a slave girl and bond maid.[31] Now, this king had another son by
his wife and cousin, and this wife wanted her own son to succeed
the king. She did everything she could to get rid of Ẓāfir, but Ẓāfir
was well aware that his stepmother was the sole cause of all his trials
and tribulations. Eventually he said to himself, "The only thing left
for me here is death."

He went to his brother.   5.2

"After tonight," Ẓāfir told him, "you will never see me again."[32]

"Why is that?" asked the brother.

"Something has happened to me," said Ẓāfir, "and I can't take it
anymore."

Ẓāfir returned home, donned a cuirass, and mounted his horse.
Lance in hand, he fled from the city into the dark of night.

He roamed the open country north and south, as ostriches do,
and when morning came he was a good distance from the city.

He continued to travel the land far and wide, through barren   5.3
sands and rolling lands, over valley and hill and dune and dell, in
land black and burned, where the mindful one feels only fright that
the horizon shows no end in sight; there the wolf finds only thirst
and even the lion fears the worst. No man, no woman, no genie or
spirit—there was nothing to hear, and no one to hear it. The only

ones to intrude on the peace were the rebel angel sons of Iblīs. As the poet said:

> A land of mirage where melancholy dwells,
>   and legions of the jinn picket,
> Wild rue grows in barren soil,
>   thorny gorse in every thicket.[33]

5.4   For five days Ẓāfir wandered through this land, and on the sixth day he found himself looking down upon a land as white as cast silver. A fresh breeze filled the air. A wadi cut through the land like the verdant valleys of al-Ḥamād, a lush green strip, with brilliant lavender flowers.[34] Fragrant musk wafted all around, and there were gushing streams and high trees with hanging branches. Animals roamed everywhere and birds sang: nightingales and partridges and pigeons and turtledoves.

Ẓāfir went down to this gorgeous, winding wadi, which resembled a snake slithering out of its skin or a sword slipping out of its scabbard. He dismounted and drank from its water. He watered his horse, put it out to graze, and unpacked his saddle and tack.

5.5   As he was about to go to sleep, he happened to notice a domed tent of white anemone on the other side of the valley. In front of it he could see a tethered horse, a hanging sword, and a spear stuck in the ground.

And here the dawn reached Shahrazād so she ceased to speak.

5.6   *Fihrās the Philosopher spoke:*

She said, Master, when Ẓāfir saw the tent he found a way to cross the river and approached, calling in a loud voice, "I give you the greeting of peace, people of this tent!"

5.7   Scarcely had he finished speaking when the sides of the tent went up, and three buxom virgins, each as beautiful as the moon, appeared and greeted him. Their necks were so luminous, their smiles so sensuous, and their vestments so fine they defied description.

46 | THE STORY OF ẒĀFIR IBN LĀḤIQ

"Good knight," they said, "Did no one warn you against entering this valley? Did no one try to stop you? By God, the mourners will mourn you and your kin will weep and wail for you. . ."

"And who will do this to me?" asked the king's son.

"The lord of this tent," they replied, "a warrior among warriors, invincible and solitary."

"What is his name and whence his fame?" asked Ẓāfir.

"His name and his story are well known. By God he brings the greatest calamity and disaster; he sends cavalry scattering and minds reeling; he is the Splitter of Skulls and the Sovereign of the Valley of the Barbarians."

While the young man was speaking to the women, a cloud of 5.8
dust appeared in the distance.

"Sir knight," they cried, "it's the warrior we just described to you! Save yourself! Get away before he gets to you!"

Scarcely had he heard their words when the warrior arrived, and when he saw Ẓāfir speaking to the women, he went into a fury. He screamed and hurled a lance, but the prince stepped aside. The lance shattered a rock and stuck in the ground halfway up the shaft.

At that, the pair went at each other. They battled with swords until they were blunted; they fought with pikes until they broke. They fought till their horses foamed with sweat and filled with fear. Suddenly, the prince let loose a furious scream that surprised and terrified the warrior. Then he charged and dealt him a blow that sliced him as neatly as a blade cuts the nib of a reed-pen.

The women came rushing out to him. 5.9

"Who are you," they asked, "who has finally rid us of this fiendish tyrant, this despotic giant?"

"What did he do?" Ẓāfir asked.

"Oh, he was an evil one," they explained. "He would kidnap all the beautiful young women he heard of and spirit them away from their fathers' palaces."

Ẓāfir dismounted. The midday heat was getting worse, so he gave the horse to one of the women, and entered the tent, which was furnished with silks and brocade. He was so exhausted that he just wanted to sleep. So he called one of the women and said to her, "Stretch out your leg so that I can lay my head on it while I sleep." She did so and he slept.

5.10 He slept until the heat of the morning sun roused him. Opening his eyes, he could see no trace of either the women or the round tent. He saddled his horse, fastened his sword to his belt and rode off.

"Power and strength come only from the Almighty God!" he said out loud.

He set off down the valley, looking to his left and his right, but saw no one.

And here the dawn reached Shahrazād so she ceased to speak.

5.11 *Fihrās the Philosopher spoke:*

The Nineteenth Night She said, Master, as he went further into the valley he found himself overlooking an immense and imposing palace. It was a spectacular structure, built on unshakeable foundations by the Amalekites and the Byzantine generals and their slaves. Next to the palace were seven domed tents of brocade. In front of each tent a sword was hung and a steed of noble stock was tethered. He crossed the wadi and went to the first one.

5.12 He called out, "I give you the greeting of peace, people of this tent! I am a stranger, far from home and wandering alone."

No sooner had the words left his mouth when the sides of the tent were lifted and out stepped a young man as slender as a willow branch or a bamboo stalk.

"Who are you who have braved the waves of the seas and the ups and downs of fate? Have you not heard of the lord of this palace and this wadi?"

"What is his name and whence his fame?" asked the prince.

"How can you not know his name," said the man, "when he is a renowned warrior and a famous chieftain? He is al-Suwaydān ibn ʿĀmir ibn Badr al-Samāʾ, Lord of the Valley of Blood, a brave and valiant warrior."

The prince looked at him.

"Young man, are you one of his men?"

"Not at all!" he replied. "We are seven brothers out to take revenge on him, since he kidnapped one of our sisters from our father's palace. Our father is a wealthy king. We will, we hope, triumph over him."

"My brothers," the prince said, "let me stay with you. I have seen something that made me mount my horse and flee like a Bedouin outlaw. I awake in one land and pass the night in another."

"Stay with us," they said. "Eat what we eat and drink what we drink, until God does what He will and «accomplishes a thing that He has already willed to be done.»"[35]

Ẓāfir dismounted and tied up his horse. He entered the tent and sat with the brothers.

While they were talking, a great scream resounded through the wadi. They went out to investigate and saw that the gate of the palace had opened. Out stepped a warrior like a mighty mountain or swollen sea, clad in grey iron and chain mail. As the poet said:

> He who goes out to fight will surely meet death
> amid dark spears, their heads like stars in brightness,
> Wearing armor, iron over iron
> like the moon rising from the doors of darkness.
> When he leans forward, sword in hand,
> It's like the tongue of dawn lambent in night's blackness.

The knight stepped to the middle of the field.

"So which of you will fight me?"

One of the brothers engaged him in combat but was quickly dispatched. A second brother came forward and he too was killed. Then a third was killed and a fourth was exterminated, a fifth was swiftly dispatched and a sixth violently brought down. Only the seventh, the youngest, remained. He wanted to fight as well, but Ẓāfir stopped him.

"Easy, my son," said Ẓāfir. "You are still young and don't know the ways of war."

He donned his armor and covered his face. He mounted his horse and rode at the warrior with a scream that shook the earth and the mountains. They charged and battled, and clouds of dust stretched over them like a tent, until night fell and they withdrew to safety.

And here the dawn reached Shahrazād so she ceased to speak.

5.16

The Twentieth Night

Fihrās the Philosopher spoke:

She said, Master, the prince went back to the tent where he had left the boy and found him weeping for his brothers.

"Don't worry," he said, "I swear by the One who splits the morning sky[36] and moves the winds that I will avenge you and rid you of this dishonor. I will see to it that you capture this warrior who killed your brothers and take him back to the land of your father as your prisoner."

They passed the night talking and when the blessed morning came, the prince was woken by the sound of hooves. He jumped up in fright and ran outside, where he found the boy butchered in a pool of blood. Long was Ẓāfir ibn Lāḥiq's despair, then he said to himself, "Power and strength come only from Almighty God!"

He rose, donned his armor, and mounted his horse. With his hand on the hilt of his sword he rushed out only to find the warrior, the lord of the palace, in front of the tent.

5.17

When the warrior saw him he said, "Does one who seeks vengeance sleep? Or feel secure in the desert? Were it not for the dishonor, by the Lord above, you'd already be dead. So come to the battlefield, and I swear upon my honor that I will give you a fight that will turn the hair of a newborn babe white and shock the bravest warrior."

Then they went at each other and fought a long battle. Horses neighed and bridles flailed, and above the din all you could hear was the striking of swords on helmets like a blacksmith's hammer on iron. The battle intensified until midday, when the prince let loose a great scream and charged like an eagle swooping from the clouds. He grabbed the warrior at the waist and lifted him out of the saddle, like a sparrow caught in an eagle's talons. He dragged him from left to right and back again, shaking him furiously until his turban fell off. Eighteen locks of black hair fell loose—it was a young woman as radiant as the moon, the most beautiful woman ever created by God.

Ẓāfir put her back on her saddle and said, "A girl with breasts and a slit and a woman's crooked ribs, fights with the warriors?"[37]   5.18

She looked at him. "And who are you?" she asked.

"I am Ẓāfir ibn Lāḥiq, lord of prosperous cities and resplendent palaces. I am traveling through these lands."

"You can rejoice," she said to him, "for God has given you all the wealth, benefits, and slave girls that you could want."

She took him by the hand.

"I know now that you truly are a brave warrior." she said, "You are the only one who has ever defeated me."

"How did you come to be alone in this palace?" he asked.

"My father was a great warrior who had no son," she said, "so he named me al-Suwaydiyyah ibn ʿĀmir, as if I were a man, and taught me the arts of the horse and the fight and the raid in the black of night, spearmanship and swordsmanship, and dueling with knights and warriors. So I am as you see me now."

Then she took his hand and led him into the palace, where he saw   5.19 great wealth and many treasures. They withdrew to a chamber and spent the night together, and he discovered that she was a virgin pure.

Ẓāfir stayed in her palace for a period of time, but eventually said, "I want to return to the city of my father."

"God willing, I'll come with you," she said.

And here the dawn reached Shahrazād so she ceased to speak.

Fihrās the Philosopher spoke: 5.20

She said, Master, the woman gathered all the treasure they could   *The* carry, left someone else in charge of the palace, and rode off with   *Twenty-First* the prince. They traveled far and wide for many days, until they   *Night* came to a place overlooking the Valley of the Barbarians, where he had fought with the Splitter of Skulls. They went down into the valley and let their horses graze on the slopes until night fell. Then they slept.

5.21   The prince awoke to feel the heat of the sun on his face. He looked for the woman, but there was no trace of her. He found his horse had been tethered, and he got up, frightened and confused. He wandered through the open country like an ostrich, seeking but finding nothing.

"Good God!" he said. "Just when you think things could not get any worse!"

After about a mile into the valley he saw a solitary shepherd tending his sheep. He greeted him.

"Tell me, shepherd," he asked. "Does anyone live here?"

"No," said the shepherd, "there's just us."

"Who is 'us'?" he asked.

"I live here in this wadi with my father. He's an old man now," he said. "There used to be a great warrior who lived here. They called him the Splitter of Skulls, but God sent a demon from the jinn to kill him, so now we are free of him."

5.22   "Do you know of anywhere around here that is inhabited?" Ẓāfir asked.

"There is a palace known as the Palace of Lights fifty miles away from here," he said." But it is protected by a magic spell for forty miles all around. As soon as the sun rises, it burns anyone who happens to be within forty miles of it. Nobody knows how to get in, but there's a great warrior who lives there, a brave and bold one. His name is Sayf al-Aʿlām ibn Khaḍḍāb al-Dimāʾ,[38] Lord of the Palace of Lights."

The Prince said to himself, "Be it as high as the sun, or as deep as the grave, I swear upon my honor that I'll make it there."

Then he said goodbye to the shepherd and headed along the wadi, moving swiftly until nightfall. He unpacked his saddle and tack beneath a tall tree and went to sleep.

He was awoken by a roar and a growl. He opened his eyes and saw an enormous, terrifying lion. The lion pounced, but Ẓāfir dodged out of the way.

And here the dawn reached Shahrazād so she ceased to speak.

Fihrās the Philosopher spoke:
She said, Master, the prince saw the lion pouncing and dodged out of its way. Seeing that the lion was confused, he rushed it and thrust his sword through its skull right down to the backbone. The lion collapsed in a pool of blood, dead.

The prince got back on his horse and rode off, when suddenly a great scream echoed through the wadi. He turned toward the sound and saw the point of a lance as bright as a lamp coming at him. The scream had come from a knight who was now trying to spear him. The prince dodged the lance and it stuck into the earth half the way up the shaft. He was taken aback but, putting his hand on the hilt of his sword, he went at the rider, and they battled until midday. Then prince Ẓāfir managed to hook the knight's stirrups with his own; he grabbed his opponent's chain mail by the collar, threw him from his horse and knocked him against the ground. The turban fell from his head and revealed locks of hair, black as the night. It was a woman!

"Who are you, you motherless creature?" he exclaimed.

"I am the one who came to you in the tent," she said, "and the one who stole from you the girl al-Suwaydiyyah ibnat ʿĀmir, who is now in my palace. I am the one called Sayf al-Aʿlām. Now let me go. As you'll see, God has given you riches you will not believe."

And here the dawn reached Shahrazād so she ceased to speak.

Fihrās the Philosopher spoke:
She said, Master, Ẓāfir stood up and let her go, even though he had meant to kill her. She rode off on her horse, with Ẓāfir alongside her, until they reached a mighty, towering mountain with a cave in the middle. They entered the cave and turned a corner. Farther and farther underground they went, until they emerged at a pool of

water where there was a number of skiffs. They embarked and the woman rowed until they arrived at the gate of a great palace.

5.26   He turned to her and asked, "Now, what is your real name?"

"My name," she said, "is Shams al-Ḍiyā'[39] daughter of Khaḍḍāb al-Dimā', and this palace is known as the Palace of Lights, because a spell protects it for forty miles in all directions. It is made from crystals, and if you don't know this and look at it, you're incinerated as soon as the sun appears, because the crystals are so bright. It was built by the jinn for Ṣakhr ibn Iblīs the Elder."

She led the prince by the hand into the palace, to a grand salon with eighty marble pillars, furnished with silk and brocade. There she sat him on a bench and said to a slave girl, "Bring me al-Suwaydiyyah and the girls we took from the Valley of Barbarians."

They soon arrived in the finest clothes, looking most beautiful, and they greeted and welcomed the prince. He spent a number of days with them. He married the daughter of Khaḍḍāb al-Dimā', and stayed with her, eating and drinking, for a whole month.

Then she went to her father and killed him.

5.27   She made the prince ruler of the territory, and all the tribes submitted to him. He mustered a tremendous army the like of which had never been seen before.

He pitched tents for a great festival and slaughtered cattle and sheep, butchered camels, and poured wine. He went home and made peace with his brother, who upbraided him for leaving and told him that his mother, the one who had tried to get rid of Ẓāfir, had died.

He stayed with his brother for several days, then left and returned to his palace and his army and stayed with his slave girls.

He sent an envoy to the palace of al-Suwaydiyyah bint ʿĀmir to bring back all its treasures and made one of his soldiers governor of the region. And thus he continued, eating and drinking to his heart's content, until there came that from which there is no fleeing, and praise be to God, Lord of all being.

The Story of the Vizier and his Son

She continued: They say, Your Majesty, that when the Caliph Hārūn   6.1
al-Rashīd[40] arrested the Barmakids, there was one among them
who managed to flee: an elderly vizier named Muḥammad who had
a son named ʿAbdallāh.

The vizier and his son traveled to Basrah, where they boarded a
ship bound for India. The winds were blowing favorably when they
came upon an enormous black mountain rising up out of the sea.
Darkness was approaching, and they had run out of fresh water, so
they stopped at this mountain isle to replenish their supply. They
explored the island until nightfall, when they decided it was time to
return to the ship.

And here the dawn reached Shahrazād so she ceased to speak.

Fihrās the Philosopher spoke: 6.2
She said, Master, when darkness came they started to go back to the   *The*
ship, but as they were making their way they heard a great commo-   *Twenty-Fourth*
tion coming from the sea. A four-legged beast had thrust its head   *Night*
out of the sea. It reached into the ship and snatched a number of
crew. Cries and shouts of "God be glorified!" and "There is no God
but God!" rang out through the night, until they finally set sail from
the mountain.

Further out at sea, somewhere in the middle of the ocean, they
were hit by a fierce wind and the sea turned rough and heavy. The

ship was smashed to pieces, but the vizier's son survived by clinging to a plank. He was tossed and buffeted all night by the waves. By the time the blessed morning came, he had been washed up on the shore of a remote island in the middle of the ocean. He got up and went to look for something he could eat.

6.3 He found many trees and fruits on the island so he ate the fruit and drank the water. In the middle of the island, he also discovered a deep well, where he found some clothes, which he put on. He stayed on the island for the rest of the day.

When the blessed morning came and the sun rose in the sky, he looked out to sea and spotted a small boat with ten men onboard crashing through the waves toward the island. The vizier's son found a spot where he could watch the men without being seen. They brought a man, shackled hand and foot, out of the boat. They lay him on a board and raising it over their heads took him and dropped him into the well. Then they returned to their boat and sailed away.

6.4 The young man took some thin twigs from the branches of a tree, fashioned a stout rope, and lowered himself to the bottom of the well. There he found the old man, beseeching God for help.

"Excuse me," he asked, "are you still alive?"

"Of course I'm alive!" he said. "And now I'm blessed! Who are you?"

"I was shipwrecked and nearly perished," said the young man. "But I made it to this island. I saw what those people did to you, so I came down here to find you."

6.5 "My boy," said the old man, "get me out of here and I will get us off this island and make you a rich man."

So the youth untied the old man and helped him up out of the well. He brought him some of the fruit he had been eating and they survived like this for several days.

One day there were white birds all over the island. The old man turned to the youth.

"Good news!" he said. "Tomorrow morning, God willing, a large number of boats will arrive to take us away from this island. If God the Exalted, by His power and His strength, wills it."

And here the dawn reached Shahrazād so she ceased to speak.

Fihrās the Philosopher spoke:

She said, Master, the youth then inquired of the old man how he came to know this.

"I know this and more important things besides," he answered. "I read in a book how to interpret omens from watching birds. When I saw the island full of birds, I knew that it would soon be full of men."

And sure enough, when blessed morning came the island was surrounded by ships and boats and was soon full of men.

Onshore the men explored the island and met the old man and the vizier's son. They asked them what they were doing there. Their story filled the men with sympathy and they gave them both a berth onboard. After several days the winds blew favorably, and they set sail across the dark and distant sea for many days and nights until a great city, teeming with people, hove into view.

The old man and the youth disembarked on the coast, and the old man led the youth to an inn and took a room. Then he procured an inkwell and a piece of parchment, on which he wrote a letter and handed it to the youth.

"Take this letter to such-and-such a place," he told him. "And ask for So-and-So, and give it to him. If he asks you about me you can tell him what happened and let him know where I am."

The young man did as he was told straight away. He found the man in question and gave him the letter.

"Young man," the man said after reading it, "where is the man who wrote this letter?"

"He's here in the city. I can take you to him if you wish."

"Yes, please do so."

When the man saw the old man he threw his arms around him and they greeted each other warmly.

"Master," the man said, "I didn't think you were still alive—God be praised!"

6.9   He went away and returned with food and drink for the two of them, and they all ate together. They talked for a while, and then the old man made a request.

"I would like you to buy me a ship," he said.

"Very well," said the man and departed, leaving the vizier's son with the old man.

"Young man," said the old one, "go to the market and buy two raṭls of red brass. Bring them to me along with some coal."

6.10   He did as he was told, and the old man lit the coal under the brass until it glowed white. Then he took some dust and threw it onto the brass, where it transformed into pure gold.

At this point the man returned.

"Sir," he said, "The ship is ready, as you requested."

The old man gave him the gold. He took it to the market, and returned shortly with a large amount of money.

"Buy whatever provisions the ship will need," the old one instructed him.

So the man bought them a slave and a servant, and then he bade them farewell and went on his way.

"If you have the patience," the old man said to the vizier's son, "God will make you a very rich man."

6.11   They put out to sea, and when they were far from the city the old man turned to the youth.

"Son," he said, "do you know my story?"

"No, uncle," said the youth.

"I was once the king of that city, and you know what happened to me. That man was my closest confidant, but I am just an old man, as you can see. Old and weak. Now I would like to give you something in return for what you did for me."

And here the dawn reached Shahrazād so she ceased to speak.

She said, Master, they sailed far out to sea for twenty days and came across a huge statue rising up into the air.

The old man turned to the youth.

"Son," he said, "this is the first of the seven statues built by Dhū l-Qarnayn, eternal peace be his, when he entered the Sea of Darkness."[41]

On they went past statue after statue until they had sailed past all seven. The last was joined to a large island, where they disembarked and made their way to the seventh statue. As they approached, the figure seemed to stand up ready to throw its spear at them. The earth shook under their feet and they heard a great cry. The old man beat a retreat with the youth right behind him.

They decided to approach the idol from a different angle, where they found a small door. The old man opened it and pulled out three keys.

He took the youth by the hand and went back to the ship and told the crew not to leave until they returned. Then they explored the island. At midday, they came upon a towering palace built by Persian kings in days long past. The palace was encircled by a small river flowing fast, in a circle, turning like a millstone.[42] Six spears were planted in the middle.

The old man turned to the youth.

"How can we find a way into that palace?" he said. "There must be a trick."

They approached the water and heard a loud cry.

"What's that?" asked the young man. "It sounds like an eagle!"

"My boy," the old man replied, "at the palace gate stands a mechanical bird in the shape of an eagle, and when someone comes up to the gate, it cries out, just as you heard. That's why it's called the Palace of the Eagle."

The old man went up to the door where he dug a hole as deep as a man is tall. There he uncovered a marble tablet with a large bolt. He turned the bolt and it began to rotate.

"Look at the water!"[43] he called to the youth. "If you see anything happen, tell me!"

He turned the bolt until the water was calm and a brass bridge appeared, rising up above the water. When the youth saw this he called the old man, who stopped turning the bolt, and came to the bridge. He crossed it together with the youth.

As they approached the palace door, they saw these verses engraved in marble:

6.15
> Enter the palace at your own risk;
>> all who enter here are deluded.
> He whose time has come can do nothing
>> but entrusts himself to the One whose fear is mandated.

And here dawn overtook Shahrazād so she ceased to speak.

6.16 *Fihrās the Philosopher spoke:*

The Twenty-Seventh Night

She said, Master, the old man opened the door. With the youth right behind him, he made his way towards the center where they beheld an awesome, towering palace, built on a foundation of solid rock. Inside it housed baths and chambers and salons, domes and arches and hallways, gardens and pools above which mechanical figures and automata and lions spouted water from their mouths. There were raised sitting rooms with doors of red sandalwood covered in gold leaf, the furnishings were of silk brocade and the beds were covered in pillows and cushions of many colors to dazzle the eyes. It was a lesson for those who take heed; a warning to those who would be warned, for it was all covered over with the dust and sand that fate and time had brought.

6.17   The old man opened the door to one of the rooms and found the room full of gems and precious stones. There were also a number of beds, and there appeared to be people lying on them. If you saw them, you would swear they were alive.

In a second room a lion stood to the right of a bed of gold, studded with precious stones, a serpent to the left. On the bed lay a person whom you would have sworn was sleeping, but who in fact was not even alive.

At his head stood an emerald tablet with the following words written in gold:

"I am Thaʿlabah ibn ʿAbd Layl ibn Jurhum ibn ʿAbd Shams ibn Wāʾil ibn Ḥimyar ibn Yaʿmur ibn Qaḥṭān ibn Hūd,[44] eternal peace be his. I am five hundred years old. I planted trees and dug waterways, but was beguiled by this earthly abode, until my time was up, and the Mighty God passed His judgment on me. If you can understand, take heed! The one who sees my state will not be tempted by this world."

6.18

In yet another room, they saw a bed surrounded by hanging candles of gold and silver adorned with more stones. On the bed lay a person who appeared to be sleeping, but who in fact was not even alive. There was a stand in front of him with a book on it that he appeared to be reading. His eyes seemed fixed on the page. The figure wore a crown adorned with gems and precious stones. On his forehead shone a ruby so clear and bright and big that it illuminated the entire chamber.

The old man turned to the youth.

"Stay where you are," he said. "I am going to take his crown and that ruby that's on his head."

And here the dawn reached Shahrazād so she ceased to speak.

Fihrās the Philosopher spoke:

6.19

The Twenty-Eighth Night

She said, Master, five steps led up to the bed where the crown and the stone were. When the old man took the first step the figure in the bed sat up. At the second step the figure closed the book before him. At the third step he took a bow and held it out by his side. At the fourth step he took an arrow and drew the bow. When he was about to take the fifth step the figure began to tremble and his legs shook. When the old man retreated the movements slowed down. He tried the last step once again, but the figure in the bed stood up and fired an arrow at the old man, who dropped dead on the stairs.

6.20   When the vizier's son saw this he feared for his life and rushed to recover the old man's body, but then a lion pounced on it from underneath the bed and began to devour it. The youth shook with terror, fell to his knees, and lost consciousness.

When he came to, he got to his feet and began to recite the Qur'an and to glorify and praise God, proclaiming, "There is no god but He." While he was doing this he heard a voice reciting these verses:

> Were it not for your reciting the Qur'an,
> you'd never set foot on this land.
> The rebel jinn reign here, and
> dread of their arrows is ever at hand.
> I have some advice for you, which those
> whose time is not yet come need to understand.
> Take what has been provided, but do not return
> even if hope calls you back to make a further demand.

6.21   The sound of these words soothed his soul. He took back to the ship such jewels of the highest value as he could carry. He used the keys to open the doors of the sitting rooms, where he found treasures that beggared all belief. He took what he wanted back to the bridge and crossed it. He closed the palace doors and turned the bolt on the tablet. The bridge disappeared back under the water. He returned the keys to the statue and then set sail on his boat, back to Basrah across the dark and distant sea for many days.

He disembarked with his wealth and treasure, and used them to buy houses, estates, gardens, slave girls and horses. He sent his servants out across the seas to conduct trade on his behalf.

And so he remained, living a most comfortable life, until there came to him that from which there is no fleeing, and praise be to God, Lord of all being.

The Story of King Sulaymān ibn ʿAbd al-Malik

She continued: They say, Your Majesty, that when Sulaymān   7.1
reached the age of seven, he already spoke with wisdom, composed poetry, and knew all kinds of things. He learned the arts of
the horse and the fight and the raid in the dark of night, spearmanship and swordsmanship, and how to duel like a knight and warrior, until he was ready to hunt lions. He was a sign and a lesson
from God.

When he reached the age of sixteen, he was a man of great force
and strength, but he was also the most handsome and generous of
God's creatures. His father was overjoyed to behold him.

"My son," he said, "tell me what you wish for—anything—and I
will give it to you."

"Father," replied Sulaymān, "I would like you to build me a
palace with rivers running through it."

"And you shall have it," said his father.

He sent for his master builder, and then brought men from all the   7.2
cities and towns who built a palace the likes of which had not been
seen before. When it was complete, the father held a great festival
there and everyone, from both the city and the countryside, joined
the feast.

Sulaymān was sitting one day in the upper chamber of the palace looking down into the courtyard, marveling at the whiteness of the marble. Two ravens appeared. They fought one another and fell in the middle of the courtyard, and their blood flowed across the white marble floor. Sulaymān gazed at it.

"I wonder," he said to himself, "Did God ever create a girl with skin as white as this marble, with hair as black as those ravens and with cheeks as red as their blood on the marble floor?"

And here the dawn reached Shahrazād so she ceased to speak.

7.3

The Twenty-Ninth Night

Fihrās the Philosopher spoke:

She said, Master, Sulaymān ibn ʿAbd al-Malik summoned his companions and ministers and told them what was on his mind.

"If there's a girl like that anywhere," they told him, "Abū Ḥazm would know."

So Sulaymān sent for Abū Ḥazm and told him about the girl he was looking for.

"Your Majesty," said Abū Ḥazm, "I know of a girl like the one you describe—the most beautiful woman in the world. She's the daughter of a king, and kept out of sight—so she's out of reach. You have a better chance of flying up to heaven."

"And why is that?" asked Sulaymān.

7.4

"It's almost impossible to get to her," he said. "Her father rules over a great kingdom—he has a hundred thousand swordsmen at his beck and call. He has given his daughter control over her own affairs and she will only marry the man she desires or the man who defeats her in battle, and she is a fearsome opponent."

Sulaymān looked at him.

"Abū Ḥazm," he said, "Tell me, where can I find her, how can I meet her?"

"I think you should send her a gift. If she accepts it, there might be some hope."

"Whom should I send as messenger?" asked the prince.

"Send ʿAbdallāh ibn Baṭṭāl," said Abū Ḥazm. "He is brave, handsome, and eloquent."[45]

Sulaymān had fallen in love with the idea of this girl; not even the seven seas could put out the fire that burned in his heart. He summoned ʿAbdallāh ibn Baṭṭāl.   7.5

"I hear and obey only God before you, Master," said ʿAbdallāh.

Sulaymān ordered a steed of noble stock be brought for him, and then composed a letter to the girl's father, stating his wish to become his son-in-law. This he sent along with a gift of jewels, rubies, emeralds, and Indian herbs, and a thousand fine camels and a thousand Christian slaves clad in silk brocade, carrying lances and shields of antelope skin.

When the gifts were ready, Sulaymān went out with his companions and, giving ʿAbdallāh his orders, bade him farewell.

ʿAbdallāh traversed the earth far and wide until he arrived at the city of Namāriq. The inhabitants came out to meet him, and gave him a great reception.

"From where have you come and where are you headed?" they asked him.

"I have come to you as a messenger on behalf of the Commander   7.6
of the Faithful, ʿAbd al-Malik ibn Marwān and his son Sulaymān,"
he replied.

"Are you threatening me with this mention of ʿAbd al-Malik and his son?" asked King Namāriq.

"Your Majesty," said ʿAbdallāh, "my sole purpose is to ask your daughter's hand in marriage for the son of ʿAbd al-Malik."

"Is his son at all like you? I swear upon my honor that you'd already be dead were it not that kings do not like to kill messengers! Go back to your master and tell him that I am coming. Within the year he will see me with ten thousand horsemen on ten thousand bay horses, and ten thousand more horsemen on ten thousand piebald mounts and another ten thousand on black steeds and ten thousand more on roans. I will kill his father ʿAbd al-Malik and seize his land. I will raze Damascus so that future caravans will pass and say, 'On this spot there once stood a city called Damascus.'"

And here the dawn overtook Shahrazād so she ceased to speak.

Fihrās the Philosopher spoke:

She said, Master, and thus did the king give his response to 'Abd al-Malik's letter, having already taken the gifts. 'Abdallāh ibn Baṭṭāl went on his way.

When the princess heard news of the visit, she sent a thousand horsemen after 'Abdallāh, with orders to take him prisoner or to bring back his head. When 'Abdallāh noticed the horses on his trail, he had no doubt that they were going to attack him, so he turned off the road, and the horsemen could find neither hide nor hair of him. He made straight for Damascus.

Sulaymān was in the upper chamber of his palace when he looked out and caught sight of 'Abdallāh ibn Baṭṭāl heading towards the palace at great speed, screaming "Help, Your Majesty, help!"

7.8 Sulaymān ordered that he be brought inside, greeted him, and listened to what had happened. Sulaymān's father, 'Abd al-Malik was informed and he asked him, "What do you want to do, then?"

"I want to take the field against them," he said, "even if they are as numerous as Muḍar."

So his father put under his command forty thousand armored horsemen, brave men who had crossed deserts and desolate regions, and gave them weapons and money. His sons Sulaymān, al-Walīd, and Maslamah would lead them.

'Abd al-Malik bade his sons farewell and for three whole days they traveled far and wide, over barren sands and rolling lands, over valley and hill and dune and dell.

7.9 On the fourth day a female gazelle appeared in front of them and Sulaymān, keen to hunt, took off after it but could not catch it. Finally he gave up the hunt and returned to where his army had been, but found neither hide nor hair of them.

He was looking high and low when he espied something bright and shining in the distance. He headed towards it and saw that it was a green, shimmering river. Fragrant musk, or perhaps crushed ambergris, falling from the sky seemed to be wafting from its banks.

As Sulaymān contemplated the beauty of the valley that stretched in front of him, he was overcome by the midday heat, and he headed down to the river, which resembled a snake slithering out of its skin or a sword slipping out of its scabbard. A dense forest rose around him as he approached the river and he walked past tall trees where the birds sang and the waters were clear and calm.

He longed for the water. He dismounted and dived in, pouring the water all over himself. But something wasn't quite right. As he dressed and hopped back on his horse, he saw it: an enormous, terrifying lion, with murder in its paws and knife-like jaws, had come out of the wood towards him. Sulaymān couldn't control himself—he cried out. Enraged, the lion attacked, intent on devouring Sulaymān, but he dodged nimbly out of the way, then dealt the lion a blow that sliced it as neatly as a blade cuts the nib of a reed pen. 7.10

And here the dawn reached Shahrazād so she ceased to speak.

Fihrās the Philosopher spoke:

She said, Master, Sulaymān left the dead lion and went back up the valley, where he noticed a palace with a domed tent of red silk in front of it. At the entrance to the tent a sword hung and spears had been thrust into the ground. He made for it. 7.11 *The Thirty-First Night*

"I give you the greeting of peace, people of the tent," he called out in a loud voice.

No one answered. As he was waiting there, he heard a plaintive cry, so he dismounted and, with a hand on the hilt of his sword, he lifted one of the flaps and went inside.

In the middle of the tent there was a young woman of blinding beauty, like the full moon at night or a gazelle in flight. Closer inspection revealed she was hanging by her own hair.

"I give you the greeting of peace, young lady," he said. "I can't help noticing that you are hanging by your hair—Who has done this to you?"

7.12   "Oh you poor fellow," she said, "didn't you see the warning telling you to stay out of this valley? Did no one try to stop you? By God, you will be mourned by your mourners and your kin will weep and wail for you! Save yourself before you suffer the greatest calamity and disaster!"

"And who will make me suffer that?" asked Sulaymān.

"A warrior among warriors, invincible and solitary," she told him. "He is called Mudhill al-Aqrān,[46] and he has a black slave named Dawwās.[47] He's out hunting right now."

"And what is your name, young lady?" he said.

7.13   "My name is Laylā, daughter of Bāsiṭ al-Liwāʾ,[48] lord of the Fortress of al-Najm and the Valley of Rukbān. This warrior captured me when I was out with my slave girls and brought me here. He wanted to deflower me, but I refused, so he tied me up as you can see."

Sulaymān felt sympathy for her and untied her.

"One must fight fire with fire," he said.

While he was speaking he heard a great cry and, turning around, he saw a huge column of dust rising in the distance. An enormous black slave appeared from below the cloud. He was like a gigantic palm-tree or a mighty tree-trunk, with lips that drooped and eyes that glowed. He was leading a camel weighed down with prey from the hunt: rabbits, wolves, onagers, gazelles, and suchlike. For all his haste, the slave saw Sulaymān and the girl by the door of the tent. He dropped the camel's reins and grabbed the hilt of his sword. With a great cry that shook the earth, the slave went at Sulaymān, brandishing a hooked club in his hand. Sulaymān dodged and the blow missed its mark. They fought on for a good length of time.

7.14   During the battle, a horseman suddenly appeared from the wood, like a mighty mountain or a swollen sea. The sight of him threw Sulaymān into an uncontrollable rage. He attacked the slave with a blow that sliced him as neatly as a blade cuts the nib of a reed pen. The horseman screamed horribly at the sight of the dead slave. He charged with a thrust of his lance. Sulaymān clung to his horse, screamed and yelled, and moved left and moved right. For a long time they battled, but finally the prince hooked the warrior's stirrups and then attacked him with a blow that sliced him as neatly as a blade cuts the nib of a reed pen.

And here the dawn reached Shahrazād so she ceased to speak.

Fihrās the Philosopher spoke:

She said, Master, the prince dismounted, collected everything in the tent and loaded it onto the camel. Then he and the girl mounted his steed and rode far and wide until they came to a mountain fortress that loomed out of the dust and appeared to hang from the clouds. Built out of solid rock by the Amalekites, the Byzantines, and their generals, it had been untouched by time or calamity. Brass poles extended from it and a host of troops surrounded it.

The girl, with the prince hard behind, took a road as thin as a sandal strap or an ant track. As they approached the fortress, the girl's father, Bāsiṭ al-Liwāʾ, came out, dressed in the garb of mourning.

Sulaymān greeted him.

"Why are you dressed for mourning?" he asked.

"I had a daughter," he replied, "and she meant the world to me. But some nights ago she was taken away."

"Would you know her if you saw her?" asked Sulaymān.

"Sir Knight," said the father, "of course!"

Sulaymān pointed to the girl, who lifted the veil from her face. She threw herself into her father's arms and told him what had happened and how the prince had saved her.

The father turned to Sulaymān.

"And who would you be?" he asked.

"You don't know me?" said Sulaymān.

"No, I don't think so," said the father.

"I am Sulaymān ibn ʿAbd al-Malik ibn Marwān."

7.15

The Thirty-Second Night

7.16

7.17

"Quiet!" hissed the father. "Let people hear your name and you will die! What has brought you here?"

So Sulaymān recounted his story. "And by God I must find her, even if she's as high as the sun or as deep as the grave."

"Be patient," said the father. "I might have a way for you to get to her, God willing."

"How am I to reach her when her father has heard that I am coming with forty thousand horsemen?"

7.18 "I will take you to him," said the father, "and when he asks your name, tell him you are Asad ibn ʿĀmir."

"Very well," said Sulaymān. And he stayed that night as his guest.

In the morning the old man and Sulaymān rode out to the land of al-Azāriqah.[49] Fate delivers its decrees and the world keeps turning. Sulaymān saw a land unlike any other, a land beautiful and white, where fresh breezes wafted perfume on the air far and wide, where the beauty of the flowers would leave you tongue-tied. In the middle stood a city that spread from the upland to the plain. In front of the city stood a fortified palace, surrounded by an army that seemed to surge like the sea: all you could see were shining coats of mail and glittering helmets. They heaved and moved like the waves but among their number not a single soul would declare the unity and might of God.[50]

And here the dawn reached Shahrazād so she ceased to speak.

7.19 *Fihrās the Philosopher spoke:*

The
Thirty-Third
Night

She said, Master, the gate of the city opened when Sulaymān and the old man arrived and out strode five hundred slaves, all of them as big as mountains, with sunken eyes and protruding teeth, massive heads and black, scowling faces. Their mouths gaped wide like open wells, their teeth were sharp as knives and their arms like the masts of ships, their fingers curved like bull's horns. Their shoulders were raised, their ears large and cavernous, their jaws were like wineskins and their nostrils like bugles. They were terrifying to behold—just one look at them would cause souls to perish; their cries would stop the beating of hearts. At their head was a black slave, frightful as a jinni demon, who held a brass shield in one hand and a camel-driver's crooked rod on his shoulder. He had teeth made to shred and crush, a head like a shield, and a face like a whetstone. His cry was like the roar of thunder, his eyes like bolts of lightning. Behind this slave were ranged two hundred mounts, each ridden by a slave girl, surrounding a great elephant, carrying a seat on brass poles. On the seat was the girl Qamar al-Azhār,[51] surrounded on all sides by slave girls with long- and short-necked lutes and drums and flutes.

Sulayman was astonished at this spectacle and especially at the girl in the center, as beautiful as the full moon. The gate opened as they approached and Qamar al-Azhār entered with her slave girls close behind.

7.20

When she had gone into the palace, her father, King Namāriq, sent for Basiṭ al-Liwā', lord of the Fortress al-Najm. Bāsiṭ al-Liwā' led Sulaymān by the hand and together they appeared before the king and greeted him.

"What news do you have of Sulaymān ibn 'Abd al-Malik?" the king asked the old man.

"May God preserve you, Your Majesty, but this horseman here knows more than I do," he replied.

"And who might he be?" asked the king.

"He is my cousin by blood, and my equal in deed," said the old man.

"And his name?"

"Asad ibn 'Āmir."

"My good man," said the king, "have you news of 'Abd al-Malik ibn Marwān and his son Sulaymān?"

"Majesty, I can only tell you about Sulaymān. I left him in the valley of al-Zarʿ with a huge army. He was planning to attack you."

King Namāriq ordered that they be given food, drink, and shelter, but when they retired from the king, a warrior came up and seized Sulaymān.

7.21

"Do kings like to be lied to?" he demanded. "You are Sulaymān ibn 'Abd al-Malik ibn Marwān!"

Sulaymān was stupefied.

And here the dawn reached Shahrazād so she ceased to speak.

Fihrās the Philosopher spoke:

She said, Master, the warrior lifted his veil and—lo and behold!—it was 'Abdallāh ibn Baṭṭāl!

"Surprised?" he said. "Anyway, just go with the old man so that you can find out what this king is up to."

So Sulaymān and the old man were taken to a tent of silk, where a messenger from Qamar al-Azhār appeared before them.

"Where is your cousin?" he asked the old man, Bāsiṭ al-Liwāʾ.

"He's right here."

The messenger turned to Sulaymān. "The mistress would like you to come and speak to her."

"Very well," he said.

The old man turned to him.

"Yes, go with the messenger," urged the old man.

7.23   So off Sulaymān went. He was given an audience and greeted her, but she did not know that he was Sulaymān.

"Young man," she said, "What is your name?"

"My name is Asad ibn 'Āmir."

"Asad," she said, "have you seen Sulaymān?"

"Yes, I have seen him."

"Describe him to me, so that I can picture him in my mind."

Sulaymān described him and added, "He looks a lot like me."

She ordered that food and drink be brought, and she addressed him again when he had eaten.

"Go and get some rest," she said, "and come back to me tomorrow, God willing."

7.24   He returned to the old man's tent and spent the night there.

When the blessed morning came, she sent for him again.

"Tell me more about Sulaymān," she said.

So he described him and added, "There is no greater horseman alive today."

"Is that a threat?" she asked. "Because I swear upon my honor that I will give him a fight that will turn the hair of a newborn babe white and shock the fiercest warrior."

She ordered food and drink, and he ate and drank while she remained behind the curtain.

Then they both heard great cries that shook the earth.   7.25

"What's going on?" she exclaimed.

A slave girl rushed in shouting, "Help! Help! O my mistress, the soldiers of Sulaymān have us surrounded!"

The woman turned to Sulaymān.

"Asad," she said, "be patient and you will see what can be born of women." Then he departed.

When the blessed morning came, the girl ascended to the upper chamber of the palace. She looked out and saw a sea of bright banners, fluttering flags and turbans and crowns of every hue. She saw horses on all sides: the greys were dressed in the glory of the morning; the jet-black steeds wore darkness like a cloak; the bays were like fire-scorched chemises; the steeds with forelocks and tails tipped with white shone brightly like the sun; the piebalds were a mixture of day and night, the roans mixed their wine with fire.[52] The earth seemed to quake beneath them.

Upon arrival, they pitched their tents and the huge army surged   7.26
like surging swollen sea. The girl was astonished.

Everyone spent the night on guard.

And here the dawn reached Shahrazād so she ceased to speak.

Fihrās the Philosopher spoke: 7.27

She said, Master, Sulaymān stepped out of the old man's tent and   *The*
went to inspect his army. The guards swooped on him, but then   *Thirty-Fifth*
they quickly realized who he was and kissed the ground before   *Night*
him. His brothers and companions gathered round. He put Jābir ibn
'Āmir in charge of the army and chose him to go into battle with the
princess. Then he returned and spent the night in the tent of Bāsiṭ
al-Liwā'.

7.28   When the blessed morning came, the battle lines formed and the mangonels and catapults were set up. Bows were strung and arrows distributed. The men donned their armor and their helmets. They girded themselves with swords of Indian steel and shields of antelope skin and wore chain mail like that of King David. Then they mounted Arabian horses. The land seemed to swell with waves of people.

King Namāriq organized his troops and his companions and they prepared for battle.

In the middle of all this activity, the palace doors opened and the princess rode out, armed to the teeth, on a long-necked, piebald mare that trampled everything in her path. The people said of this horse: "Guide the mare and she goes lightly; let her loose, she flies like lightning." No one would be able to overtake her.

The princess wore a coat of Davidian mail, and had an ancient helmet[53] of brilliant gold on her head; she wore three turbans and had a sword of Indian steel, with a ten cubit spear in her hand. She rode into the center of the battlefield and called out: "So where is your leader? Where is Sulaymān ibn ʿAbd al-Malik?"

7.29   Scarcely had she finished speaking when Jābir ibn ʿĀmir came out to face her. She went at him with a ferocity that would turn black hair white. He turned and fled from her, but she kept after him, striking his head with her spear until she had forced him off the battlefield. Then, weak and tired, she returned to the palace.

When Sulaymān appeared before her, she said, "What do you think, Asad? What do you make of this courageous Sulaymān you told me about? I gave him a fight that turned his hair white."

"Not so fast," said Sulaymān. "That wasn't Sulaymān, that was just one of his men. If you were to face him, you'd think you'd suffered the greatest calamity and disaster ever to befall you."

7.30   She stood up and sat down again in agitation. "Is that a threat? Because I swear upon my honor that I would deal with you right now were you not a guest of our cousin Bāsiṭ al-Liwāʾ!"

Then she sent him away and remained in her palace, infuriated but unaware that Asad was in fact Sulaymān. The next morning . . . .

And here the dawn overtook Shahrazād so she ceased to speak.

Fihrās the Philosopher spoke:
She said, Master, Sulaymān returned to the old man's tent.

"I will fight her tomorrow, God willing."

"Do as you will," replied the old man.

He rejoined his army and spent the night with his brothers. When the blessed morning came, he donned his armor and covered his face, took up his weapons and mounted his steed. He rode onto the battlefield between the two lines and moved between the two sides. He was dressed in the same clothes as Jābir.

Finally the palace gate opened and the princess emerged, armed to the teeth and riding a jet-black mare that moved faster than birds can fly and swifter than ostriches can run. She rode onto the battlefield and called out, "Where is Sulaymān ibn 'Abd al-Malik?"

Scarcely had she finished speaking when Sulaymān advanced and gave her a fight the likes of which no one had ever seen. The princess realized that she was powerless against him so turned and retreated in defeat, but he kept at her, striking her head with his spear until her helmet came off and he struck a blow to her skull. Amid the chaos of dust flying and people screaming, her father's horsemen made to attack, but she waved them off.

"Stay where you are," she commanded.

Sulaymān returned to his army and the princess to the palace. He changed back into his own clothes and was on his way to the old man's tent when a messenger appeared and asked the old man, "Where is Asad ibn 'Āmir? The princess wants to see him."

So Sulaymān accompanied the messenger to the palace. He and the princess greeted each other, and she spoke.

"Asad," she said, "I know that you are well informed about Sulaymān: he did something terrible to me today. He would have killed me if I hadn't fled."

"Didn't I tell you that the one you fought yesterday was not Sulaymān? That it was just one of his men?"

At this the princess emerged from behind the curtain.

"Sulaymān," she said, "do you think you can fool me, pretending that your name is Asad?"

He wanted to get up and leave, but she gave a cry and forty armed guards rushed in, ready to chop his head off. The princess gave another cry and they put down their swords and lifted their face-coverings to reveal forty young women, each as beautiful as the full moon.

7.34   The princess turned to Sulaymān.

"Surprised?" she said. "I knew as soon as I laid eyes on you that you were Sulaymān. But treachery is not a quality of kings. I hereby announce that tomorrow morning there will be a battle that will melt iron and send shivers down the spine of even the hardiest warrior."

She called for food and drink and they ate and drank. Then she addressed him with words softer than butter.

"Sulaymān," she said sweetly, "give me your hand. There is no disbelief after belief: I bear witness that there is no god but God, and Muḥammad is the messenger of God." And so she became a Muslim.

And here the dawn reached Shahrazād so she ceased to speak.

7.35   *Fihrās the Philosopher spoke:*

The Thirty-Seventh Night   She said, Master, then the princess said to Sulaymān: "O Commander of the Faithful,[54] I want to ask you about what prevents a man from listening to his heart. Will you not recite a song for me?"

"Yes, of course," said Sulaymān. And he recited:

> He weeps tears and blood out of longing,
>   he's so lovesick, he cannot taste sleep,
> The most debased of lovers—
>   witness his sighs, long, and his moans, deep.
> Be merciful to your supplicant and
>   before it's too late, intercede and his trysts keep.

Then the princess took the lute and tuned it and began to sing with pure heart and eloquent tongue:

God knows, and the stars attest,
My love denies me sleep and rest.
Both moon and stars by your beauty surpassed,
you're all that's truly the best.

Then the princess sent him away until the next day.   7.36

Back in the tent, the old man saw that Sulaymān was completely drunk.

"Sulaymān," he cried, "What's going on?"

He told him all that had happened between him and the princess, and spent the rest of the night there.

When the blessed morning came, he rose and donned his armor and covered his face. Mounted on his steed, he rode out to his troops and onto the battlefield. Then the palace gate opened and the princess rode out on a steed of noble stock. She wore three turbans of different colors wrapped round her head and a belt of snakeskin round her waist. In her hand was a beechwood spear. She advanced onto the battlefield.

"So where is your leader, Sulaymān ibn ʿAbd al-Malik?" she called.

Scarcely had she uttered these words, when Sulaymān rushed   7.37
forth with a great cry, and the two of them gave battle. The battle went on, but eventually Sulaymān hooked his stirrups on hers, grabbed her by the arm, and unseated her from the saddle. Then he put her back on the saddle again.

In the midst of this, there arose a great cry over the land far and wide, so loud that people thought that the earth was shaking, the mountains crumbling, and the trees toppling. Then there appeared a spearhead, like a lamp, or a young crocodile ready to snatch men's souls, and a horseman swooped down on the princess and snatched her away, carrying her out into the open country.

7.38   When the people saw this, all hell broke loose. Sulaymān took
off after the horseman. When Sulaymān had caught up with him,
the horseman uncovered his face. It was his father, ʿAbd al-Malik
ibn Marwān! He was overjoyed, and each was delighted to see the
other.

The two of them approached the army and gave the girl back her
horse and sent her back to her palace. Then the troops of ʿAbd al-
Malik arrived and filled the land far and wide.

The girl, sent back to her father's palace, asked him, "Father, can
you fight against the rising tide?"

7.39   "What are you getting at?" he replied.

"Make peace with them," she said, "and marry me to Sulaymān,
because he is a fearless king who commands respect."

"Is your mind made up?" her father asked.

"Yes, for I vowed to marry only the man who could defeat me on
the battlefield, and that is Sulaymān."

"Then I will do what you ask," said the king.

In the morning gifts were brought from all over to the encampment of ʿAbd al-Malik ibn Marwān.

And here the dawn reached Shahrazād so she ceased to speak.

7.40   *Fihrās the Philosopher spoke:*

The   She said, Master, then King Namāriq, father of the girl, appeared in
Thirty-Eighth   his finest garments, preceded by slaves dressed in tight caftans with
Night   gilded belts around their waists, and spears and shields of antelope
skin in their hands.

The princess sent for Sulaymān and his father ʿAbd al-Malik ibn
Marwān and they met with her father. They greeted each other, and
King Namāriq accepted Islam and held a great celebration. Cattle
and sheep were slaughtered and the wine flowed freely; there
was music from lutes, short-necked and long, from timpani and
drums, and delightful distractions and diversions were to be had
everywhere.

Sulaymān married the princess. She was a great beauty, like the finest, smooth cotton. Her pupils played coquettish games, and the full moon wandered bewildered above her necklaces.

She stayed with him, eating, and drinking, for thirty days. Then   7.41
Sulaymān the son of ʿAbd al-Malik departed for Damascus where he held a great reception attended by all and remained there with the princess, eating and drinking to his heart's content, until there came to them that from which there is no fleeing, and praise be to God, Lord of all being.

Dīnārzād spoke: "Shahrazād, my sister, won't you tell His Majesty another one of your excellent stories?"

"Very well," she said.

The Story of Maslamah ibn ʿAbd al-Malik ibn Marwān (God Show Them Mercy)

8.1 They claim, my King, that Maslamah went out hunting one day with a group of his companions. Somewhere outside Damascus, they spotted a group of gazelles and Maslamah went after one. The chase was long and exhausting, and when it was time to return to his companions, he could find no trace of them. Darkness fell, and he spent the night in the desert.

8.2 When the blessed morning came, he mounted his horse and began to roam the open country as ostriches do, and came to a hill. Up he climbed, and, stretched out before him, he saw a valley full of fruits and trees. The heat of the sun had become unbearable so he headed for it. He dismounted in the valley, and took shelter in the trees.

Something caught his attention. He looked round and saw a girl, the most beautiful of God's creatures, dressed in long-sleeved robes of silk brocade and carrying a bamboo basket, picking blossoms from the trees. When he espied her, he tethered his horse and crept towards her, stealthily, like a shadow. He grabbed her and put his sword to her throat.

"Who are you, girl?"

8.3 It turned out she was a Byzantine. She said to him, "Listen, let me go, and I'll lead you to the most beautiful girl in all of Christendom. Her name is Maria and she's the daughter of ʿAbd al-Masīḥ, who rules one of the Byzantine cities. Her cousin wanted to have her, so her father sent her to live with one of the monks. His name is San'ān."

And here the dawn reached Shahrazād so she ceased to speak.

Fihrās the Philosopher spoke:

She said, Master, Maslamah got on his horse and traveled with her until he found his companions. They rejoiced that he was safe, but he said to them:

"Don't get settled! We are going with this girl!"

So off they went to the monastery, attacked it, and entered by force. Inside they discovered twenty girls, including Maria. They killed the monks and returned to their homes.

Maslamah took Maria back to his palace. He entrusted her to his mother, and she stayed with her for three months.[55] Then he wanted to have her, so she was brought to him in a wedding procession, dressed in the finest raiment, surrounded by slave girls with lutes, short- and long-necked, timpani and drums.

On the way, they heard a great cry. A man in full armor, armed to the teeth, unsheathed sword in hand had attacked them. He grabbed Maria and the slave girls fled, leaving her to him.

When Maslamah heard this he clutched the hilt of his sword and went out to the courtyard where he came upon a Christian youth; he and the girl were holding on to each other's hands tightly.

When the youth saw Maslamah, he let go of his sword.

"And who might you be?" asked Maslamah.

"This girl is my cousin," the youth replied, "and I was married to her. When her father heard that she'd been abducted, he sent a message to me, saying, 'The Muslims have taken your cousin— she is with Maslamah. Bring her to me or die trying to save her.'[56] So here I am. Kill me or pardon me, do as you wish. I am your prisoner."

"Girl, is this your cousin?" Maslamah asked her.

She said, "Yes, he is."

So Maslamah granted her to him. He gave him a steed of noble stock and gave the girl a horse as well, along with clothes and money, slave girls and servants, and he sent escorts to accompany them back to their country.

8.7 The Christian took the girl to bed,[57] and she made a vow that whether she gave birth to a girl or a boy she would give it to Maslamah.

One day about seven years later, Maslamah and his companions were in the countryside and stopped for a rest. Maslamah went to relieve himself, but by the time he returned his companions had gone and he could find neither hide nor hair of them. He traveled on, not knowing where he was going, and came to a great mountain, at the foot of which lay a pleasant meadow with fruit trees and running springs. He could not see anyone there so he got down from his horse, drank from the spring and then fell asleep.

8.8 He awoke to find spears pointed at his chest. A thousand armored Christians had surrounded him. They said:

"Where are you from?"

"From Damascus."

"Have you any news of Maslamah ibn ʿAbd al-Malik?"

"When I left him he had marched from Syria against the Christians."

8.9 They seized him, bound him, and took him to the land of Byzantium, where they brought him before their queen. Lo and behold, it was the same young woman! Her father had died and she succeeded him. She had given all her men and her warriors the order that if they took Maslamah prisoner they should bring him to her.

And here the dawn reached Shahrazād so she ceased to speak.

8.10 *Fihrās the Philosopher spoke:*

The Fortieth Night

She said, Master, the woman recognized Maslamah the moment she saw him. She sent the others away and disappeared for a while, before returning with an old woman. She asked her:

"Is he the one, is he the Maslamah who treated me as you described?"

Then she released him, gave him a cloak, kissed his forehead and sent him to the official guest quarters. Her husband was out hunting, so Maslamah enjoyed her hospitality until he returned. When he got back she told him the news, and he went in to see Maslamah and kissed his forehead. Maslamah then remained with him for a full month, eating and drinking.

8.11

Then one day the young woman brought him a girl who was among the most beautiful of God's creations.

"Your Majesty," she said, "This is my daughter, and she is now your servant. I made a vow on the day you acted with such kindness—that whether I bore a girl or a boy I would give it to you. God has blessed me with this girl, so take her as a gift from me to you."

Maslamah accepted the girl, along with the queen's gift of two hundred Christian slave girls, many rare treasures and exquisite garments. The queen also gave him a steed of noble stock and sent her warriors to escort him back to his country. Back in Damascus, he took the girl to bed and remained with her, eating and drinking to his heart's content, until there came that from which there is no fleeing, and praise be to God, Lord of all being.

8.12

The Story of Gharībat al-Ḥusn
and the Young Egyptian

9.1   They say, Your Highness, that there once was a handsome young man who lived in the city of Cairo.[58] This young man was very fond of reading and, one day, while he was sitting by the door of his house reading from a book, a young woman passed by. She was as beautiful as the full moon at night or a gazelle in flight. She raised her veil and said to him, "Young man, are you the one who has vowed to avoid women?"

9.2   He looked up, and the sight of her made him buckle and swoon. The woman continued on her way. The young man got straight to his feet and followed her until she entered a house and closed the door.

The youth was in a state of bewilderment; not even the seven seas could put out the fire that burned in his heart. He returned home, reciting these verses:

> Like the moon among the stars she walks,
> > with the stars of Orion plaiting her locks.
> She is watered by the eastern breeze,
> > and sways like lissome branches in the trees.
> She smiles, and her perfect red lips show
> > where the white and the yellow of the chamomile grow

She handles my yearning heart like a toy,
  like a bird in the hands of a playful boy.

And here dawn reached Shahrazād so she ceased to speak.

Fihrās the Philosopher spoke:

She said, Master, when the youth finished his recital, he fainted and fell to the ground in front of his house. A servant came out and brought him inside. His father, meanwhile, was at the market, and heard the cries.

"What's going on?" he asked.

"It's your son," they told him. "He's gone mad."

Now this merchant was a wealthy man, but there was no one on earth dearer to him than his son. He left immediately and brought his son electuaries and potions. The name of the son, by the way, was ʿAbdallāh ibn Muḥammad al-Miṣrī.

"My son," said the father, "What is the matter? May God bring our hearts together."

"I am dying," said the youth, "there can be no doubt."

His father did not leave his side, caring for him until he might once again open his eyes. Many days passed without the young man eating or drinking at all. So his father summoned a wise physician who was well acquainted with all maladies and medicines.

The doctor examined him and turned to his father.

"Abū ʿAbdallāh," said the doctor, "your son is in love, drowning in the sea of passion. His liver is weak—I can tell from his urine. You must look after him, before he perishes."

When the doctor left, the merchant turned to his son. "My son, tell me whom you have fallen in love with, for I swear by the Lord, «the One who brings forth life»,[59] if I have to spend all of my wealth to make you happy, I will do so."

So he told his father what had happened with the girl.

The father asked around and made inquiries and eventually found out who she was. He asked for her hand on behalf of his son.

The girl's father was not wealthy, so he consented graciously, but also said, "Listen, I have vowed that I will not celebrate this occasion with a feast, so just send a mule and a servant for her tonight."

"Very well," the young man's father agreed.

Then the girl's father began to get his daughter ready and the young man's father paid her bride price. The young man's father went back home and his son awoke from his stupor at the news.

9.6   At the agreed time, the young man's father sent a mule, a servant,[60] and some clothing to the girl's father. The girl's name, by the way, was Gharībat al-Ḥusn.[61] The servant was about to leave, but realized she had left something behind, so she went back inside, and left the girl at the door.

Now, the Master of the Unknown does as He wills. The ruler of Cairo and Alexandria happened to have sent to the Caliph al-Muʿtaṣim one hundred slave girls mounted on one hundred mules. They happened to pass by the young woman just as she was waiting on her mount by the door. She was caught up in the group as it passed and joined them with no idea where she was going.

When the servant came back out, she found no one there. There was neither hide nor hair of the bride! The servant fled in panic and nobody knows where she went.

9.7   Some time later, the servant had still not returned, so the young man went out to look for the girl, but in vain. She was gone again. Once more he fell into a swoon and tore his clothing. His soul was crushed.

Meanwhile in Baghdad, the slave girls were brought before al-Muʿtaṣim. He counted them and realized there was one extra. He made inquiries about her and she told him her story. Full of sympathy at her plight, he ordered that she be taken to his sister's palace.

"Take this girl and keep her with you," he told his sister. "If someone comes looking for her, give her back to him, if Almighty God wills it."

And here the dawn reached Shahrazād so she ceased to speak.

She said, Master, al-Muʿtaṣim's sister installed her in one of her apartments. Meanwhile the young man, her would-be husband, went days without eating or drinking. Then one day a group of merchants arrived; he asked them for news of his bride, and they told him about her. He repeated the news to his father.

"Father," he said, "This grief has gone on too long."

The father got his son ready for the journey, and the young man left, traveling far and wide, high and low. He entered Baghdad and settled in its best merchant inn where he rested and recovered.

9.9

Then he went out into the city, seeking news of her, until he came to the perfumers' market. He made inquiries and was told that the page boys from the palace came here frequently to buy perfume and camphor.

So the young man opened a shop and stocked it with perfumes, and then he sat there buying and selling. His charm and generosity meant that people began to frequent his shop. The palace servants heard of this and they would come to him each day, when he would lower prices of goods for them and give them what they wanted at no cost. When he got to know the servant in charge, he plied him with gifts.

9.10

"Listen, young man," the chief servant would say, "just let me know if there is anything I can do for you."

One day the youth said, "Actually there is something you can do. It would mean everything to me, and it would not be too difficult for you."

"Tell me, what is it?" he asked.

He told him his story, and his friend promised to bring him and the girl together.

One morning several days later, the friend came to the young man, who had passed a restless night, lost in his thoughts.

9.11

"Get up—and get yourself ready."

He gave him some women's clothing to put on, then placed various kinds of merchandise on a bamboo tray. He lifted it onto his head and went to the door of the palace. He got the youth, disguised as a girl, permission to enter, and sent him in via one of the palace porticoes.

"Now," said the friend, "head for the middle apartment—that's where you'll find your girl."

9.12   "May you be blessed for what you've done for me," said the young man, and then he was left alone. He forgot all about the chamber and had no idea where to go. As he stood there he heard a voice recite these verses:

> A torrent of tears that drenches the lover
>> is sole witness to what is in my heart
> My heart's delight now keeps me awake,
>> passion my only ally against fate's bitter smart.

The young man followed the voice into a room, but it was not the one his friend had told him to enter. Inside he saw slave girls as beautiful as gazelles, in the company of the sister of al-Muʿtaṣim.

And here the dawn reached Shahrazād so she ceased to speak.

9.13   *Fihrās the Philosopher spoke:*

She said, Master, when the young man entered the room, al-Muʿtaṣim's sister saw him, and said to her girls, "Who is this man who shows himself to us?"

9.14   The young man froze, speechless. The woman noticed his beauty and his good looks, and something struck her heart, like a cool draught in a parched throat. She ordered the slave girls to bring him near.

"Who are you, young man, and what is your story?"

"My story," he replied, "is such-and-such."

So the woman, the sister of al-Muʿtaṣim, whose name was Rīm al-Quṣūr,[62] ordered Gharībat al-Ḥusn to be brought. When she saw Muḥammad the Egyptian in the room she threw herself into his arms and kissed his forehead.

The sister of the king invited them to eat and drink, and the wine cups made the rounds until their souls were at ease, their cheeks were flush and their minds were calmed.

Then the girl burst into verse:

> This is the spring, these are its flowers,
>> the trees are in full bloom, with blossoms entwined.
> So drink to the memory of the beloved, and sing,
>> for he is gone, and this is all he's left behind.

When she had finished, the young Cairene took up the lute and tuned it, then began to recite:

> My regard for the beloved is gentle,
>> but the burden of separation is great.
> I can't express the iniquity I suffer,
>> but God knows I'm treated with an unjust fate.
> I had said prayers of mercy for those tortured by love,
>> till I was afflicted, now it is I who for prayers of mercy must
>> wait.

When he had finished reciting, he and the girl continued drinking till nightfall. Drunkenness got the better of them, and the young Cairene went to bed with Gharībat al-Ḥusn and Rīm al-Quṣūr, the sister of al-Muʿtaṣim, all of them having had their fill of wine.

As fate would have it, that night it occurred to the Caliph al-Muʿtaṣim to visit his sister, for he had not seen her for some time. When night had fallen, he put one hand on the hilt of his sword and picked up a candle with the other. Without informing anyone in the palace, he went to her chamber and found the door open, which was unusual.

"She must be asleep," he said to himself. He entered and found
the slave girls sleeping and the candles in place. Now al-Muʿtaṣim was also feeling the influence of some wine, so he felt drowsy and went to the bed and pulled back the curtain. He saw three people

sleeping under a single sheet, with drops of sweat running down their faces like pearls on pomegranate flowers. As the poet said:

Two lovers—why does this bounty
    the harmony of their beauty increase?
When the day is drunk, so it is said,
    they hold their breath and from life cease,
Until they meet under cover of night
    when the lover's arrival is celebrated, and they embrace in
        peace.[63]

At first, al-Muʿtaṣim thought they must be slave girls, so he pulled the sheet away and saw the young man from Cairo in the middle. He put his hand on the hilt of his sword and was about to kill the young man. But then he stopped himself, and went to his mother's apartment. He woke her up by putting his hand around her throat.

"Were it not for God's command to honor one's parents,[64] I would kill you first by God!" he said.

9.17   "My son," she said, "what is the matter?"

"Get up and see for yourself what's happened to us."

He told her what had happened and she went with him to the chamber. She saw the two women with the young man between them. She woke them all up and said to the youth, "What has made you do this?"

"My story is a strange and wondrous one," he replied.

"Never mind about that," interrupted al-Muʿtaṣim, "because by God you are not going to live another day. But tell me what you are doing here."

So the youth told him his story, and when al-Muʿtaṣim's mother heard it she felt sorry for him.

"My son," she said to al-Muʿtaṣim, "do not be hasty. God does not act in haste."

"So what should I do?" he asked his mother.

"I think you should give each of them some money and send them back safely to their homeland."

And here the dawn reached Shahrazād so she ceased to speak.

Fihrās the Philosopher spoke:

She said, Master, al-Muʿtaṣim ordered that they be given money and a mount each, and sent with them an escort to take them all the way home.

They traveled back to Cairo, and inside the city the young man greeted his father and also married the sister of al-Muʿtaṣim. He held a great banquet and remained with the two women in the sweetest and most comfortable life until there came to them that from which there is no fleeing, and praise be to God, Lord of all being.

The Story of the Young Egyptian and his Wife

10.1   She said: They say, Your Majesty, that there once was a very hand-some, very wealthy young man from a good family who loved the refined company of literate people and who gave shelter to the weak and the poor.[65] At his salon he was generous to all. His father had left him his wealth, and he had married his cousin. He built a house in the city of Cairo on the bank of the Nile—no other house overlooking the river was as tall as his. It offered views of all the land. He loved his wife very much, and God had blessed them with a son.

10.2   Now the young man was friends with a nobleman, who paid him a visit at his shop one day and offered him an Iraqi apple.

He refused to take it, and said "This is the kind of apple only lovers keep!" and he went on with his business of buying and selling. A servant, meanwhile, had brought the young man's four-year old son to see him, and the nobleman gave the apple to the boy without the father's knowledge. The boy accepted the apple and put it in his pocket. Then the servant took him back to their house where the boy played with the apple for a little while, then gave it to his mother, who took it and placed it under her pillow.

10.3   The merchant returned home at night and got into bed to sleep. He felt a lump under his head, so he lifted the pillow and found the apple. He took it and said to himself, "This is the apple that my friend offered to me, the apple I didn't accept. Oh, no! He's been with my wife! It is as the poet says,

> Many an apple I've wanted to eat,
>> the knife ready to cut it into strips,
> Then I've compared it to my beloved's cheek
>> and gave it to her freely, taking a tithe of kisses from her lips

"I swear, she won't live another day!"
And here the dawn reached Shahrazād so she ceased to speak.

Fihrās the Philosopher spoke:

She said, Master, the merchant took the apple, hid it, and called his wife.

"I feel anxious. I'd like you to make me a bed in the upper storey, so I can look out on the Nile. Maybe that will help me relax."

She rose and went to prepare the bed, with no inkling of what was going on—the One who knows the unknown will do as He will. They went to the upper storey, where the young man opened the window.

"Put your head out and take a look," he said to his wife.

When she had her head out the window, he picked her up by the legs and threw her into the Nile.[66]

As fate would have it, however, there happened to be a fisherman below the window. When the woman fell into the water—and this was in the black of night—he noticed something splashing around in the water. He hauled the woman on board his boat and took her to his home.

The fisherman lived on the banks of the Nile twelve miles distant from the city, but he used to visit that spot regularly because there were so many fish there.

The next morning, the young man came down from the upper storey into the main part of the house where he found his son crying.

"Why are you crying?" he asked.

"I gave my mother an apple," said the boy, "it was given to me by Uncle So-and-So at your shop, and now I don't know where she hid it."

10.6   The young man was full of regret at what he had done, but regret was of little use. He did not tell his son or his wife's family what had happened.

One day, he was sitting in his shop reflecting on these matters, when he saw one of the hawkers holding his wife's dress in his hands.

He took it from him and said, "Take me to the owner of this dress."

The hawker took him to the fisherman.

"How did you get this dress?" the young man demanded.

"It's mine," said the fisherman.

"Tell me the truth," said the young man, "and I'll give you the dress and what it's worth."

10.7   So the fisherman told him his story from beginning to end, and the young man looked after him as his guest for three days. Then he took his cloak and his mule and went with the fisherman to his village. The fisherman ushered him into his house where he saw his wife. He threw himself into her arms and confessed what had happened.

"I only did what I did out of jealousy," he told her.

"Cousin," she replied, "may God forgive all that has passed."

The young man spent the night as the guest of the fisherman.

10.8   Just before dawn, he turned to the fisherman and said, "I would like to go now."

"If you insist," said the fisherman. "Now is the best time, because during the day Bedouins waylay people on the road."

"May God bless you for this," said the young man.

And here the dawn reached Shahrazād so she ceased to speak.

10.9   *Fihrās the Philosopher spoke:*

She said, Master, the young man rode his steed, with the woman mounted behind him. When they were about two miles from the village, thieves attacked them and ran off with the woman while he lay unconscious on the ground. One of them also took an Iraqi kerchief that he had wrapped around his head. They took the girl and the spoils and left him there.

When the young man came to, he shook the dust from his head and returned home. He told no one what had happened.

He returned to his shop and carried on buying and selling, all the while worrying about the fate of his wife. One day as he was sitting in his shop, he saw his kerchief in the hawker's hand. 10.10

"Where did you get that kerchief?" he asked. "Who gave it to you?"

"A Bedouin gave it to me," said the hawker.

"Bring him to me this instant!"

He greeted the Bedouin and addressed him. "Listen, brother of the Arabs, do you know me?" 10.11

"No," he said, "at least I don't think so."

"I am So-and-So."

"And who is So-and-So?"

"The one you deposited 3,000 dinars with." (This was a ruse on the young man's part.)

Then the Bedouin said, "Ah yes, that's right, so you are."

Then the merchant said to him, "Listen, brother of the Arabs, where did you get that kerchief?" 10.12

"By God," said the Bedouin, "that was all I got for my share."

"How is that?" asked the merchant.

"One day I joined my brothers on the highway to rob and hunt and we came upon a city type with a woman, so we killed him and took her, and drew lots for the woman and her clothes. I drew the kerchief."

The young man addressed the Bedouin and said, "Come with me so I can give you your money."

"May God bless you for this," said the Bedouin.

The young man took him home, and led him to a room in the depths of the house. 10.13

"Go on in," he said.

The young man's plan fell into place. As the Bedouin entered the room, he rushed at him with a lance, saying, "I swear by the Lord, «Splitter of the morning sky»,[67] that if you don't write to your brothers telling them to bring me the woman . . ." and he made as if to kill him.

10.14 "Wait!" the Bedouin said. "Bring me ink and paper."

The young man brought ink and paper and his captive wrote a letter to his brothers saying he was being held ransom for the woman. "When you receive this letter, send her right away to Cairo to the house of So-and-So."

And here the dawn reached Shahrazād so she ceased to speak.

10.15 *Fihrās the Philosopher spoke:*

The Forty-Seventh Night

She said, Master, he handed the letter to the young man and described where his brothers lived.

"Send anyone you want to deliver it."

10.16 So the young man took the letter and sent one of his slaves to deliver it. The slave made inquiries about the brothers and when he found them, gave them the letter. When the brothers learned what had transpired, they gave the woman all her clothes, set her on a mount, and brought her home.

She accompanied the slave straight back to her husband and they told each other what had happened. He asked about the Bedouins and how they treated her.

"They treated me most honorably," she replied.

So he let the Bedouin out of the chamber, gave him the kerchief and a few dinars, and sent him on his way. And thus he shared with his wife the sweetest and most comfortable life until there came that from which there is no fleeing, and praise be to God, Lord of all being.

Then the King said, It's all over unless you tell me more of your amazing stories.

And Shahrazād said, Very well . . .

The Story of the King and his Three Sons

She continued: They say, Your Majesty, that there once lived a   11.1
mighty and powerful king whose dominion stretched far and wide
and who had three sons.[68]

In his old age, when his bones grew frail and his back stooped
more and more, he summoned his viziers and men of state.

"My sons are adults," he said. "Find me a king who has three
daughters so I may marry my sons to them."

An old man stood up. "Your Majesty," he said, "in the land of
Fars lives a king who has three daughters, the most beautiful in the
world."

When the king heard this he summoned his sons. He left one of   11.2
them in charge of the kingdom, and went to arrange the engage-
ment. He traveled far and wide and came to a high hill, with a cave
in the middle. It was night, so he made for the cave, to sleep there.
When he got there he dismounted, laid his leather shield on the
ground, and slept upon it.

He awoke to find a lion crouched over him. The lion killed him
and ate his horse.

His sons waited and worried when the king did not return at the
appointed time. When they had finally given up hope, they met to
talk about what they should do.

"My brothers," said the eldest, "there is no word from our father. I say we put someone in charge of the city and go looking for him in the land of the Persians."

"You are quite right," they agreed.

11.3   So they put someone they trusted in charge of the city and traveled far and wide in search of their father.

By night, they were near the cave where the lion had eaten their father. They dismounted and drew lots to see who would stand watch that night. The lot fell to the eldest.

As his brothers slept, he kept watch, patrolling the cave with his hand on the hilt of his sword. Without warning, the lion appeared. It was truly terrifying—it seemed to be as big as a mountain. The prince saw it coming for the kill, but he dodged to one side and dealt the lion a blow that split it as neatly as a blade cuts the nib of a reed pen. He took its head, stuffed it in a bag and left its remains in a corner. Then he kept watch over his brothers until morning.

And here the dawn reached Shahrazād so she ceased to speak.

11.4   *Fihrās the Philosopher spoke:*

The Forty-Eighth Night   She said, Master, when the blessed morning came, the brothers rode out again through the land, far and wide. The others knew nothing of the killing of the lion. When night fell, the middle brother kept watch while the eldest and youngest slept.

During his watch, he noticed a light in the distance. He followed it, and discovered that the light came from a candle inside a large cave. In front of the candle sat a girl as radiant as the full moon, as perfect as the lunar orb. A black man, as tall as a palm tree, was sleeping with his head on the girl's thigh. She had tears in her eyes.

11.5   Silent as a shadow, the young man sneaked in and dealt the black man a blow that split him as neatly as a blade cuts the nib of a reed pen.

"Who are you?" asked the girl. "Who has God sent to save me from this horrible fiend? Are you human or jinni?"

"I'm human," he replied. "And who are you, young lady?"

"My name is Ẓabyat al-Quṣūr,[69] I am a princess, daughter of the king of the Land of al-Nawāwīr."

"And where does he live?" he asked.

"Beyond this hill you see before you. I'll tell you what happened—I went out with a group of slave girls when this warrior carried me away and brought me to this place."

The young man led her by the hand to her father's palace. He knocked at the gate and the doormen came out.

"Who is it knocking at the king's gate in the dead of night?" they demanded.

"I have important words for His Majesty," he said.   11.6

Permission for him to enter was granted. He appeared before the king, greeted him and recounted the story of what had happened to his daughter. The king thanked him for what he had done and said, "Young man, I would like you to marry her."

"By all means, Your Majesty," said the young man, "but there is something I must do first, before I return."

"Very well," said the king, and gave him his signet ring. The young man returned to his brothers and watched over them for the rest of the night. They had no inkling of what had happened.

When the blessed morning came, they rode far and wide until   11.7
nightfall. The youngest brother kept watch while both his older brothers slept. At the onset of darkness, he went on patrol, with his sword and shield and as he did so, he noticed a light in the distance. He made for it, and discovered a cave with a fire burning inside. There were ninety-nine men around the fire.

And here the dawn reached Shahrazād so she ceased to speak.

Fihrās the Philosopher spoke: 11.8

She said, Master, the young man infiltrated the men and found out   *The*
that they were thieves. They had food and were dividing it into   *Forty-Ninth*
ninety-nine portions. Each thief took a portion as did the young   *Night*
man, so the leader found himself with none.

"Comrades," he said, "there is someone here who should not be."

11.9   They counted the portions of food. There were ninety-nine.

"Pick them up," ordered the leader. They did so and once again the leader had no portion.

"Didn't I tell you there was an extra person here?" said the leader.

Their hands rushed to their swords and they began the hunt for the extra man.

"Stay where you are!" called the king's son. "I've come to join you. I must tell you—I am the greatest of thieves!"

11.10   His words delighted the thieves who let him join their meal.

"Young man," they said, "tonight we are going to rob the palace of King So-and-So." This was the king whose daughters the brothers wanted to marry.

"I know better than anyone how to get in," he told them.

So they went to the palace and began to tunnel through its walls. When the work was completed, the king's son entered the palace through the tunnel, then called to his companions.

"This way!"

In they went, one after the other, and, as each one emerged from the tunnel, the youth lopped off his head, right down to the last man. Then he climbed back through the tunnel, sealed it up and returned to his brothers. He spent the rest of the night on guard.

11.11   When the blessed morning came, they rode to the city. They found the gates locked and a swarm of excited people milling about. The brothers asked what was amiss and learned that during the previous night something had happened in the palace of the king, whereupon a proclamation had been made: "O people! Anyone who can inform the king of what happened in his palace last night will have half of his kingdom!"

At this the brothers sought permission for an audience with the king, and it was granted. They greeted him, and he asked, "And who might you be?"

"We are the sons of King So-and-So."

The eldest brother then stepped forward. "This is what happened to me," he said, and produced out the lion's head which he
put before the king.

Then the middle brother stepped forward. "This is what happened to me," he said, "and I returned the girl to her father. This is
her father's ring."

Then the youngest brother stepped forward. "Master," he said,
"this is what happened to me last night here in this very castle. I was
the one who killed the thieves."

The king was astonished at this.

"You have spoken truthfully," he told him.

And here the dawn reached Shahrazād so she ceased to speak.

Fihrās the Philosopher spoke:

She said, Master, the king ordered that they be welcomed as his
guests. They made inquiries after their father and searched for him
but could find no trace of him.

They enjoyed the king's hospitality for a number of days and then
the king married his daughter to the youngest brother. There was a
great feast and the king bestowed great riches on him.

The middle brother left to marry the girl he had saved, while the
eldest brother remained with the king and the youngest returned to
his father's kingdom. Their kingdoms were next to each other, and
so the brothers lived the sweetest of lives until there came to them
that from which there is no fleeing, and praise be to God, Lord of
all being.

The Story of the Young Man and the Necklaces

12.1   Then the storyteller said: They say, Your Majesty—and God knows best—that once in Baghdad there lived a young man who was the son of a merchant. His father died, and left him great wealth, and he ate, drank, and was merry until nothing remained—not even a single gold dinar or silver dirham.[70]

When he had nothing left, he went to see the friends he used to drink and carouse with, but they brushed him off and ignored him. He returned to his mother and told her what had happened.

"My boy," she said, "I was afraid this would happen. But I have no coins, gold or silver. All I've got is this rug that we sleep on."

12.2   She gave it to him and he took it to the market where he sold it for a dinar. He had started home, coin in hand, when a broker appeared, crying, "Who wants to buy something that will make him rich this very night? Buy my wares!"

The young man approached him and asked, "What is it?"

The man produced a large knife. The young man, whose name was 'Alī ibn 'Abd al-Raḥmān al-Bazārī,[71] paid a dinar for the knife and went back home.

"What did you do with the money you got for the rug?" asked his mother.

He told her he had bought a knife. "And what are you going to do with that?" she asked.

"I heard the broker saying 'Who wants to buy something that will make him rich this very night? Buy my wares!' So I bought it."

The young man waited till nightfall, when he took the knife and went out into the dark where night had covered everything in a black cloak. He went through the alleyways to the palace of al-Ma'mūn, where he tried the door and found it open: the guards were fast asleep. 12.3

"Tonight," he told himself, "I will either become rich or die."

He entered the palace, and made his way from room to room. The light revealed a delightful garden planted with all kinds of fruits, surrounded by elevated apartments and domes of sandalwood, with iron windows looking out on to it and birds nesting in the trees. A waterwheel of aloewood overlain with glittering gold lifted the water up and poured it down again. It was as the poet said:

> A wineskin empty and dry,
>> that wept tears from a lover's eye.
> It moans and sighs, as do I:
>> My lover is gone—now from fear's wounds I die.[72]

And here the dawn reached Shahrazād so she ceased to speak.

Fihrās the Philosopher spoke: 12.4
She said, Master, the youth hid in the trees until the whole palace was sound asleep. Then he went through the rooms until he came to one where he could smell food. He was hungry, so he went in and he began to eat the white bread and other fare he found there. *The Fifty-First Night*

While he was eating, he heard a noise behind him. He turned to see a black slave with a sword in one hand, and in the other the hair of a slave girl as beautiful as the full moon at night or a gazelle in flight. The black slave dragged the girl into a room where he threw her to the floor, and pinned her down, sitting on top of her chest.

"If you don't let me take you," he told her, "you won't live to see the light of day."

THE STORY OF THE YOUNG MAN AND THE NECKLACES | 103

"By God," she replied, "cut me into pieces, if you want, but you will never have me! You evil slave—you'll never get what's meant for the Commander of the Faithful!"

12.5   The slave got ready to kill her, but the young man pounced on him with the knife he had been carrying, driving the blade between his shoulders until it protruded from his chest. The slave fell to the ground, dead.

The girl got up and threw herself into the arms of the young man.

"I've been blessed!" she exclaimed. "Who are you? Are you human or jinni?"

"I'm human, of course!" he replied. "I slipped into this palace but I am no thief! It was God in His Mercy who sent me to you. My story is this . . ." And he told her his story.

"What's your name?" she asked.

"My name is ʿAlī ibn ʿAbd al-Raḥmān al-Bazārī."

"And where do you live?"

"In Such-and-Such a place."

"Stay where you are until I come back."

12.6   Some time later she returned radiant like the sun when it appears from behind the clouds. She gave him a thousand dinars and said, "Young man, this is part of your reward. Every day I'll seek you out with whatever gifts and treasure I can."

Then she whisked him secretly out of the palace and hid the dead slave in a closet.

The young man went back to his mother and found her crying for him. She hugged him when she saw him and he gave her the sack with the money.

"My son," she cried, "where did you get this?"

"It's a blessing," he replied. "«God provides for whomever He will without reckoning.»"[73]

And here the dawn reached Shahrazād so she ceased to speak.

Fihrās the Philosopher spoke:

She said, Master, the night passed, and when the blessed morning came, there was a knock at the door. The young man opened the door to a black servant.

"Sir," she said, "are you ʿAlī ibn ʿAbd al-Raḥmān al-Bazārī?"

"Yes," he replied. She gave him a thousand dinars.

And so it continued: each day the slave girl sent him some gift or other.

One day she happened to prepare a grilled lamb with loaves of white bread for him. Inside the lamb she placed four necklaces, each one worth a whole treasury. She set the lamb and the loaves on a bamboo platter and covered it with a silk cloth.

"Go now and take this to ʿAlī's house," she ordered her servant.

The servant went to the young man's house. In the street she passed by some of his former friends and drinking companions who, smelling the lamb, followed her and saw that she was going to ʿAlī's house.

She knocked on the door and he came out.

"Sir," she said, "Take this present."

He took the platter and the servant returned to the palace.

His friends came up to him and said, "Ibn ʿAbd al-Raḥmān! This food that servant brought you smells delicious—maybe you'd like to share it with us!"

"By God," he said, "none of you is going to set foot in my house."

"Then how about letting us into the front room, no farther?" they rejoined.

So he led them into the front room and put the platter in front of them. He went inside to get some water, not having any idea what was inside the lamb. His companions lifted the kerchief and noticed that the lamb was stuffed with something, so they opened it up and found the necklaces hidden inside.

At the sight of this, they exclaimed, "By God, necklaces like these can only come from the royal palace! He must be carrying on with one of the king's slave girls—let's go tell the Commander of the Faithful what he's been up to!"

So they took the necklaces to the king's palace.

"We have counsel for the Commander of the Faithful!" they cried out.

12.10 The chamberlain appeared. "And what is this counsel of yours?"

They told him. He secured the king's permission for an audience, so they went in and greeted the king.

"Your Majesty," they said, "We were eating at the house of ʿAlī ibn ʿAbd al-Raḥmān al-Bazārī when we found these necklaces hidden inside a roasted lamb that someone in the palace had given him." And they handed him the necklaces.

Meanwhile ʿAlī knew nothing of what was happening. When he came back with the water, he found no trace of his guests. So he took the platter inside and placed it in front of his mother. They began to eat and all the while his former friends were on their way to the king.

12.11 At the sight of the necklaces the king changed color, for he knew that they could only have come from the slave girl. He commanded a group of slaves to bring the young man before him.

The young man was still eating with his mother when he suddenly found himself surrounded by the slaves who shackled him and dragged him outside. They took him to the king and sat him down. The king demanded, "Who gave you these necklaces?"

"May God make the Emir prosper!" said the youth. "In a hadith the Prophet says that gifts should be accepted! I was given a gift, and I accepted it!"[74]

"But who gave you this gift?" asked the king.

12.12 "I was sitting at home when I heard a knock at the door. A servant was carrying a platter on her head containing roast lamb and white bread. Then these people arrived and asked to share it, so I let them into the front room and went in to get them some water. When I came back, they were all gone. I used to drink and carouse and get up to all sort of things with them. Now they eat my food, and look at what I get in return!"

When the king heard these words he stood up quickly and went to the slave girl, the owner of the necklaces.

"Do you recognize these necklaces?" he asked her.

"Yes," she said.

And here the dawn reached Shahrazād so she ceased to speak.

Fihrās the Philosopher spoke:

She said, Master, the king then said:

"Who put them inside the roast lamb and gave it to a young man, a merchant's son?"

"I did," she said.

"And why was that?"

"May God make the Emir prosper!" she said, "This is what happened to me . . ." And she told him the story of how the young man had killed the black slave. She led them to the place where she had hidden the body so the king could see the corpse. Then she showed him the marks on her back where the slave had struck her with his sword. "I simply had to repay the young man somehow, as you can see."

He left her and asked the young man to tell him his version of events, which was exactly the same as the slave girl's story.

The king gave the slave girl to the young man, and passed judgment on his companions: expulsion from the city and exile from the land. He also seized the wealth and the possessions they had received from the young man who became a regular attendee at the king's salon until there came to him that from which there is no fleeing, and praise be to God, Lord of all being.

The Story of the Four Companions

13.1   The girl spoke: They claim, O blessed king, that in the time of Hārūn
        al-Rashīd there lived four companions: a thief, a tracker, a carpen-
        ter, and an archer.[75] They came to Baghdad and lodged together in a
        house. Now the houses in Baghdad had iron windows, and one eve-
        ning when they were sitting down to eat, the window came crash-
        ing down. They jumped up and went to see what had happened. Lo
        and behold, there was a young woman as beautiful as the full moon
        when it rises.

13.2   "Who are you?" they asked her.

        She did not answer.

        The companions turned to each other and each said: "She's
        mine!"

        And here the dawn reached Shahrazād so she ceased to speak.

13.3   *Fihrās the Philosopher spoke:*

The   She said, Master, when each exclaimed, "She's mine!" the eldest
Fifty-Fourth said, "Listen—I'll tell you what we should do."
Night
        "Very well," said the others.

        "We'll lock the girl in one of the rooms and leave her there till
        tomorrow morning, God willing. Whoever among us proves him-
        self the most skilful and the most clever will win her."

        "Excellent idea!" they agreed.

So they put the girl in a room and locked her in. Thus they passed 13.4 the night. In the morning they opened the door, but found no trace of the girl.

"I'll find out where she's gone," said the tracker.

He searched for an hour.

"The girl's been kidnapped by a jinni demon," he announced. "If she had been abducted by a human, I would have seen his tracks. Come with me and I'll show you, because by God whether she's gone way beyond the sun or as deep as the grave, I am going to win her."

He followed the tracks until they came to the seashore.

"She went out to sea here," said the tracker.

At this they turned to the carpenter. 13.5

"So what about these skills you claim to have?" they asked.

"I'll show you," he said. And he built them a boat.

They sailed in the boat across the sea to a towering mountain isle that looked as if God Himself had chiseled it. They dropped anchor and secured the boat. It was now the tracker's turn.

"So what about these skills you claim to have?" they asked.

"I'll show you," he said.

The tracker went ashore and followed the tracks to a cave, where 13.6 they discovered the girl and a demon lying with his head on her thighs. The demon was asleep. He went back to his companions and told them what he saw.

They turned to the thief.

"So what about these skills you claim to have?" they asked.

"I'll show you," said the thief.

So up he went to the cave. The young woman was still there. He managed to get the demon's head off her thighs without waking him, and then he took her down to the boat. She boarded and they set sail. The demon awoke and, when he could not find the girl anywhere, let out such a loud scream it shook the mountain. He soared into the air, and from his vantage point on high he could see the girl in the boat. He rushed down towards it, intending to drown them all.

13.7   But the companions said to the archer: "So what about these skills you claim to have?"

"I'll show you," he said.

"Kill that demon for us!" they exclaimed.

He put an arrow to his bow, and aimed at the demon. He fell to the sea, dead.

Then they argued over who had done what with his trademark skill and each them declared, "She's mine!"

"Would you accept the judgment of the Commander of the Faithful Hārūn al-Rashīd?" asked the thief.

13.8   "And how are we supposed to get him to judge?" asked the others.

"I'll get you in to see him," said the thief, "and whomever he judges in favor of, the girl is his and he takes her."

"Agreed," they said.

And here the dawn reached Shahrazād so she ceased to speak.

13.9   *Fihrās the Philosopher spoke:*

The Fifty-Fifth Night

She said, Master, they crossed the sea all the way to Baghdad, took lodgings and secured the girl, with an iron lock, in a room. When night had covered everything in a cloak of darkness, they headed to the palace.

13.10   The thief found a way to get them into the palace, and brought them to the king's salon where Hārūn al-Rashīd, reclined on his throne, with Sahl the storyteller talking to him. Then the king fell asleep, as did Sahl.

The thief got up and carefully carried the storyteller behind the door. Then he came back and put himself in Sahl's place.

The king awoke from his slumber.

"Tell me a story, Sahl," he said, thinking that the thief was Sahl.

"Very well," said the thief. "Master, there were once four close companions: a thief, a carpenter, an archer and a tracker. It so happened that . . ." And he recounted their tale just as it occurred.

13.11   "The thief brought his companions to your salon, leaving them at the door, and he went in and removed me from my place. Then he sat where I was supposed to be, and told you stories. So which of them, in your judgment, should win the girl?"

"I could only rule in favor of the thief!" said the king.

Then the king fell asleep again, so the thief carried Sahl back to his place and rejoined his companions.

"You are not going to get the girl until he judges one more time!" they told him.

Then the king awoke from his slumber.   13.12

"Sahl," he said, "tell me the story of the thief, his companions and the girl."

"Which thief is that, Master?" asked Sahl.

"The one you were just telling me about a little while ago."

"By God," said Sahl, "I have never told you any story about a thief! I think it must have been something you saw in a dream."

"That is possible," said the king.

Then Sahl told him another story and the king once again fell   13.13
asleep and Sahl slept as well.

The thief crept back into the room, removed Sahl and took his place once more. The king awoke and said, "Sahl, tell me a story."

"Yes," he said. "O Commander of the Faithful: the story you asked me about, the story of the thief, his companions and the girl, has come back to me. There once were four close companions, and it happened that . . ." He told him the story from beginning to end.

"And the thief entered your salon and took me from my place   13.14
and stole the hat off of my head, and replaced it with one made from palm leaves. Then he took the ring from your hand and put in its place a ring made of reeds, and then he sat and told you stories. Now who, in your judgment, should get the girl?"

"The thief who took you from your place," he said.

The thief told more stories until the king fell back asleep. Then   13.15
he returned Sahl to his proper place, took his hat from his head and replaced it with one made from palm leaves. He took the ring from the hand of the king and replaced it with one made of reeds. When he got back to his companions, he said, "Now are you satisfied?"

"Yes, absolutely." they said, "Anyway, if anyone of us were to try to take her, you'd steal her from him!"

And here the dawn reached Shahrazād so she ceased to speak.

Fihrās the Philosopher spoke:

She said, Master, when the thief and his companions had left, the king awoke from his slumber.

"Sahl," he said, "tell me the story of the thief."

"What thief, Master?" asked Sahl.

"The one you told me about—how he carried you from your place, and took the hat off your head, and replaced it with one made of palm leaves, and how he took the ring from my hand and replaced it with one made from reeds."

"By God, Master, I have never told you any such story."

13.17   But then Sahl felt his head and found he was wearing a hat made from palm leaves. "Commander of the Faithful and Lord of the Kaaba! I've been robbed!"

The king looked at his hand, and there on his finger was a ring made from reeds. He threw it away and seized his sword, uttering a great cry that reverberated through the palace. The slaves gathered around him with their maces of iron and their swords. They searched the palace from one end to the other, but found no one. The king was astonished.

13.18   When the blessed morning came, the king ordered the crier to proclaim through the alleyways of Baghdad: "O people! The man who can tell the king what happened last night in the palace shall have a guarantee of safety, and he shall also receive five hundred gold dinars."

The crier walked through the alleys of Baghdad and came to where the thief and his companions lived. When the thief heard the crier he went outside.

"I can tell the king what happened last night in the palace," he said.

13.19   So the thief was brought before the king.

"Master," he said, "last night in the palace the following events took place," and he related the rest of the story and returned the ring to the king and the hat to Sahl. The king was astonished at his story and his cunning and his God-given talents so he granted him his safety and the thief repented of his ways. The king then gave him the money and recorded his name in the register of storytellers. He also gave him the girl. There he remained, eating, drinking, and living a life of luxury until there came to him that from which there is no fleeing, and praise be to God, Lord of all being.

The Story of the Prince and the Seven Viziers[76]

14.1   Then she said: They say, Your Majesty, that there once lived a mighty, courageous king called Sayf al-Aʿlām.[77] Great kings feared him, and lesser kings bowed before him. But King Sayf al-Aʿlām was unhappy because he did not have a son. He summoned his physicians, astrologers, and wise men, and they read lines in the sand, studied the stars, and tried to divine his fortune.

"Your Majesty," they concluded, "a male child will soon be born to you. He will bring you great joy, God willing."

14.2   So the king would eat only the finest foods and finally a son was born to him, a son more beautiful than any of his time. The king held a great celebration at which all the people from both city and the countryside feasted. Then he summoned the astrologers.

"I want you to study my son's stars," he told them, "and tell me what fortune awaits him."

The astrologers went to work and soon reported back to the king, "Your Majesty! Your son will have a long life, but when he is twenty years old, a terrible thing will happen to him and you will fear for his life."

The king was astonished at what the astrologers told him.

And here the dawn reached Shahrazād so she ceased to speak.

Fihrās the Philosopher spoke:

She said, Master, then the king sent his son first to Qur'an school and then, when the boy was twelve, turned him over to a tutor. However, amazing as it sounds, the boy learned nothing.

The king became concerned at his son's inability to learn, so he summoned the scholars from each province.

"I want to know what you think about my son," he told them when he had brought them all together. "Is there any one of you who can teach him? I'll give him all the wealth and treasure he desires."

There were one thousand scholars seated before him, and four of them stood and each said, "I will instruct him, Your Majesty."

Sindbad, his first teacher, stood up.

"Your Majesty," said Sindbad, "I will teach him what no one else here can teach him."

He turned to the other scholars present and asked, "How do you propose to educate the young man?"

And each gave the king an account of what he would do.

"That's it?" said Sindbad. "I've already instructed him in all that you've said and he didn't learn a thing. I always knew that none of you was more learned than I, so it is I who will teach him."

Sindbad continued: "The heart is master of the limbs, the hands, the feet, the tongue, and the eyes and ears, for if the heart doesn't learn a thing, then the rest of body won't learn it either."

An Elephant's Education[78]

"I have heard, Your Majesty, that there was once a king who liked elephants. A young elephant was captured for him and given to the trainer, the keeper of the elephants.

"'Teach it well,' he was told.

"'I shall.'

"When the elephant had matured the king asked about it.

"'It is just as you wanted, Your Majesty,' the trainer said.

"'Can I ride it?' asked the king.

"'Yes, if you wish.'

"'Bring it to me.'

"The trainer brought the elephant but when the king mounted it and was securely seated on its back, the elephant took off at a gallop and the king was barely able to hang on. It would not stop and finally the king fainted from exhaustion.

"Eventually the elephant seemed to remember its stable and returned to it. When the king, badly shaken, regained consciousness, he ordered that the trainer be killed.

"'Please, not so fast!' pleaded the trainer.

14.7 "He picked up a piece of iron that he held in the fire until it became white-hot, approached the elephant and said, 'Take hold of it.'

"The elephant took hold of the hot iron. 'Throw it,' commanded the trainer.

"The elephant threw it.

"The trainer turned to the king.

"'Your Majesty, I have taught it every action it performs with its foreleg, but there is no way to get to its heart.'

"So the king pardoned him and let him go and he remained in his service."

And here the dawn overtook Shahrazād so she ceased to speak.

14.8 *Fihrās the Philosopher spoke:*

The Fifty-Eighth Night She said, Master, when Sindbād had finished his parable, the second teacher got up.

"I'll teach this boy in one year what you haven't been able to teach him in twelve."

When the king heard that he called to Sindbād and said, "And how long will you teach him for?"

He said, "In six months there will be no one more learned than he, and if I don't keep my word, then take my life as well as all that I possess."

14.9 Then Sindbād continued, "A land without kings or scholars or merchants or physicians is no place to live. But all of these are found in your land, praise be to God. I have been told, Your Majesty, that monarchs are like fire: keep your distance, and you'll be safe; get close, and you'll get burned. If a man gets close to a king, he will always fear for his life; if he keeps his distance, he'll live a pleasant life. I have only one condition."

"And what is that condition?" asked the king.

"Do not do unto others what you would not want done to yourself." 14.10

"And who is capable of that?" asked the king.

"You, Your Majesty," replied Sindbad.

So the king wrote out a contract, and had it countersigned by witnesses. He turned the boy over to Sindbād after stipulating the month, day, and time he would bring him back, education completed.

Sindbād took the boy home with him and had an underground 14.11 palace of dappled marble built for him, with plaster representations of the sciences, from grammar, belles-lettres, and poetry to jurisprudence and such. Then he turned to the boy, "This is where you will sit until you have learned everything I'm going to teach you."

He sat with him and taught and tutored him. Food and drink and whatever else they needed was brought to them. When the time was up, the boy had learned everything Sindbād had taught him. The king was informed, and overjoyed, he summoned Sindbād to appear before him.

"Your son has been an excellent student," said Sindbād. "God willing, he will come to you tomorrow at the second hour of the day."[79]

The king was delighted to hear this and Sindbād returned to the 14.12 boy.

"I shall bring you back to your father tomorrow, God willing, but tonight I must look at your stars."

That night, he looked at his stars and saw something ominous.

"Your stars tell me that you are not to speak for seven days. If you speak, I'm afraid you may be killed."

Here the dawn reached Shahrazād so she ceased to speak.

Fihrās the Philosopher spoke:

She said, Master, at the words of his teacher the prince dropped what he was holding and said to his teacher, "I'll do whatever you think. I'm at your mercy."

"I promised your father that I'd bring you back tomorrow," said Sindbād, "and I cannot go back on my word."

The next day, at the appointed time, he said to the boy, "Go to your father by yourself, but don't utter a single word for seven days, until I come to you."

"Very well," said the youth.

14.14 So off he went alone to see his father, who sat him down beside him and tried to talk to him, but got no answer. He asked him what he had learned but the boy would not speak. Sindbād was summoned, but was nowhere to be found.

"What do you think about the boy's behavior?" he asked his entourage. "You try talking to him; maybe he's forbidden him to speak to me!"

They tried to get him to say something but still he would not utter a word.

"Your Majesty, we think that Sindbād tried to teach him but couldn't get him to learn anything, and so when the time was up, and afraid of the scandal, he gave him some drug that would stop him speaking."

This thought upset the king even more.

One of his slave girls, a beautiful and beloved favorite, saw this, and said to him, "Your Majesty, leave me alone with him. Perhaps he will tell me what is going on, since he's always enjoyed my company."

14.15 "Go ahead and try," said the king.

Off she went with the boy to her residence, where she spoke but he did not. So she said to him, "You are ignorant, but I am going to offer you something you cannot refuse. Your father is getting old and weak. What do you think about killing him—I'll figure out a way for you to do it, and then you will be king and I your queen?"

The prince became so angry when he heard this that he forgot the pledge to his teacher.

"By God," he exclaimed, "I wouldn't go along with you even if I were ignorant, so how could I agree now, when God has granted me knowledge and learning that I did not have before? I am not supposed to talk for seven days, but when they are over, I'll speak and you'll know my response to what you propose."

When the slave girl heard what he said, she knew that she was finished. Using all her wiles and cunning and skills of deception, she screamed, scratched her face and tore her clothes.

14.16

When the king heard the slave girl's screams he got to his feet and rushed to see her.

"What's going on here?" he demanded.

"This boy here, the one you claimed could not speak, has tried to seduce me!" said the slave girl, "but I refused, so he clawed my face and tore my clothes and tried to kill me!"[80]

The king was extremely jealous and protective of his women and when he heard this, he flew into such a rage that he forgot his love for his son.

He ordered that his son be put to death.

And here the dawn reached Shahrazād so she ceased to speak.

Fihrās the Philosopher spoke:

14.17

She said, Master, the king ordered that his son be put to death.

Now this king had seven viziers, men of learning and letters, wise and experienced. They conferred among themselves, "If we do nothing and leave the king to his own devices, he will kill his son. He will regret it but the blame will fall on us: he'll say, 'How could you have let me kill my own son?' And we will look bad and suffer because of it."

One of the viziers said, "I'll delay the killing for today, but keep the boy with you until I come back from the king."

The vizier left and went to see the king.

14.18

"Your Majesty," he said, "it is inappropriate for kings to take action without counsel. A king should be patient, and not act rashly." Then he recited:

> Better to be patient than to rush;
>> strive to forgive, from morning to dusk.
> Act not in haste but with intelligence,
>> and don't kill your son without evidence.

When he had finished his recital, he told a story:

LION TRACKS[81]

14.19   "I have heard, Your Majesty, that there once was a king who tended to take a great liking to whatever he was shown. He was sitting in his tower one day when a beautiful woman passed by, and he liked what he saw. He summoned her husband and sent him away on a mission, and then visited the woman's house and demanded her for himself.

"'Majesty,' said the woman, 'I am your servant. Anything you wish from me, consider it done.'

14.20   "She brought him a book belonging to her husband, on the subject of the prohibition of forbidden acts and grave sins, and the legal judgments thereon.

"'Look at this until I come back,' she said.

"The king opened the book and started to read about sin and the evils of consorting with women who belong to other men. He began to regret what he had intended to do and so he left the woman and returned to his palace. However, he had forgotten one of his slippers in the woman's house.

"When her husband came back home, he saw the king's slipper in his room. He recognized it, and knew that the only way this slipper could have turned up in his house was if something was going on between his wife and the king.

"He left his house but spoke to no one, out of fear of the king. He did not go near his wife and shunned her for many days.

"The woman sent a message to her family: 'My husband has abandoned me!'

"Her family came and brought a claim against him to the king.

"'May God make the Emir prosper!' they said to the king. 'We gave a piece of land we had to this man so that he could live there and cultivate it. He lived there for a long time but then one day he left and has not come near it since. He should either come back and till the land, as he used to do, or he should return it to us.'

"The king turned to the woman's husband.

"'What do you say in response?' he asked.

"'They have spoken truthfully, Your Majesty,' said the man. 'They gave me the land and I tilled and cultivated it until one day I came home to find the tracks of a lion on my land. So I never went back, out of fear of the lion.'

"'What you say is true,' said the king, 'but I swear upon my life that although the lion entered, he did no harm, because what he found there was a pit that would lead him to ruin were he to till that soil. So he left it alone. Your land is yours, cultivate it and have no fear.' The man was relieved to hear this, and so he returned to his wife."

Then the vizier said, "Now I will tell to you a story I heard about the crafty wiles of women."

THE HUSBAND AND THE PARROT[82]

"They say, Your Majesty, that there once was a man who was mar- ried to a beautiful woman. He was fiercely possessive of her and would not even allow himself to travel because of his jealousy. This situation continued for a long time, when eventually he purchased a bird known as a parrot. He placed it in an iron cage and taught it to speak.

"The bird's task was to inform him on his return of everything that went on in the house."

And here the dawn reached Shahrazād so she ceased to speak.

Fihrās the Philosopher spoke:

She said, Master, "Then the man went on a journey. In his absence his wife took a lover. The bird saw everything they did.

"When the man returned from his trip, he called to the bird and asked it to report. The bird informed him of what it saw, and so the man shunned his wife and did not go near her.

"The wife assumed that it was her servant who had told him her secret and struck the woman, demanding, 'Why has my husband shunned me? It must have been you who told him what I did!'

14.25   "'By God,' the servant replied, 'I didn't say anything! It must have been the bird who told him!'

"So that night the wife went to the parrot and began to spray water on it through a sieve and used an Indian mirror to shine light on it, while the servant turned a grindstone until the blessed morning came.

"Then the man came to the bird and said, 'Tell me what you saw last night.'

"'How could I even open my eyes last night with all that thunder, lightning, and rain?' replied the bird.

14.26   "When he heard this the man said to himself, 'The bird must have lied to me about my wife! What rain was there last night? Everything it's told me is false!'

"So the man set the bird free and destroyed its cage. He made up with his wife and was happy with her.

"And I've told you this story so you would know that the wiles of women are great!"[83] said the vizier.

When the king heard this he rescinded the order to kill his son.

On the second day the slave girl came crying to the king.

"A king should not pardon his son when he should be killed!"

THE FULLER AND HIS SON[84]

14.27   "I heard of a fuller whose son used to go down to the river with him. The son would play in the water and the father would not try to stop him. One day he went too far from the bank and started to drown.

The father went to save him but the boy clung to him and they both drowned. And you, Your Highness, if you do not see that justice is done to me with regard to your son, what happened to the fuller will happen to you. You will perish for what he has done."

When the king heard this, he reinstated the order that his son be killed.

The second vizier came and ordered that the boy be kept in custody. Then he had an audience with the king.

The Loaves of Bread[85]

"Your Majesty, if you had one hundred sons, it would not be right to kill a single one of them, but you have only one son. He who acts in ignorance will regret it when it's too late.

14.28

"It is said that in bygone days there was a traveling merchant who was very careful and restrained in what he ate and drank. He visited a city and sent his servant to the market to buy something to eat. While the servant was doing the rounds of the market, a slave girl appeared, carrying two delicious loaves of white bread. The servant bought them both and presented them to his master.

"The merchant enjoyed them so much he said to his servant, 'I want you to buy two loaves from that slave girl every day.'"

And here the dawn reached Shahrazād so she ceased to speak.

Fihrās the Philosopher spoke:
She said, Master, "The servant would go to the market each day for his master and buy two loaves from the slave girl. But one day he went and she wasn't there. Several days passed before he met her again, and when he did he asked her, 'Why aren't you making those loaves anymore?'

14.29
The Sixty-Second Night

"'Sir,' she said, 'the man we make the loaves for has gone to rest.'

"So the servant returned to his master and told him what the slave girl had said.

"'Bring her to me,' he instructed.

"She came before him and he asked her how she made the loaves.

14.30

"'My lord had a sore on his back,' she replied, 'and the doctor said to take good quality flour and mix and knead it with butter and honey and place this mixture on the sore, to heal it. So I did, and when I removed the poultice I made two loaves and baked them, as you know, and your servant would buy them from me. But my lord's illness ran its course and he breathed his last so I don't need to make anything for him anymore.'

"When the merchant heard this he burst out in a loud wail, and asked the servant, in despair, 'I can clean my mouth and my body, but how can I wash my insides?'

14.31   "I have told you this story so that you kill your son in haste, for a woman will ruin your life just as one ruined the merchant's life."

"Then he recited these verses:

> Take your time, don't be too hasty for what you want.
>> Be merciful, and you will be tried with mercy
> He who sows good deeds will thrive;
>> he who defies time will enjoy no safety.
> The hand of God controls all;
>> be harsh, and you will be tried harshly.

The Lady and Her Two Lovers[86]

14.32   "I have also heard men say that the crafty wiles of women is a subject that defies description.

"For example, there was a married woman who took a lover, one of the king's officers.

14.33   "One day he sent his servant to see if the woman's husband had left or not, but when the servant entered the house the woman liked what she saw. She offered herself to him, and he gladly accepted.

"But his master, the woman's lover, realized that the servant was taking too long, so he set out after him. When he arrived, the woman hid the servant in a closet. She ushered her lover in, and he asked about his servant.

"'He came and asked if my husband was here or not and then left in a hurry,' she said.

"The lover stayed and satisfied his needs. But meanwhile, the husband arrived home. The woman could not bear the thought of him finding her like this, but at the same time, she was afraid to put her lover in the closet along with the servant. 14.34

"'Take your sword in hand and stand at the door of the salon,' she said to her lover, 'and abuse and threaten me, then leave and do not speak to my husband.'

"He followed her instructions and left, sword in hand. The woman's husband tried to question him, but he departed without saying a word. He went in to his wife and asked her, 'What is going on with that man?'

"'His servant ran away from him,' she said, 'and asked me for help and I let him into the house. His master followed him here and was going to strike him with his sword, but I wouldn't let him into my room.' 14.35

"'So where is the servant?' asked her husband.

"'He's in the closet,' she replied.

"Her husband went to see if the master had gone. He had. The husband came back inside, went to the closet and said to the servant, 'You can leave now, your master has gone.'

"I am only telling you this story so that you are not taken in by the words of women and so that you won't listen to what they say." 14.36

When the king heard these words he rescinded the order to kill his son.

On the third day the slave girl arrived with a knife in her hand and said, "Your evil viziers are stalling you—they just want to see me found guilty and destroyed! I'll kill myself with this knife and my sin will be on your head! I would rather do that than do what your son has done. You must not listen to your evil viziers!"

And here the dawn reached Shahrazād, so she ceased to speak.

Fihrās the Philosopher spoke:

She said, Master, then the slave girl said, "Your Majesty,"

THE PRINCE AND THE OGRESS[87]

14.38 "I have told you about the king's vizier. This king had a son who loved the hunt and the chase. The king, though, would not allow it, and this became the source of much grief for the son.

"'Ask my father's permission to go hunting,' the son asked the father's vizier, 'and you will be doing me a great favor.'

"The vizier asked and received permission for them to go hunting.

"The son set out with the vizier and an onager ran past. 'Go get it!' said the vizier.

14.39 "The vizier stayed where he was, and the prince went after the animal, but every time he managed to get close, it ran even further away. In the end he had traveled a great distance in pursuit. He was now a long way from where he had left the vizier and had no idea which way to turn. He was sure that this was going to be the end.

"While he was occupied with these thoughts, he suddenly caught sight of a girl in the middle of the path. She was crying.

"'Who are you?' he asked the girl. 'And what on earth are you doing here?'

"'I am the daughter of the king of Such-and-Such a land,' she said. 'I was traveling with my family, on a mule. We had set out for Such-and-Such a place. I dozed off and fell off my animal but no one noticed. By the time I came to, my people had gone on ahead without me, and I didn't know which way to turn. So I walked until my feet almost fell off and I didn't know where on God's earth I was.'

14.40 "'I too am a son of the king of the land of So-and-So,' he told her. 'If you want, I can take you with me and then I can marry you.'

"'Yes,' she said.

"He took her by the hand and sat her behind him on his horse. From time to time he would steal a glance at her, and at one point she said to him, 'Look here, I need to get off, let me down.'

"So he helped her dismount and she went behind some ruins. The king's son stole a peek at her and what he saw was an ogress and a ghoul. The ogress said to the ghoul, 'I've brought you a human.'

"'Take him into the other ruin and I'll come and get him,' the ghoul said.

"She came back out and got up behind the young man.

"She noticed he was shaking with fear and asked why he was so afraid.

"'It's betrayal I'm afraid of,' he replied

"'What betrayal?' she asked.

"'The one I fear in my heart,' he said.

"'Seek help from God,' she told him.

"'I will.'

"He lifted his hand to the sky and said, 'O God, deliver me from this ogress and protect me from her evil!' She toppled to the ground, and the youth fled back to his own people, his mind reeling from all that he had endured.

"I have told you this story so you will know that your viziers are an evil lot. Do not accept what they say, and if you don't save me I'll kill myself."

And so the king ordered that his son be killed.

And here the dawn reached Shahrazād so she ceased to speak.

Fihrās the Philosopher spoke:

She said, Master, when the king had ordered that his son be killed *The* the third vizier ordered the boy to be seized and then went in to see *Sixty-Fourth* the king. *Night*

"Are you going to kill your own son for the sake of a slave girl, when you don't even know whether she is telling the truth or not?" he asked.

The Drop of Honey[88]

"I have heard, Your Majesty," he went on, "that a group of villagers fought and killed each other for a drop of honey. What happened was that a man filled a container with honey and went to the market to sell it, accompanied by his dog. At the shop, he took the honey out for the shopkeeper to taste and a drop fell to the ground.

14.45 "Along came a wasp and landed on it. Now the shopkeeper had a cat, and the cat pounced on the wasp, the dog pounced on the cat and bit it and killed it. The owner of the cat raised his staff, struck the dog and killed it. Then the owner of the dog and the owner of the cat attacked each other. In the middle of all this some people from this village and some from that approached, and started fighting with each other. In the end there were no survivors.

"I've told you this story so you will not kill your own son for the sake of a slave girl, when you don't even know if she is telling the truth or not. From many a trifle there has come much evil."

The Woman Who Made Her Husband Sift Dirt[89]

14.46 "On the topic of the cunning and wiles of women, I have also heard the story of the man who sent his wife to the market with a dirham to buy some rice. She gave the dirham to the rice seller who measured the rice out for her, and said, 'Rice only really tastes good with sugar. Do you have any sugar?'

14.47 "'My God, no,' she said. 'I don't have any sugar.'

"'Why don't you come into the back of the shop here with me,' he said. 'You give me what I want, and I'll give you a dirham's worth of sugar?'

"'Fine,' said the woman.

"So he weighed a dirham's worth of sugar, and she tied it up in a cloth with the rice, then she accompanied him into the backroom, leaving the cloth with the rice and sugar in the shop. The shopkeeper's servant replaced what was in the cloth with dirt and tied it back up as it was.

14.48 "The woman took the cloth home, thinking it contained sugar and rice. She was in the storeroom getting the pot to cook the rice, when her husband opened up the cloth and found the dirt.

"'What have you done?' he exclaimed. 'What's this dirt you are bringing home?'

"She knew right away that she had been fooled. So on the spot she came up with a ruse of her own. She brought out a sieve instead of the pot.

"'I was on my way to the market when I was knocked down by a mule,' she told him. 'As I fell, I dropped the dirham. I looked everywhere for it but I couldn't find it, so I gathered up all the dirt so I could sift through it. I thought perhaps God would return the money to me that way.'

"And her husband believed her story and began to sift through the dirt.

"I have told you this story so that you will not act on the word   14.49
of a woman and will understand that the wiles of women are great, and that their craftiness cannot be matched."

When the king heard this he rescinded the order that his son be killed.

And here the dawn reached Shahrazād so she ceased to speak.

Fihrās the Philosopher spoke: 14.50

She said, Master, on the fourth day the slave girl appeared before   *The*
the king with a knife in her hand and said, "Your Majesty, if you do   *Sixty-Fifth*
not do right by me against your son I will kill myself. I beseech God   *Night*
to save me from your evil viziers, just as He helped the king's son to triumph over the vizier."

"How is that?" he asked.   14.51

She said:

THE ENCHANTED SPRING[90]

"They say, Your Majesty, that a king once arranged to marry his son   14.52
to the daughter of another king. This king invited his future son-in-law to come and stay with them for some days, at the end of which, God willing, he would send him back.

"The king ordered his son to go and sent one of his viziers with him. They were both very thirsty when they came to a spring.

"Now, it so happened that any man who drank from this spring, would turn into a woman, and any woman who drank from it, would turn into a man. The vizier knew this but the king's son did not.

"'Stay here until I return,' said the vizier.

14.53 "The vizier left the king's son, who grew terribly thirsty and took a drink from the spring. He was turned into a young woman. He was distraught and devastated by this transformation. A jinni in human form found him sitting there in a state of confusion.

"'Who might you be?' asked the jinni. 'Where have you come from and where are you headed?'

"'This is my story,' said the king's son, and explained that he was heading for the land of his father-in-law, the king. 'I came to this spring with the vizier, and I was thirsty so I drank the water and then I changed into a woman!'

14.54 "The jinni felt sympathy for him and said, 'I'll take your place as a girl and make you a man, so that you can go and consummate your marriage, but then you must come back and change into a woman again.'

"'Very well,' said the king's son.

"They agreed on the plan and fixed a time for the return. Then the jinni showed the prince the way and off the prince went to the city, where he made love to his new wife.

"When the agreed time was up, he returned to the spring, and saw that the jinni was pregnant.

"'How can I take your place when you're now pregnant?' cried the prince. 'When I left you, you were a virgin!' They fought, and the king's son was the victor.

14.55 "He returned home and, bringing his wife to his father, told him what had happened. The king ordered that the vizier be put to death.

"And so likewise, I beseech God to save me from your evil viziers. I will kill myself because of the wrong he has done me, and my sin will be on your head!"

And so the king ordered that his son be put to death.

The fourth vizier ordered that the boy be seized and appeared before the king.

"Your Highness," he said, "it is better not to act with haste and without consultation. If not, you will regret it, just as the bath-keeper regretted what he did."

"And how was that?" asked the king.

THE PRINCE AND THE BATH-KEEPER'S WIFE[91]

"Your Majesty," began the vizier, "a prince once went to the baths   14.56
to wash and get clean. He was a fat boy—so fat you could hardly see his penis. When he undressed the bath-keeper saw him and wept. He felt sorry for the boy.

"'Why are you crying?' asked the king's son.

"'I look at you,' he said, 'and I can't see any penis, and it looks as if you won't be able to have relations with a woman.'

"'By God,' said the youth, 'my father wants me to marry, but I don't know if I'm able to do it or not. Take this dinar: bring me a beautiful woman, and I'll see how I do.'

"The bath-keeper took the dinar. Now, this bath-keeper had a   14.57
very beautiful wife, and he said to himself, 'I'll just keep the dinar for myself and bring him my wife, for he's not going to be able to do anything with her.'

"So he brought his wife to the king's son in the baths, and went to watch them through a peephole. The king's son assumed the position that a man assumes with a woman, took her and satisfied all his desires with her.

"When the bath-keeper saw this he let out an anguished wail. He rushed home, put a rope around his neck and hung himself. He died, grief-stricken."

And here the dawn reached Shahrazād so she ceased to speak.

Fihrās the Philosopher spoke: 14.58

She said, Master, then the vizier said to the king, "Here is what I am   *The Sixty-Sixth*
going to tell you about the deviousness of women and their wily ways:"   *Night*

14.59　"A husband set out on a journey. He and his wife had pledged to each other that they would not betray one another. He told her he would be away for a certain period of time, and when the time had passed and he still had not returned, she left the house to look up and down the road. A man saw her and tried to seduce her but she refused.

"This man went to see an old woman, a neighbor of the wife.

"'I've fallen in love with your neighbor,' he said, 'Can you help me? If you can get the two of us together, there's a dinar in it for you.'

14.60　"'I'll do it,' said the old woman.

"She immediately took some dough and added a lot of pepper and fat to it then baked it into a round loaf. She went to the house of the woman the man had fallen in love with. Now, the old woman had a dog, which she brought to the woman's house, and began to feed some of the bread. The dog liked the taste of the fat, but because of the heat of the peppers, tears began to stream from its eyes.

"The old woman paid her neighbour a visit, and brought along the dog, which was crying and wagging its tail. When the woman saw the dog crying she exclaimed, 'Mother![93] Why is the dog crying?'

14.61　"'My daughter,' said the old woman, 'this dog used to be my neighbor. She was so beautiful. But a man fell in love with her and tried to seduce her and she refused, so he cursed her and changed her into a dog, as you can see. And when the poor thing saw me she started to cry and to wag her tail.'

"'Oh no! A man tried to seduce me, too,' said the woman. 'But I refused and now I am afraid that he will put a curse on me and turn me into a dog! If you bring him to me, I'll give you a dinar.'

"'Who is this man?' asked the old woman, as if she had no idea.

"'So-and-So,' she told her.

14.62　"'I'll go and get him.'

"'Just as I planned,' the old woman muttered to herself as she left.

"The young woman got up, put on some perfume and got herself ready for the man, and prepared some food.

"Meanwhile, the old woman looked for the man but could not find him. 'I'll have to bring her another man, but he'll have to be more handsome than the first.'

"While she was looking for a man, the woman's husband arrived back from his travels.

"The old woman, not knowing who he was, said 'By God! This one is much better looking! He'll be a good substitute.'

"'Young man,' she said, 'How would you like some food and some drink and a pretty face?'

14.63

"'Very much,' he answered.

"'Then come with me.'

"He followed her and when he realised he was heading for his own house, he knew his wife was up to something behind his back.

"He followed the old woman to his own house. She led him into a room where the old woman said, 'Take a seat on the bed.'

"He did so. When his wife saw him and recognized him she ran to him and grabbed his beard.

14.64

"'You wicked man!' she cried. 'Is this the pact you made with me? You go following a procuress!'

"'You're the one in trouble now,' said the husband. 'What do you think you are doing?'

"'When I heard you were coming I got ready for you and fixed up my room. Then I sent this old lady out to you to tempt you, to see if you would follow her or not. And look at how quick you were to follow her! By God, I will never get close to you again, ever!'"

And here the dawn reached Shahrazād so she ceased to speak.

Fihrās the Philosopher spoke:
She said, Master, "The woman finished speaking and the man said to her, 'By God, if she had taken me anywhere but my own house I wouldn't have followed. I was afraid that you were behaving like this all the time I was away.'

14.65

The Sixty-Seventh Night

"The woman slapped her face and tore her shirt. 'So you think that badly of me?'

"And she refused to make it up with him until he had showered her with gifts and tried valiantly to please her.

"I am telling this story so you may know that the wiles of women are great."

When the king heard this, he rescinded the order that his son be killed.

THE BOAR AND THE MONKEY[94]

14.66 On the fifth day, the slave girl came before the king and said, "If you do not do right by me against those who have wronged me, if you do not give me my due, I'll throw myself in this fire,"—in front of the king was a blazing fire—"and my sin will be on your head.

"Your evil viziers will do you no good. Let me tell you, Your Majesty, about the boar that used to come to a fig tree and take the fruits that had fallen from its branches. One day it came to the tree as usual and found a monkey in the branches at the top of the trees. The monkey threw a fig down to the boar, who ate it and enjoyed it. The boar raised its head a second time and the monkey threw another fig. This went on until the veins in the boar's neck burst and it died.

"And I am afraid that you will end up like the boar, who liked the food so much that it kept on eating until its neck burst."

14.67 When the king heard this, he feared she would throw herself on the fire, and so he ordered that his son be put to death.

The fifth vizier ordered the son to be seized and appeared before the king.

"Your Majesty," said the vizier, "You are an intelligent man (God be praised!), and you know that it is better not to act hastily, before the truth is made clear."

THE DOG AND THE VIPER[95]

14.68 "I have heard, Your Majesty, that there lived a man who held a great position at the court of the sultan. He had a dog, with which he would hunt. He had taught the dog to do only what it was ordered to do, and he held nothing more dear than his dog. One day his wife set out to visit her family. As they had a small child she said to her husband, 'Stay with your son until I get back. I'll only be gone a short while.'

"The man was sitting with his son when an envoy of the king arrived. 'The king wishes to see you right away,' said the envoy. 14.69

"'Look after my son until I get back,' the man said to his dog. 'Keep your eye on the door and do not let anyone in.'

"The dog sat beside the boy. A black viper entered the house, approached the boy and was going to bite him. The dog pounced on it and bit off its head. When the man returned to his house he saw blood all over the dog's mouth and thought it had eaten his son, so he beat the dog and killed it.

"But when he went into the room he found his son alive, next to the decapitated snake. He slapped his face in despair and regret but it was too late." 14.70

And here the dawn reached Shahrazād so she ceased to speak.

Fihrās the Philosopher spoke: 14.71

She said, Master, then the vizier said to the king, *The Sixty-Eighth Night*

THE WILES OF THE OLD WOMAN[96]

"Your Majesty, on the matter of the limitless deviousness and wiles of women, let me tell you about a man who, if he heard of a beautiful woman, had to speak with her. One day he caught sight of a woman of radiant beauty. So he followed the woman and found out where she lived, then told an old woman who used to take care of such things for him about her. 14.72

"'That's the wife of So-and-So,' said the old woman. 'There's no point. She has no desire whatsoever, so don't trouble yourself.'

"'I must have her,' he said. 'Find me a way and I'll make it worth your while.' 14.73

"'If you must,' said the old woman, 'then go to the market and buy a robe from her husband.' She explained who he was and where to find him.

"The man went to the woman's husband and bargained and bought a robe from him that he took back to the old woman. She burned it in three places.

"'Sit here in this room,' she said to the man, 'and don't let anyone see you until I come back.' Then she picked up the robe, folded it and took it to the house of the merchant's wife. She knocked on the door.

"'Who's there?' asked the woman.

"'Please open up,' said the old woman.

"She opened the door, and the old woman entered.

"'My daughter, prayer time is near, and I need to make my ablutions. Could you fetch me some water?'

"The young woman got up and went to get her some water for her ablutions. The old woman took the robe and, without the woman's knowledge, quickly put it under the young woman's pillow in the merchant's bed.

"Then she did her ablutions and departed.

"The merchant came home from the market and went to bed. He felt something under the pillow. He lifted it to see what it was and found the robe he had sold to the man. He concluded that the man was his wife's lover and had forgotten it there, so he beat his wife soundly, but without telling her the reason why. She did not understand what she had done to deserve such a beating.

"He went to his shop and the woman, terribly upset, went to her family and told them that her husband had beaten her for no reason.

"She stayed with her family until nightfall, then returned to her house. The old woman heard about this and the next day she came again to the house to do her ablutions.

"'My daughter,' she said, 'What's the matter? You have changed.'

"She told the old woman her story.

"'By God,' she said, 'I really don't know what sin I've committed.'

"'Well, there's clearly something between the two of you,' she said. 'Do you know what I suggest?'

"'What is that?'

"'I know of a man, who's more knowledgeable than anyone else I know. Would you like to come with me to see him and ask him what to do? Perhaps he can help you. Maybe he could write something that would make peace between the two of you.'

"'Yes,' said the young woman.

"So she put on her best cloak and went with the old woman to the man who had bought the robe from her husband."

And here the dawn reached Shahrazād so she ceased to speak.

Fihrās the Philosopher spoke:

She said, Master, "The man approached her, clasped her in his arms, and had his way with her. She was too embarrassed to scream and so stayed silent until he had finished.

"'I'll fix things between the two of you,' he told her. 'I'll write you an amulet of love and affection.' He wrote out the amulet and gave it to her. She thanked him and returned home.

"'You did what I asked,' the man said to the old woman, 'but you've ruined things between her and her husband.'

"'No matter,' she said. 'I'll fix things up between them, just as I ruined them. Get going now. I want you to walk past her husband and make sure he sees you. If he asks you about the robe you bought from him, tell him, "I sat next to a fire and burned it in three places, so I gave it to an old woman I know, a neighbor, to take it to the tailor to get it mended but I don't know what she did with it." Then when you see me, grab me and say, "This is the woman I gave the robe to," and ask me about it. I'll take care of the rest.'

"So off he went to the market and walked past the merchant, the woman's husband, making sure he saw him. Sure enough, the merchant came up to him and asked him about the robe. He told the husband exactly what the old woman had instructed him to say.

14.76

14.77

14.78

The Sixty-Ninth Night

14.79

14.80   "In the middle of their conversation, the old woman appeared. 'This is the old woman!' exclaimed the man.

"The merchant asked her about the robe.

"'This man gave me a robe to take to get mended,' she said. 'I passed by a house I knew and went inside to do my ablutions. I put the robe under a pillow, but after washing I forgot all about it and went out. Then when I remembered it, I couldn't find the house again and I didn't know where it was.'

"'I found your robe, old woman,' said the merchant, 'and it was a big headache. You left it in my house.'

14.81   "Then he gave her the robe and went to his wife. He told her what had happened and, thus satisfied, made peace with her.

"'This is how it was,' said the wife.

"I tell you all this so that you may know that the wiles of women are great."

When the king heard this he rescinded the order that his son be killed.

On the sixth day the slave girl appeared before him with poison in her hand.

"Your Majesty," she said, "your evil viziers are just indulging you. I beseech God to aid me against them, just as He aided the thief!"

"And how was that?" asked the king.

The Lion and the Thief[97]

14.82   "They say, Your Majesty, that a great caravan camped beside a village on its route. There were thieves in the village, and on this day the wind and rain were fierce. The inhabitants of the village said to the people in the caravan, 'Keep hold of your possessions and your animals, and look after yourselves so that you do not get robbed.'

"That night a lion crept in among their mounts to get away from the cold and the rain. A thief came to steal one of the animals. The biggest and best animal he could find was the lion—but of course he did not know it was a lion because it was so dark—so he mounted it and rode off at a gallop."

And here the dawn reached Shahrazād so she ceased to speak.

Fihrās the Philosopher spoke:

She said, Master, "The thief rode the lion, and the lion said to himself, 'This is the thief[98] that the inhabitants of the village mentioned!' So he fled with the thief on his back, both frightened of each other, until the blessed morning came. The lion came to a great tree where the thief grabbed hold of a branch, and the lion ran away.

"He met a monkey, and the monkey said to him, 'Why are you so scared, lion?'

"'A thief grabbed hold of me last night,' said the lion, 'and kept me running until the blessed morning came.'

"'So where is this thief now?' asked the monkey.

"'He's in that tree,' replied the lion.

14.84

"The lion followed to see what the monkey was doing. The monkey went to the tree and saw the man up there. So he climbed up above him and motioned to the lion, who began to walk to the tree. Now the monkey had two large testicles that hung down just above the thief's head. The thief grabbed hold of them and pulled hard. The monkey screamed, lost consciousness, and died. The thief threw the dead monkey down to the lion.

"When the lion saw the dead monkey he fled, saying to himself, 'By God, I may have met the thief but it was the monkey who was killed.' So the thief came down and was saved from the lion.

"And I beseech God to aid me against your evil viziers as He aided the thief against the monkey who wanted to destroy him."

14.85

Then the slave girl took out the poison.

"I will drink this poison," she announced, "and my sin will be on your head if you do not do right by me against your son who has wronged me."

So the king ordered that his son be killed.

The sixth vizier ordered that the prince be seized, then appeared before the king.

"Your Majesty," he said, "if you did not have a son, you would ask God to grant you one. So how can you order him to be killed when you do not have any more? Is this all because of what a woman says? When you know that the words of women are untrue, and you can never tell if a woman's lying or telling the truth?"

THE KING AND THE FISHERMAN

14.86   "They say that a fisherman once brought a fish to a king as a gift. The king liked the fish, and ordered that he be given four thousand dirhams for it.

"'You shouldn't have done that,' his wife said. 'You gave a fisherman four thousand dirhams for just one fish?'

"'What can I do?' he said. 'I've ordered that he be paid and it is not right for someone in my position to go back on his word.'

"'When he comes tomorrow,' she said, 'say to him, "That fish you brought me—is it male or female?" If he says "female," then say to him "Don't let me see you again until you bring me a male!" and if he says "male," then tell him to bring you a female.'

"The next day, the fisherman came to the king and the king posed him the question the woman had told him to ask.

"'May God protect the Emir!' the fisherman replied. 'It was a hermaphrodite—neither male nor female.'

14.87   "This made the king laugh and he ordered the fisherman be given another four thousand dirhams.

"As the fisherman was leaving with his money a single dirham fell to the palace floor. He stopped to pick it up off the ground.

"The king's wife observed this.

"'I've never seen such shamelessness,' she cried. 'One measly dirham falls to the ground—one out of many, many dirhams—and this fisherman won't leave it behind for one of our retainers?'

"She informed the king of this, and convinced him that he should get the dirham back. He summoned the fisherman.

"'Have you no charity?' asked the king. 'You dropped one single dirham out of such a hoard and you wouldn't leave it behind.'

"'May God give the king strength!' said the fisherman. 'I saw that the dirham had your noble name on it, so I picked it up off the ground, to honor you. I did not want it to be trodden on.'

"So the king ordered that he be given another four thousand dir- 14.88 hams and on the gate of the city he had this written:

"'Pay no heed to the words of women! No good will come of them.'"

And here the dawn reached Shahrazād so she ceased to speak.

Fihrās the Philosopher spoke: 14.89

She said, "May God give the king strength!" said the vizier. "Let *The* me tell you what else I have heard about the wily deviousness of *Seventy-First* women." *Night*

THE ELEPHANT[99]

"They say, Your Majesty, that there was a man who farmed a plot of 14.90 land, and one day while he was out in the field, his wife prepared a meal of chicken and chickpeas for him. She put it in a basket and went to take it to her husband.

"On the way, some thieves abducted her and took her to a place 14.91 where they enjoyed her one after the other. One of them took the chickpeas that were in the basket and moulded them into the shape of an elephant, and then put them back in the basket.

"When the last thief was done with her, they left her and went on their way. She picked up the basket, not knowing what had been done, and went off to see her husband.

"'What have you brought?' he asked her.

"She set the basket before him and when he opened it he found the figure of an elephant made out of chickpeas.

"'What on earth is this?' he asked.

"She realized that the thieves must have made the elephant, and 14.92 in her wily deviousness she replied, 'I saw an elephant trampling you in a dream, so I asked an interpreter about it and he advised me to make an elephant out of chickpeas for you to eat.'

"Her husband thanked her and, thinking she was telling the truth, ate the meal.

"I tell you this story, Your Majesty, so you will know that the wiles of women are great."

When he heard this, the king rescinded the order that his son be killed.

14.93 On the seventh day the slave girl said to herself, "If they do not kill him today, he will speak and I'll be the one who'll be killed. I must kill myself before he talks."

She gathered what money she had and gave it as alms to the poor. Then she ordered a great deal of firewood, which was gathered for her. She climbed up on top of the firewood and gave the order for it to be set alight.

When the king heard this, he said, "Grab her before it's too late." And he ordered that his son be put to death.

The seventh vizier ordered the boy be seized. He appeared before the king and said, "Your Majesty, are you going to kill your own son because of the words of a woman, when you don't even know if she is telling the truth or not? A sensible man does not let a woman determine his actions."

THE THREE WISHES[100]

14.94 "They say, Your Majesty, a man once had a servant who was a jinni. He had only to ask for whatever it was he wanted. One day, the jinni servant said to him, 'I am leaving you, but I will teach you three invocations that will bring you anything you wish. All you have to do is ask.' And he taught him the three invocations.

"The man, sad to see the jinni go, went to his wife and told her the bad news.

14.95 "'This is a blessing,' she said.

"'What would you like to ask from Almighty God?' he said.

"'Well, all you men think about is women, so ask Almighty God for more penises.'

"So he asked, and his wish was answered: his body was covered with penises.

"When he saw the results, he regretted the wish.

"'Don't fret,' his wife told him. 'You have still two more wishes. Use the second wish to ask God to take them away.'"

And here the dawn reached Shahrazād so she ceased to speak.

Fihrās the Philosopher spoke:
She said, Master, "The woman said to her husband, 'Use the second wish to ask God to take them away.'

"So he asked God to take them all away, and he was left without a penis.

"He regretted this, but his wife said, 'You still have one wish. You can ask Almighty God to bring back the first one, even if it's crooked.'

"So he asked God to have it back, and it came back, bent and crooked. He had used up all three wishes, and all because he did what a woman told him to do.

"I have also been told, Your Majesty, the following story regarding the deviousness and wiles of women."

THE MAN WHO INVESTIGATED THE WILES OF WOMEN[101]

"There was once a man who wanted to know the devious wiles of women. On his quest, he came to a village, where they told him, 'You must lie in ashes for forty mornings, and eat barley bread with no salt in order to find what you seek.'

"So he did just that.

"He kept a written record of all the answers to his questions about the wiles of women so as to compose a book on the topic.

"When he returned to his own country he happened to pass by another village on the way. He saw that one of the villagers had prepared food for a feast and that all the villagers had been invited.

"The man joined the group and when the owner of the house saw him he asked, 'You there! Who might you be?'

14.98 "'A wayfarer,' the man answered, 'I've come from the land of So-and-So seeking such-and-such, and I have lain in ashes for forty mornings and eaten barley bread with no salt.'

"When the master of the house heard this, he felt pity for the fellow, and took him by the hand and brought him to his wife and recounted the man's story. He told her to feed him some good, fatty broth, something to ease his mind and relax his body.

"Then the wife asked him what he had learned. He told her that he knew the devious wiles of women, and that he had composed a book on the topic. The wife knew then that he was an idiot. She sat him down and gave him food and drink.

"'Well,' she said, 'a woman can have no secret from you, then, given what you know about their devious and wily ways. Let me tell you, my husband has not touched me for years. If you would like to come to me, have your way with me and I with you, then come on, do it!'

14.99 "'Yes, please!' said the man, already moving towards her.

"He jumped on top of her, full of desire,[102] but she screamed and kicked him off. He sat up straight, scared nearly to death, his senses gone, his mind confused and his body gripped with fear."

And here the dawn reached Shahrazād so she ceased to speak.

14.100 *Fihrās the Philosopher spoke:*

The She said, Master, "At the wife's scream the inhabitants of the village
Seventy-Third came and gathered round the man.
Night
"'What is going on here?' they demanded.

14.101 "'I gave this man some food, and he took a bite and then started choking. His eyes were bulging and I was afraid he was going to die right in front of me, so I yelled for you to come.'

"They looked at him at saw that he was pale.

"'Get him some water.'

"They went away and left him with the wife.

"'What do you think?' she asked, 'Is that in your book?'

"'By God, no it is not.'

"The man went on his way. He burned his book, convinced that   14.102
no one could ever match the wiles of women.

"I have told you this story, Your Majesty, so that you are not
seduced by the words of a woman into killing your own son."

When the king heard this, he rescinded the order that his son be
killed.

On the eighth day, as the sun rose, the young man said to himself,
"This is the appointed day, the day when my teacher will arrive. The
viziers have spoken for these last seven days, and I must thank them
for what they have done before the enemy appears before my father
and he orders me to be put to death."

He summoned the slave girl who had been serving him for the   14.103
past seven days.

"Go to the grand vizier," he told her, "and tell him to come to me."

She was so thrilled to hear the prince speak that she left right
away to see the grand vizier. She entered his palace and told him
that the prince had spoken and wished to see him. The grand vizier
took off, barefoot, to the king's son and greeted him. The prince
told him what had prevented him from speaking.

"Praise God who has, by your hands, saved me from death!" said
the young man. "To you I will always be grateful, of the bounty of
our Lord ever mindful. If God hears my hopes then you shall see
what goodness I will give you. I would like you to go to my father
and tell him that I have spoken before that enemy of God gets to him
and he orders me to be put to death."

And here the dawn reached Shahrazād so she ceased to speak.

Fihrās the Philosopher spoke: 14.104

She said, Master, the grand vizier went straight to the king, telling   *The*
him that his son had begun to speak.   *Seventy-Fourth*
    Night
    "Bring him to me right now!"

The vizier and the king's servant brought the king's son to him. When the son entered, the king greeted and embraced him, then kissed his forehead and the two of them wept.

"My son," cried the king, "what has stopped you from speaking these past seven days, when I wanted to have you killed?"

14.105   "May God protect the king," said the son. "I had made a vow to my teacher not to speak for these last seven days. But then this slave girl made me so angry with what she said that I forgot what my teacher told me. I said to her, 'I was forbidden to speak for seven days,' and once she learned this, her only care was to have me killed before I could speak and disclose her disgrace. But perhaps the king would care to gather the jurists so there will be witnesses to what I am going to say?"[103]

The king was overjoyed to hear his son's words.

"Praise God who gave you to me and did not let me kill you!" said the king. Then the prince's tutor Sindbad appeared before the king and greeted him.

"Where were you," asked the king, "these last seven days when I wanted to put my son to death because of your advice to him?"

14.106   "God be praised," said the teacher. "You are an intelligent man, and an intelligent man does not act in haste."

"Praise God who showed mercy and did not let me kill my son unjustly!" said the king. "But tell me, if I had killed him, who would be to blame? The teacher, the girl, or me? Or the astrologer who did not inform me that he saw in his stars that he should not speak for seven days?"

"Your Majesty," said one of the scholars, "the fault would not be that of the teacher, because the king made it a condition that he not be even an hour late for the appointed time. The fault would be, rather, with the king who each day ordered his son be put to death, based on the words of a woman when he didn't even know whether she was truthful or not."

14.107   "Your Majesty," said another scholar, "the king is not to blame. The blame lies with the teacher, who did not bring the boy and tell the king of what was seen in his stars, but left him alone until the seven days had passed."

Then another scholar got up and said, "The teacher is not at fault; the fault lies with the slave girl that slandered the boy and wanted him put to death for no reason."

"The king is not at fault," the second scholar said, "for I have been informed that there is no strife and discord on earth except that created by women, and that there is no wood colder than sandalwood and camphor, yet if you rub one against the other, there is fire!"[104]   14.108

And here the dawn reached Shahrazād so she ceased to speak.

Fihrās the Philosopher spoke: 14.109

She said, Master, when the scholar finished speaking, Sindbad spoke.   *The Seventy-Fifth Night*

"Your Majesty," he said, "I have passed on everything I know, all my knowledge and learning, to your son. I don't know of anyone on earth more learned than he. For that, Your Majesty, God be praised."

"And what do you say?" said the king to his son.

"The worst of people are the ungrateful," said the son, "One should do only good. I have only good to say of him, and I ask God to protect me from saying my teacher did not make every effort in instructing me. God I praise; my teacher I thank."

When the king heard this he praised and extolled God, and ordered that the slave girl who lied be brought before him.   14.110

"What caused you to act as you did?" he asked her.

"May God protect the Emir," she said. "I have learned that humans love their selves most of all. I only spoke to your son as I did to make him speak. When I saw that he was angry, I was afraid for my life, and Satan took control of me. I admit it: I am guilty."

The king ordered that she be released and pardoned her. Then he commanded great wealth and many treasures be conferred on Sindbad and the viziers. They continued to enjoy the sweetest life, until there came to them that from which there is no fleeing, and praise be to God, Lord of all being.

THE STORY OF THE KING AND THE SERPENT[105]

15.1   They say, Your Majesty, that long ago there lived a king who owned many camels, sheep, and cattle. He had a mare that was more beautiful than any other mare, but dearest of all was his camel, young, newly weaned, and magnificent. The camel would patrol and guard the sheep and cattle. The king loved this young camel dearly. On excursions, he would ride along on the mare and admire the beauty of the young camel.

No one dared approach those sheep and cattle for fear of the camel.

15.2   One day the young camel got very agitated and ran off to the steppe, and all the sheep, cattle, and camels followed suit. The king and his army, about forty thousand strong, rode out in pursuit, but all they could see were clouds of dust.

The king returned home very upset. He sent out an announcement among the Bedouin tribes:

"I shall give a thousand ounces of red gold and a thousand she-camels to anyone who brings me news of the young camel!"

But for a long period there was no news or trace of the animal.

And here the dawn reached Shahrazād so she ceased to speak.

15.3   *Fihrās the Philosopher spoke:*

The Seventy-Sixth Night   She said, Master, then one day, two men came to the king and greeted him enthusiastically.

"What brings you here?" asked the king.

"We have news of your camel and your cattle," they said.

"Where are they?" inquired the king.

"At the mountain of the serpent," replied the two men. "It is a mountain with many trees and fruits and all the animals are there. The camel guards them, but they are ruining the land and making it impossible to live there."

"If what you say is true," said the king, "you will have all that I promised." 15.4

"We'll go with you on one condition," they said.

"What condition?" asked the king.

"When we get near the mountain, we will show you where the camel is, and then we leave you," they said.

"Very well," answered the king.

The king gave them what he had promised and then, spear in hand, he mounted the mare. They rode to the mountain they had described. 15.5

"Your camel is just behind this mountain." Then they left him.

The king drew near and spotted his young camel surrounded by the other livestock.

He shouted out and the mare whinnied. At the sound, the camel approached the king, mouth open and eyes shining bright. Then the camel attacked the king and seemed to be trying to kill him. The king took flight with the camel hot on his heels and the chase continued until midday. The king was certain that this would be the end.

Then, without warning, the mare fell into a pit, an underground granary, and the king toppled over, losing consciousness. When he came to he looked around the pit and there, right in front of the mare, was a great serpent. The camel stood on the lip of the pit crying out, saliva dripping from its mouth. The serpent raised its head. It looked at the young camel. It looked at the king. Then it shot between them and bit the camel between the eyes. The camel fell down, dead.

The serpent returned to where it had been and pushed the mare up the sides of the pit.

15.6 Then it stretched out its tail for the king and cast him out of the pit. At this, the king fainted.

And here the dawn reached Shahrazād so she ceased to speak.

Fihrās the Philosopher spoke:

She said, Master, when the king regained consciousness he praised Almighty God, then mounted his mare, rounded up his livestock and headed for home. When he had gone about three miles, he saw clouds of dust and bright billows of smoke in the distance. As he got closer, they seemed to multiply, and then the wind blew them away to reveal ten horsemen who looked like angry lions. They had loosened their camels' reins and removed the spearheads from their spears. Behind them stood ten excellent mounts, each carrying an iron cage. The horsemen came forward and greeted the king.

15.8 "O brother of the Arabs," they said. "From where do you come and where are you headed?"

"I've come from the open country," he said. "These livestock here got away and I had gone in search of them."

"You must know this land better than we do," they said. "Maybe you could tell us of a good place to hunt."

"What are you after?" asked the king.

"Serpents and giant snakes," they responded.

"How much would you give if I led you to the greatest serpent you've ever seen?" said the king.

"We'll give you a thousand gold dinars."

"That's not enough," replied the king.

15.9 So they bargained, and settled on a sum of five thousand dinars. The king took the money and led them to the pit.

"There you go," he said. "Be careful!"

"Why don't you stay with us and join the hunt?" they suggested.

One of them advanced and looked down at the serpent.

"This is just what we were looking for," he announced.

They made the camels kneel, took the cages down and set up the hooks. Then they took out skins filled with grease and each covered himself head to foot in grease.

One of them went down into the pit. The serpent began to lick him with its tongue, looking to bite him in a spot not covered in grease. The man tied the serpent in chains as it kept trying to bite him but was not able to because of the grease. When the man in the pit was sure the serpent was well trussed up, he rejoined his companions. Then they set up the cage and, working together, got the creature inside and locked it.

The serpent looked at the king it had saved from the mad camel. It did not take his eyes from him, and the king began to regret what he had done.

And here the dawn reached Sharazād so she ceased to speak.

Fihrās the Philosopher spoke:

She said, Master, they passed the night there, but the king did not sleep. When the blessed morning came, the group rode off, and the king went with them. At midday, the heat of the sun began to take its toll on them, and it was time to rest. After unloading the cage, they took refuge under the shade of a tree. All this time the snake never took its eyes from the king. Once they were settled and had gone to sleep, the king lay awake, regretting what he had done to the serpent. After some thought he schemed to set the serpent free from the cage. In his determination to help, he went to the cage and opened the lock. When the serpent saw this, it went straight for the sleeping men, like an arrow shot from a bow, and killed each and every one of them. Then like a blaze of flame it returned to the king. It gave him a look full of hate and wickedness, then charged. It blew powerfully into the king's face . . . and he lost consciousness.

The serpent then went on its way.

When the king came to, he found that his face had turned black. He gathered the hunters' equipment, loaded it onto the camels and

15.11

rounded up the livestock. Then he mounted his mare and went on his way.

When he was within sight of his own tribal lands, six thousand horsemen in full armor came out, thinking that all the sheep, cattle, camels, and beasts of burden were an enemy approaching.

"You, slave," they called to him, not recognizing the king because of his black face. "Where did all these animals come from? And where is the owner of that mare? It looks like you might have killed the man who owns it . . ."

"By God," he said, "I'm no slave! I am So-and-So the king!"

"Who do you think you're fooling?" they responded. "What a lie. King So-and-So was a most handsome man."

"By God I am the king! And my sons are Such-and-Such."

They believed what the king said, and about forty thousand riders gathered around him, some in full armor, some not. A great cry rose up at his arrival. The Bedouin tribes came from all quarters and his family came to greet him and ask him what had happened. He told them the whole story of the camel and the serpent, of how he had freed it and of how it had killed the ten horsemen, from beginning to end. Everyone was astonished.

15.12 Then he turned to them.

"What do think of what has happened to me?" he asked.

A Bedouin tribal elder came forward.

"Don't you have two sons?" he said.

"Yes," replied the king.

"Send one of them to take your revenge and kill the serpent, and the other to get you some medicine."

"Very well."

He summoned his two sons and informed them of the plan.

"We accept your plan," said the sons.

He gave them two steeds and the provisions they needed and bade them farewell. The sons traveled far and wide, high and low, in search of the medicine. Eventually they came to a Bedouin campsite full of frenzied activity and teeming with people.[106] There were the sounds of riding beasts and the chatter of slaves, horses whinnying, roosters crowing and dogs barking. Horses and mules roamed freely and at ease; swords were hung up and the bows unstrung; the ornate shields were breathtaking, too numerous to count.

At the approach of the brothers, the people came out and asked them what they were doing. 15.13

"We are the sons of King So-and-So," they answered.

And here the dawn reached Shahrazād so she ceased to speak.

Fihrās the Philosopher spoke: 15.14

She said, Master, the people went to their king and gave him the news. The king ordered that the brothers be treated with honor and given hospitality, then he summoned them to appear before him.

"What has brought you from your land, away from your homes and from your father?" asked the king.

When they had told him the news, he said to them: "Your father is getting old, his bones are frail, and his mind is feeble. Stay with me until I send word to him and send the both of you back."

"That is a sensible plan," said the older brother.

"By God," said the younger one, "I am not going back until I've done what he asked of me."

So he left his older brother and mounted his steed. He rode 15.15 through the open country alone, until he came to a beautiful place, lush with plants and trees, in the middle of which stood a tower of brass. On top of the tower, built by the wise men of old, there perched a peacock with colored wings.

At his approach the peacock gave a great cry, and the door opened to reveal an old man, bent double with the burden the years had placed on him.

He greeted the prince.

"And who are you?" he asked. "Who has entered the place where none has gone before?"

"Sir," said the prince, "my story is a strange one. I am in search of medicine for my father."

"What sort of medicine?" asked the old man, and the youth told him what he was looking for.

15.16 "My son," said the old man, "the only place you'll find it is at the Palace of the Precious Stones. A woman who is half-jinni and half-human lives there—her father was a jinni and her mother human—and there is no one on earth more beautiful than she. Her name is Shams al-Thaʿābīn,[107] daughter of Sarīfān ibn Shaʿnā ibn Iblīs al-Akbar. She sleeps for seven days every month and does not leave the palace. She is never seen during this time, as she is in a very, very deep sleep. Now, in the palace there is a dome of colored brocade raised between two trees on rods of gold. What you have to do is to take some leaves from the tree on the right and pound them with some milk, then rub the mixture on the spots and blemishes on the face. Apply it once and you'll be even more handsome than before. The leaves of the second tree will help against elephantiasis, leprosy, and abscesses: you do the same as with the leaves of the first tree. But the problem, my boy, is getting to them and getting to the place with the dome. This is something that all the philosophers and sages have never figured out. Heaven is closer, and easier to reach!"

"By Him who raised the heavens without any pillars[108] and who spread the earth over frozen water," said the prince, "no one will stop me from reaching it, God willing, and may God do with me as He wills!"

15.17 "I am just a monk who lives here," said the old man, "but if you insist on going, then trust in God!"

And here the dawn reached Sharazād so she ceased to speak.

15.18 *Fihrās the Philosopher spoke:*

The Eightieth Night

She said, Master, when the monk told the prince, "If you insist on going, then trust in God," he gave him whatever provisions he needed, set him on the right path and bade him farewell.

The young man left the monk and traveled far and wide for seven days.

On the eighth day, he looked out over a beautiful white land, where a fresh breeze blew. A fertile and verdant valley cut through it. The scent of fragrant musk wafted everywhere and the land abounded in mighty forests of fruit trees, flowing fountains, and birdsong. The valley floor was covered in saffron and beautiful, brilliant flowers: roses, violets, irises, anemones, and delicate jasmine. Nightingales and partridges sang in the trees. On the side of the valley, an imposing palace reached from the dust right up to the clouds. It was recently built, with corners made of metal, splendid balconies, and fortified gates.

The prince crossed the valley and approached the palace. By the door he came across the remains of a huge tomb. Its stones had crumbled and only its outline remained, but at the head there was a marble tablet with these verses: 15.19

> Look at the ruins, how all has changed.
>> The dwellings are now empty and strange.
> Calamity's coattails dragged all over it,
>> their stones tumbled down and split.
> Its people have gone their way,
>> no tracks or traces left to display.
> When I contemplate this empty scene
>> my eyes fill with tears they cannot contain.
> If only you knew how my sadness would not abate,
>> that is all that I've seen, there is my fate.

The prince read these verses, advanced and found that the door of the palace was open. He tethered his horse, put his hand on the hilt of his sword and unsheathed it. He went through the palace, room by room, until he came to an extraordinary light that appeared from the courtyard. In the middle of the courtyard he saw a domed tent of brocade decorated with radiant gold, at the top of which shone a golden crescent with precious stones that would blind the eyes. And just as the monk had said, there was one tree to the right of the dome, and another to the left.

15.20 He approached the tent and went inside. Nothing stirred. He saw an emerald tomb, and at its head, on a tablet of red gold, this verse was written:

> For the mortal there is no kingship;
>> true kingship is His alone.

He read the tablet, then went from the tent back into the palace but met no one. He was filled with astonishment. He noticed a great salon with high walls and pillars, and curtains of silk, and went in. It contained luxurious furnishings and engravings, and in the middle he saw a bed with a canopy of white anemone covered in a netting of jeweled silk.

Here dawn overtook Sharazād so she ceased to speak.

15.21 *Fihrās the Philosopher spoke:*

She said, Master, the young man lifted one side of the canopy and peered in. He saw a bed raised on legs of gold adorned with precious stones. On top of the bed a figure slept, covered by a cloak woven with gold. He lifted the cloak and saw a girl of indescribable beauty. She shone like the full moon; the hair on her cheeks was like the poet's description:

> Let your eye wander to her face.
>> See how your Lord has wrought so perfectly,
> Her hair across her cheek,
>> like a raven's wing upon a lily.

15.22 The young man was so taken by the girl's beauty that he could not control himself. He removed his clothes and was about to get up on the bed when he heard a sound from behind the curtain. He saw a great serpent shoot out from under the bed. It was the size of a palm tree, and its mouth was open, ready to bite. He had tried to climb on the bed, but the serpent stopped him in his tracks. The prince removed his foot from the bed and moved backwards, and the serpent returned to its place. When the prince saw this, he realized that the serpent was not real; it was an automaton. He found a way to disable it, then he got back up on the bed and climbed in next to the girl. He held her in a tight embrace but she was in such a deep sleep that she felt nothing. He took her and, finding her a pure virgin, an unbroken filly, an unpierced pearl, deflowered her. He satisfied his every desire, while she lay there sound asleep.

Then he rose and dressed, and wrote a message on the wall: "This was the work of So-and-So, Lord of Such-and-Such a land!"

Then he left the girl as she was, and went to the tree the old monk had described, took the leaves he needed and went back to the monk in the tower. He passed the night with the monk and told him about the girl. 15.23

The next day he said farewell to the old man and headed for home, quite pleased at his success. He came to the camp where he had left his brother. He asked for his brother and the people of the area came out to meet him, his brother among them. They fêted his safe arrival and he enjoyed their hospitality for three days.

On the fourth day, he and his brother mounted their steeds and headed home.

Just before they arrived, they stopped to rest. As it was near the end of the day, they took out some food and sat down to eat and drink.

The younger son told his brother everything. He told him all about the girl and the tree and showed him the leaves he was bringing to their father.

Upon hearing this, his brother thought, "If he turns up with the leaves and I have nothing, what will my father think of me? My brother will reap all the rewards!" Thus he began to plot against his brother. 15.24

After their meal, the younger brother slept, while the older one got up and took the leaves. Then he tied his brother to a nearby tree as he slept.

"I am going to leave you here for the wolves and wild beasts to devour," he said. He left him there, and went to his father.

He sent a messenger on ahead and his father and family, people, and companions all came to meet him. He dismounted and went to speak with his father on his own. He told him the instructions he had heard his brother give, and handed him the leaves. The father soaked them in accordance with his son's instructions, and then applied them to his face. The blackness cleared up and his face reverted to its normal color.

In celebration, the king held a great festival and slaughtered camels and cattle. But then he asked his son about his younger brother.

"I left him in the land of the Tribe of So-and-So," he replied, referring to the place where he himself had been.

And here the dawn reached Sharazād so she ceased to speak.

Fihrās the Philosopher spoke:

She said, Master, when the king heard this he swore an oath to himself that when his younger son arrived, he would seize and crucify him. Of course, he did not know all that is unseen, and the Master of the Unseen does as He wills and ordains.

Now we resume the story of the younger brother, bound to the tree. At nightfall, as the air turned cold, he awoke to find himself tied up. He was in no doubt that this was his brother's doing.

In the morning some birds tried to approach. He screamed at them but more and more turned up. He was sure that that they would devour him and this would be the end of him.

He remained tied to the tree, beset with birds for almost half the day, when God sent a caravan his way. The young man shouted loud and long. The people of the caravan heard him, and stopped and looked.

"Who are you?" they asked. "And who did this to you?"

15.26   "I am a stranger," he told them. "Bandits attacked me and stole all I had and tied me up like this, as you can see."

They untied him and took him with them to his father's lands. They camped nearby and the prince, recognizing the area, left them and made for the palace. When he entered, his father looked at him but did not greet him. Instead, he ordered that he be tied up and beaten with iron rods. He ordered one of his slaves to call the Bedouin to witness the crucifixion of the prince. For ten days the crier sent out the message, and then on the eleventh day, large crowds of Bedouins had assembled.

The king ordered his son to be crucified on the trunk of a tall palm tree. They tied him up, and then the king summoned his older son.

"You kill him yourself," the king told him.

Lance in hand, he moved forward to kill his brother, out of pure evil and spite. 15.27

But then a great cry filled the air. The mountains and all who were on them shook terribly.

As the Bedouins looked up at the sound, there appeared, as swift as a gale or the sudden hand of fate, a horseman, a mountain of a man. Behind him flags fluttered and banners waved. Horses appeared from every direction.

The horseman stood before them, attired in coats of mail, an ancient shining helmet on his head, with two lances in one hand, and ten-cubit spears in the other. With his troops at his back, he looked at the crucified man on the palm tree and at the crowd beyond. He let out a scream that sent the nearby Bedouins scattering. Then he attacked the deceitful elder brother and struck him down dead with a single blow. He directed another thunderous scream at the Bedouins, uncovered his face and looked up at the crucified prince.

"Do not fear, peerless and matchless prince!" said the horseman. 15.28

It was none other than the young woman, Shams al-Tha'ābīn, mistress of the Palace of the Precious Stones. She chopped down the palm tree, set her lover free, and clasped him to her breast.

She wrapped the prince in a cloak, mounted him on her horse, and took him back to her people. Then she returned to attack his father's people. Only a few were spared. She took his father captive.

They scattered and sought refuge in safe places, mountaintops, and deep valleys.

She made the prince ruler, rounded up all the deserters from his father's army, and brought them before him.

"Do with them as you wish," she said.

He pardoned them.

Then he freed his father, who had not known of his brother's envious treachery and betrayal.

He told his father what had happened with the girl.

"My boy," said the father, "your brother deceived us—praised be God who has punished him for what he did."

Then the young woman remained there with the prince until the people eventually came back, and she granted them indemnity.[109] She let the king have his own land, to rule as he pleased, and she went back to her palace with the prince. They were married, and she appointed him as ruler over her land, and he lived with her a life of sweetness and luxury until there came to them that from which there is no fleeing, and praise be to God, Lord of all being (and eternal peace upon His messengers).[110]

The Tale of the Ebony Horse[111]

Shahrazād spoke: They claim, blessed king, that there once lived a king whose domains stretched far and wide. He was a just ruler to his subjects. Arabs and non-Arabs alike feared him and brought him gifts; whole nations made way for him. All men grovelled before him. He was cultured and eloquent and loved the company of the learned; scholars and wise men gathered around him as they had done for no king before him.

16.1

He held two feasts a year: The Feast of Joy and the Feast of the Autumnal Equinox. At the end of the feast it was his custom to open the door of the palace to courtiers and commoners alike, and listen to their requests. Each would greet him in a manner befitting a king, and each would present him with whatever gift his circumstances would allow. He would accept the gifts, which would be placed in his treasury, and would reward everyone handsomely.

16.2

But what he loved most of all were gifts that had some wizardry to them.

And here the dawn reached Shahrazād so she ceased to speak.

Fihrās the Philosopher spoke:
She said, Master, during one of the feasts, three sages came to the king: an Indian, a Greek, and a Persian. Each had so many riches that he needed camels to carry it all.

16.3

The Eighty-Third Night

16.4 Each one of them bore a great gift, showing the wizardry of his craft. Now, it was the custom of this king that, if given something he liked, he would grant the giver a wish and see that it was carried out.

The king ordered that the sages be admitted, and the first to come forward was the Indian, who gave him a brass figure in the form of a man, a trumpet to its mouth.

The king was delighted.

"O learned sage," he said, "what does it do, this statue with the trumpet?"

The sage had been most ingenious in making this device.

"You put this statue at the gate of the city," he told the king, "and if any spy, enemy, or evildoer enters, the statue will sound the trumpet. Then you can capture the intruder and do with him what you will."

16.5 The king was overjoyed at these words. He ordered the statue be brought up for the Day of the Test, which was the third day of the feast. It was his custom on the Day of the Test to try out each of the gifts he had received. If he found that it truly worked, he would bestow all manner of honors and favors on the giver.

Then he gave the order for the second sage, the Greek, to come in. He entered and placed before the king a tray made of red gold in the center of which stood a peacock, surrounded by twelve chicks, all of them beautiful in form and pleasing to the eye.

The king was delighted at the sight and thought it excellent.

"O learned sage," he said, "what's so special about these peacocks?"

16.6 "Your Majesty," said the Greek sage, "you place them before you, and every hour of the day one of these little birds flies up. This is what they do, at the end of every hour, bird after bird, until the day is done. And then at night, when an hour of the night has passed, one of the birds flies down, and so on, every hour until the night is over. At the end of the day and at the end of the night too, the peacock will whistle. When a month is up it will give a loud whistle and open its mouth, and in its mouth you will see the new moon. Thus you will know that that night is the start of the next month."

"If what you say is true," said the king, "and I see what you describe, I will grant you your dearest wishes."

Then he ordered the device to be taken up to the treasury.

And here the dawn reached Shahrazād so she ceased to speak.

Fihrās the Philosopher spoke:

She said, Master, the peacock was taken away and the king gave the order for the third sage, the Persian, to enter. He was an old and ugly man. He greeted the king and placed before him a horse of ebony, with a saddle of gold, and reins of pearls and precious stones, the likes of which no one had ever seen.

The king and everyone else in the room were amazed at the sight, and his royal heart filled with joy.

"O learned sage," he said, "I've never seen anything like this horse! What miracles does it perform?"

"May God give the fortunate king strength," said the sage. "This is no ordinary horse that you see. In a single day and night it will carry its rider as far as a swift steed could carry him in an entire year."

When the king heard this he said, "If you speak the truth, then you may have from me whatever you wish."

Then the king ordered the horse to be taken up to the treasury for the Day of the Test, and the three sages left, the king having promised them all great rewards.

On the Day of the Test the king sat on his throne, placed his crown on his head and ordered his ministers and men of state to assemble. When they had arrived and taken their places, he summoned the three sages and ordered that the statue, the peacock, and the horse be brought out.

"If what you have said is true," he told the sages, "then you shall have whatever you desire."

The king ordered that they begin with the statue holding the trumpet. He tried it out, found that it worked exactly as the sage had said. The king was overjoyed.

"Ask me for whatever you desire," he said to the sage.

"Your Majesty," he said, "I wish to marry your eldest daughter and to be your son-in-law."

"And you shall have what you desire," said the king.

16.9   Now, the king had three daughters and one son. The daughters were watching their father from behind a curtain set up so they could look on without being seen. When the eldest saw this she was thrilled that she would marry such a refined, cultured, and highly intelligent sage.

The second sage, the Greek, came forward and brought out the tray. The king tested it and found that it worked exactly as the sage had described.

"Ask me for whatever you desire," he said to the sage.

"Your Majesty," he said, "what I desire is that you bestow upon me the same favor you granted my colleague, and marry me to your middle daughter."

The king agreed to this.

When the king's middle daughter looked at the sage she was overjoyed. He was perfectly handsome.

16.10   Then the third sage, the Persian with the horse, came forward and kissed the ground before the king.

As the horse was brought out, the king addressed him.

"O learned sage," he said, "I would like to see if this horse will really carry its rider as you say!"

"Yes, Your Majesty," said the sage. Then he hopped on the horse, reached out his hand and turned the pin that made it rise. This horse had a pin on the right side that made it ascend, and another on the left that made it descend.

At the turn of the pin, the horse began to move, and the wind filled it up inside until it rose up into the air. This was how the horse worked: the more it filled with wind, the higher it rose. Then the sage turned the other pin to make it descend, and down he came before the king, who was enraptured.

"What a sage you are!" exclaimed the king. "A master of your craft! Ask me for whatever you desire! No one has ever given me anything like this!" 16.11

"May God strengthen you!" said the sage. "I wish that you would allow me to join my companions and marry me to your youngest daughter, and make me your son-in-law."

And the king agreed.

And here the dawn reached Shahrazād so she ceased to speak.

Fihrās the Philosopher spoke: 16.12

She said, Master, when the king agreed to give his youngest daugh- *The* ter to the sage who had brought the horse, this daughter, the most *Eighty-Fifth* beautiful of all her sisters, as radiant as the sun, took a look at him *Night* and saw that he was an ugly old man. She was terribly upset at this, burst into tears, and slapped her face in despair.

Her brother, who loved her dearly, sauntered in and, seeing her 16.13 in this state, asked her, "Sister, why are you crying? It's a day of joy!"

"My brother," she said, "How can I not cry? Our father has just given me to that ugly old man!"

"Don't cry," he told her. "No need for sadness: I'll save you from him and I'll undo whatever our father has planned."

Then he hurried to his father.

"Father," he asked, "how can that ugly old man deserve to marry into our family?"

"By his wizardry and his mastery of his craft," answered the king.

"What wizardry?" he asked. "What craft?"

"My son, this horse you see here," said the king, "can fly with its rider way up in the sky! Just like a bird!"

The youth looked at the horse.

"I'll test it and see if he's telling the truth."

He came forward and mounted the horse, but he could not get it 16.14 to move. He gave it a kick, but the horse remained still.

"This horse doesn't do anything!" exclaimed the prince.

The sage got up and went over to it. He turned the ascent pin and the horse began to climb. The prince was so astonished that he forgot to ask how to make it descend, and the sage, enraged by the prince's words, neglected to tell him about the descent pin.

The prince turned the ascent pin and the horse began to move and buck; its middle filled up with wind and it took off into the air.

The king watched as the horse disappeared from sight. When the prince had been gone for some time, he said to the sage, "Very well. Now bring back my son."

"Impossible!" said the sage. "You'll never see him again."

16.15   "And how is that?" demanded the king.

"Your son was so amazed and in such a rush," answered the sage, "that he did not ask me how to make it come down. He will keep going up, higher and higher, until the winds carry him away to his death. Unless, of course, God inspires him and he finds the descent pin, in which case he will be saved."

The king's expression changed at these words. He threw off his crown and fell to the ground in a faint. They splashed water on his face to wake him, and no sooner had he regained consciousness than he ordered that the sage be put in prison. In despair for his son, he grieved and wore only garments of wool,[112] and refused to eat and drink.

16.16   As for the prince, when he realized that he was himself going higher and higher, he began to regret what he had done. Realizing that there must be some means of making the horse go back down, he looked all over and soon enough found a small pin on the left side. He turned it and the horse went down. Then he turned the first pin and the horse began to rise again. So he now understood that the left pin was for going down and the right one for going up. Relieved, he started the horse's descent, and down, down he went, all day long until nightfall.

And here the dawn reached Shahrazād so she ceased to speak.

She said, Master, the prince looked down and saw a city of white marble, with streams and fruit trees.

"I wish I knew what city that is," he said.

He continued his descent and landed on the roof of the most beautiful palace ever seen.

"I wish I knew whose palace this is," he thought.

Then he circled around, looking to the right, then to the left.

"I won't find anywhere better than this to spend the night," he said to himself. "At first light I'll get back on my horse, go back to my father and tell him what I've seen."

And as he looked at the horse he thought: "If Almighty God returns me safely to my father, I swear I will reward that Persian sage!"

Night had fallen, so he sat down and drowsiness overtook him. But he was too hungry to sleep.

"Surely there must be something to eat and drink in this palace!"

Leaving the horse on the roof, he went down into the palace. His walk led him to a great chamber covered with silk brocade and ornamented with red gold. He stood there stunned, not knowing which way to turn.

He heard snoring. A slave was there fast asleep, with a sword next to him, and a candle in a golden candelabra and a huge golden bowl filled with food in front of him.

He entered the chamber and ate and drank his fill. Thus fortified, he said to himself, "By God, I am not going to leave this palace until I've seen what's inside it."

He crept towards the sleeping slave and took his sword. He made for a light he could see shining in another chamber. Inside he saw candles, and a bed on four legs of gold in the middle. A figure lay on it, asleep.

"That must be the lord of this palace," he thought.

Upon closer inspection he saw that it was a girl, as radiant as the shining full moon, covered by a fabric of red gold. At the sight of her he lost his mind and cared for nothing else. He climbed up on the bed and sat by her head, contemplating her beauty. Unable to control himself, he kissed her forehead.

The girl awoke, saw him and sat upright.

"Who are you and how did you get in here?" she demanded.

And here the dawn reached Shahrazād so she ceased to speak.

Fihrās the Philosopher spoke:

She said, Master, then the girl asked him, "Are you human or jinni?"

"Young lady, lower your voice!" he said, "We mustn't wake the eunuchs!"

16.22 "Who are you?" she asked. "Are you the one my father has chosen for me to marry? Did he tell you to come in here like this?"

"Yes," said the prince.

The girl was overcome with joy and delight, for she saw how handsome and attractive he was.

Her slave girls heard them talking and they sat upright, transfixed by the beauty of the young man.

"Is there anyone more handsome than this young man my father has chosen for me to marry?" the princess asked them.

"How did he get in here?" they asked.

"By God," she said, "all I know is that I woke up and there he was, sitting next to me. I asked him who he was and what he was doing here and he said, 'I'm your husband.'"

16.23 But then one of the slave girls said, "I swear he's not the one your father chose for you yesterday because that one's not even fit to be this man's slave. I know him, the other one, and when he left your father, he made a poor exit.[113] But this one is right for you, and you are right for him."

Meanwhile, the slave had woken up and, looking for his sword, found it missing. He went in to the slave girls as they gleefully gossiped about what had happened. Then he found the prince and the young woman sitting together on the bed, and he said to the prince: "If you are a jinni, then she is forbidden to you, but if you are human, then the girl is fit for no one else but you."

"I am human just like you," said the prince.

The eunuch left and went to tell the king what had occurred.

"Damn you! How did he get in?" exclaimed the king.

"I don't know," said the slave.

When the king heard this he got up and rushed to the slave girls.

"What is going on here?" he demanded.

16.24

"We don't know," said the slave girls. "We just found him sitting next to her with a sword in his hand."

The king made for the bed, threw back the curtain and—lo and behold—a youth, as beautiful as the full moon at night, was sitting there with his daughter.

The king drew his sword and made to strike. When the youth saw him he asked the girl, "Who is this?"

"That's my father," she answered.

At this, the youth got up and let out a loud cry that shocked the king.

He tried to be polite: "Are you human or jinni?"

"Were not for the honor of your daughter," the youth answered, "I'd make you join those whose time has come and gone. How could you think I could be a jinni or a demon? I'm of royal blood and will inherit power and dominion!"

16.25

And here the dawn reached Shahrazād so she ceased to speak.

Fihrās the Philosopher spoke:

She said, Master, these words filled the king with fear.

"If you are as you say," he said to the youth, "then how is it that you entered my palace without my permission and entered the women's quarters? Now, I will order my slaves to kill you."

16.26

The Eighty-Eighth Night

The prince laughed.

"What's so funny?" asked the king.

16.27

"Your lack of sense," said the prince. "Where are you going to find a better husband for your daughter, one with more money and more men?"

"Look, I would have liked to give her to you. But we would have had to do it properly, with witnesses present, so there would be no scandal."

"Very well," said the prince. "But let me tell you that the smart thing to do is to leave me here till tomorrow. In the morning, come out with all your troops and all your soldiers and order them to meet us on the battlefield. If they win and I am defeated, so be it; if I win and defeat them, I alone will take your daughter."

16.28 The king was astonished at these words. He put down his sword and the prince did too, and they sat down and talked for a while. Then the king ordered his slave to go to the vizier and tell him to prepare the troops. The eunuch rushed to the vizier with the order, and the vizier commanded the soldiers to mount right away. When the blessed morning came, the king rode out and presented the youth with a steed of noble stock, but he refused to mount it until he had seen the king's troops and what he was up against.

The king ordered a herald to proclaim: "You people who gather here! There has come to me a young man of intelligence, refinement, and eloquence the likes of which I've never seen! He has asked for my daughter's hand, and doing battle with you will be his bridal price, so behold your opponent!"

Then he said to the youth, "And behold yours!"

"Fine, but my own horse is on the roof of the palace," said the youth.

The king did not take this seriously. "Your horse has climbed up on the roof, has it?"

"Send some of your slaves with me," he replied.

So he did so, and they went up onto the palace roof, where they found the horse. They carried it back down to the king, who was flabbergasted.

"This is madness!" he said to himself.

16.29 The youth mounted the horse and turned the ascent pin. Necks craned as the horse flew up high into the sky, between the heavens and the earth.

When he saw what was happening, the king shouted "Get him before he escapes!"

"May God give the king strength!" they said, "But how can we catch a flying jinni? Let us give praise and thanks to God for saving us from him!"

And here the dawn reached Shahrazād so she ceased to speak.

Fihrās the Philosopher spoke:

She said, Master, the troops returned in dismay, and the king went back to the palace where he found his daughter sad and distraught, pining for the prince. Her condition was so severe she had taken to her bed. Her father saw how bad she was and kissed her forehead.

"God has relieved me of that sorcerer," he said. He tried talking with her but her sadness only got worse, and she vowed to herself that she would not eat or drink at all until reunited with the prince.

As for the prince, he soared homeward through the sky but his thoughts were with the beautiful girl. When he landed and entered the palace, his father, who had been grieving for him, jumped up and embraced his son. His mother and sisters were all overjoyed at his return.

He asked them about the sage.

"He is in prison," they told him.

His father ordered that the sage be released, and gave him wealth and favors, but did not marry him to his daughter. This made the sage furious.

The prince told them about what he had seen in the palace of the king, and how he wanted to return. But they warned him not to go back there.

"By God," he said, "I have to do it!"

He stayed with his father for three days. On the fourth he took what provisions he needed, mounted the horse and took off on into the sky. When his father saw him fly away, he regretted having let him go.

16.32   The horse flew and landed on the roof of the girl's palace. The young man waited there until nightfall and then, certain that everyone was asleep, came down from the roof and crept to the girl's room in the harem. The doors were open and a candle burned within. He went to the girl and woke her up with his kisses. When she saw who it was she sat up and returned the kiss.

"Look, I'm madly in love with you," he told her, "but you saw how your father treated me. I left my family and came back for you. If you are ready to come with me, now is the time; if not, I'll leave you and go back to my own people."

"Life is not worth living without you," she said.

The prince got up and she followed. He went up onto the roof, mounted the horse and seated her behind him, pulling her close. He turned the ascent pin and the horse carried the two of them aloft.

16.33   The slave girls awoke and could find no trace of the princess, so they began to shout and cry. The king was roused from his slumber.

"What has come over you?" he asked them.

They told him about his daughter, and he struck his face and tore his clothes in grief.

Meanwhile, at a good distance from the city, the prince asked the girl, "Would you like me to take you back to your palace?"

"No," she replied. "I'll never leave you."

And here the dawn reached Shahrazād so she ceased to speak.

16.34   *Fihrās the Philosopher spoke:*

The   She said, Master, at her words the prince's love for her grew even
Ninetieth stronger. They flew to the city of his father where the youth landed
Night   in a garden close by and where he left the gardener in charge of the girl and the horse. He wanted to show her how his father's kingdom compared to her own father's realm.

"Stay here," he said to her, "while I go and tell my father that you've arrived, so that our women and eunuchs can come to meet you."

She was very happy with this. So he went to see his father, who greeted him warmly.

"Did you bring the girl?"

"Yes," replied the prince. "I've brought the girl. I left her in the garden and I'd like to show her your kingdom, and for you to have your troops ride out in their best dress."

"It will be done," said the king.

Immediately the king gave the order for the people to festoon 16.35 the city and mount their horses. He and his son rode out in all their finery. The slave girls, the virgins, and the eunuchs carried censers containing different types of perfume. The whole city was gathered there to watch.

The prince returned to the garden but could not find either the girl or the horse. He let out such an anguished scream that he fainted.

When he came to, he cried, "If only I hadn't left her!"

He summoned the servants of the garden.

"Tell me who came here after I left," he asked them.

"May God strengthen the king," they said. "Only the Persian sage 16.36 entered. He was gathering herbs."

The prince realized that the sage must have abducted the girl. And that this is in fact what had happened: after the prince's departure from the garden, the sage happened to hear that the girl and the horse were in the garden and so he planned his ruse. He picked his herbs until the guardians no longer paid him any attention, then he looked for the girl. He found her awaiting the return of her prince. He kissed the ground before her and she asked him who he was.

"I am a messenger of the prince," he replied. "He sent me to bring you to another garden, one closer to the city."

"Well," she said, "he certainly couldn't find a messenger uglier 16.37 than you. He's falling short in his work."

"I assure you, young lady," said the sage, with a laugh, "that he would not have sent me if I were not this ugly to look at. He's far too jealous and protective for that."

The girl believed him, so she got up and the sage mounted her behind him on the horse. He turned the ascent pin and the horse flew away with them until they were a good distance from the city.

And here the dawn reached Shahrazād so she ceased to speak.

Fihrās the Philosopher spoke:

She said, Master, when the girl saw that they were high in the sky, she asked, "Can this really be where your master sent you?"

"God curse the man you speak of!" he said.

"I think you've tricked me!" she exclaimed.

"He's not my master," said the sage. "That was just a ruse." And he told her his story, just as it happened. "And now I've got both you and the horse."

When the girl heard this she slapped her face in anguish and tore her clothes.

"Oh, if only I had stayed with my father! If only I hadn't gone off with the prince!"

16.39   On they flew to a great meadow near a city, where they landed.

The king of this city happened to have gone out for a walk that took him past the meadow. He noticed the girl, the old man, and the horse, and saw that the girl was crying.

"See what is the matter with that girl, the one who's with the old man," he ordered his slaves.

So one of the slaves went and asked her what the matter was, but the old man interjected, "Look here! She's my wife."

"Liar!" said the girl. "You kidnapped me out of evil and spite!"

The slave reported this to the king, who ordered that the sage be put in prison, and the girl and the horse brought to his palace.

But he did not know the secret of the horse.

16.40   The king asked the girl about the horse but she gave nothing away. He ordered that a special room be readied for the girl, one richly furnished with colored brocade. She was to have whatever she wanted and a eunuch to attend to her. Then he tried to seduce her, but she refused and threw herself to the ground as if possessed.

He left her for several days and then tried to seduce her again, but she did as she had done before. When the king saw her condition, he ordered that she be tied up, but he was deeply troubled.

As for the prince, when it became clear to him that the sage had taken both the girl and the horse, he grieved terribly and took to wearing wool in penance.[114] Eventually, he took what money he needed and, bidding his father farewell, went out to search the cities and citadels for his beloved.

He roamed from one city to the next until he reached the most distant lands, but still he heard nothing of her. He would arrive at a city and enter, disguised as a merchant, but the only news he ever heard was that her father still grieved for her. So on he would go until eventually he arrived in a city where he heard a group of merchants talking about the girl, the horse, the sage, and the city they were in.

When the prince heard what she was doing he was overjoyed. He traveled far and wide to the city where the girl was being held.

He tried to enter the city, but it was the king's custom that all strangers would be brought before the king and asked who they were, from whence they came, why they had come, and what was their trade.

And here the dawn reached Shahrazād so she ceased to speak.

16.41

16.42

Fihrās the Philosopher spoke:
She said, Master, the prince came to the gate of the city at the time of the evening prayer, so they took him to the prison to wait until he could be brought before the king and questioned in the morning. Everyone in the prison was amazed by the sight of his perfect beauty.

Food was provided and placed before them. They began to eat and the youth joined them. When their meal was over, they were talking and asked the youth who he was and what he was doing.

"I am from Fars, the country of the Persian kings," he said.

16.43
The Ninety-Second Night

16.44   Some of them laughed. "Young man," they said, "we've all heard the stories people tell, and nobody is a greater liar than that Persian[115] who is with us here, and no one more repulsive."

"How is that?" asked the prince. "What lies did he tell you?"

"He claims to be a sage," they told him. "The king went out hunting one day with his companions and found him sitting there with a girl and a wooden horse. He said she was his wife, but she denied it, saying he'd kidnapped her. The king took her back to his palace and tried to seduce her, but she refused. Now she's possessed and the king has promised half his wealth to anyone who can treat her. And the sage is in here but he refuses to eat or drink—says he's too heartbroken."

16.45   The prince was overjoyed at the mention of the girl, but kept it to himself and talked with them until the blessed morning came. Then he was taken before the king, whose men told him that the youth had arrived the previous evening.

"And who are you, young man?" asked the king. "What country do you come from, and what is your trade?"

"O fortunate king," said the youth, "my name and my country are Persian; as for my profession, I am a physician, knowledgeable in medicines for the sick and the possessed. I travel the lands so that people may benefit from the knowledge I possess, and in the word of mighty and glorious God, «Above every man of knowledge is One who is All-Knowing.»"[116]

16.46   The king was overjoyed at these words.

"Wise physician," said the king, "you have come to us at just the right time. I have a girl who is disturbed, and if you can cure her, I will share all of my kingdom with you."

"I will do my best, and to God I leave the rest," said the youth. "Describe the girl's case and how this jinni took hold of her."

So he described her case and how he had taken her away from the old sage.

"And what did you do with the horse?" asked the youth.

"It's in my treasury, but we don't know whether it is useful or dangerous."

"I think," the prince thought to himself, "that I should examine the horse before anything else, because if something has happened to it, I'll need a different plan to get out of here."

"I would like to see the horse," he told the king. "It may help me to figure out what's wrong with the girl." The king quickly took him by the hand to the treasury where the horse was kept. The prince walked around it and checked its movements. Everything was in order. He knew then that his plan was going to work.

16.47

"Could I see the girl now?"

They took him to her. At the sight of the prince she threw herself to the ground and began to wail. This was her way of keeping the king away from her. When the prince saw her, he almost collapsed from joy. He approached her.

"I seek God's protection from the accursed Satan!" he said. "In the name of God, the Merciful and Compassionate!"

She struck her face and screamed even louder, complete deception on her part, for she was so relieved to see the prince. All the while he made signs to her, urging her, "More!"

16.48

"Your Majesty," he said, "do not let her screams frighten you. I will cure her, God willing."

And the king thanked him.

And here the dawn reached Shahrazād so she ceased to speak.

Fihrās the Philosopher spoke:

16.49

She said, Master, the king made generous promises to the youth who went to see the girl.

The Ninety-Third Night

"Bring me a chicken plucked and boiled, and another roasted, with lots of spices!" he demanded.

They brought what he asked for and the prince bound her hands and began to feed her. He ate with her and told her quietly what he intended to do. He promised to save her. For three days he stayed with her, and on the fourth day the king came to him.

"It's time for me to have a look at her," he said.

16.50   The young man accompanied the king and the girl turned pale at the sight of him.

"I seek God's protection from the accursed Satan!" cried the prince. "In the name of God, the Merciful and Compassionate! O you blessed child, be still!"

She bowed her head to the ground. In his delight the king rewarded him with a fine robe of honor and a thousand dinars. Then he released her from her bonds and ordered that she be taken to the baths. After her visit to the baths, he dressed her in fine clothes and jewelry.

But when the blessed morning came, she threw herself to the ground just as before and one of the slave girls rushed to tell the king she was screaming and deranged.

The king was horrified. He ran to the girl and tried to speak to her. But she only screamed more and more.

16.51   "You're in trouble now! What is this?" he asked her physician.

"Do not get excited, Sire," he said. "I will look at her stars tonight and then I'll know how she's doing. God willing, let us leave it until the morning."

When the blessed morning came, the king asked, "Doctor, what did you learn from her stars?"

"I saw that an evil jinni took possession of her in the meadow where you found her with the horse and the old man. She can only escape from it in the very place where it first possessed her. This is what the stars tell me."

"Very well," said the king, and he ordered her to be brought out to the meadow, where a tent of white silk was pitched for her. A thousand horsemen surrounded the meadow and guarded her for the remainder of the night.

16.52   When the blessed morning came, the prince-physician said to them: "Bring me the horse that was with her when you found her. This is what we have to do."

The king ordered the horse be brought to the meadow. When the girl saw the physician conjuring and reciting spells she threw herself to the ground.

And here the dawn reached Shahrazād so she ceased to speak.

Fihrās the Philosopher spoke:
She said, Master, the prince mounted the horse, placed the girl behind him, and then tied her to him with his turban. He was so overjoyed he could hardly believe it. So was the girl. He moved the ascent pin and the horse began to fill with air.

He turned to the king. "Long may your realm and your hospitality continue! Farewell!"

And up he soared into the sky. The king and men of state looked on as he disappeared from sight. When the king despaired of ever seeing the two of them again he wept and wailed, then fainted. The men of state gathered around him and sprinkled water on him to revive him.

"May God give Your Majesty strength." they told him. "That thing flew away like a bird; there's nothing to be done. It's beyond you."

With their continued reassurance he recovered somewhat.

Then he returned to his palace in tears, hopelessly depressed, and just a few days later, he was dead.

And here the dawn reached Shahrazād so she ceased to speak.

Fihrās the Philosopher spoke:
She said, Master, the prince mounted the horse and they flew off into the sky, all the way to his father's city. On the roof of the palace, the youth dismounted and helped the girl down. He took her by the hand to his father. When the king saw his son, he jumped up and threw his arms around him. His mother and the women came and embraced him. Everyone in the palace greeted him and the girl. Then his father sat him down beside him and he told his father of all that had happened while he was away.

"Father," he said, "I endured it all for this girl."

"Praise be to God," said his father, "who has rescued the both of you."

16.56   Then the prince sent a message to the girl's father telling him what had happened and asking for her hand in marriage. The arrival of the messenger with the letter gave the king her father great joy. His sadness left him and he rewarded the messenger and treated him with honor. He wrote back to say that he was delighted by the marriage of his daughter to the prince and he held a magnificent celebration. When the messenger returned with a gift from the king, the prince and the girl were overjoyed. The king held a great celebratory feast for his son. He fed all the people, from the city and the countryside, for a whole month. The girl was dressed in the finest raiment. The young man took her and found her untouched, a virgin. And thus they remained, eating and drinking to their hearts' content, until there came to them that from which there is no fleeing, and praise be to God, Lord of all being.

The Story of the King and the Gazelle[117]

Then she said, They claim, Your Majesty, that a king once went out   17.1
hunting one day with his viziers and his men of state. While they
made their way through the open country, a gazelle appeared before
them. Its face was radiant with beauty; it wore a necklace of jewels,
bracelets of gold, anklets of silver, and a raiment of green brocade.

When the king saw how gorgeous and beautiful she was, he said
to his viziers, "That gazelle is meant for a king—see that it doesn't
get away!"

So they let the dogs and the hawks loose after it, but when the
dogs caught up with it they held back and kept their distance. The
king was astonished.

"Chase it," he said to his vizier. "Maybe we can catch it."

So off they went after the gazelle, but it ran fast ahead of them.

They had stayed on its trail all day when it led them to a vast   17.2
meadow where trees and fruits abounded. Amid the grazing camels
and cattle and sheep, there stood a great palace, the likes of which
no one had ever seen. The king and the vizier rode up to it and
contemplated its beauty and perfection. Then a young man clad in
green came riding out of the palace on a steed of noble stock.

When the gazelle saw the young man it drew its legs together and   17.3
leapt up on the saddle beside him. He put his arm around it, then
rode into the palace.

The king was astonished at this.

"Your Majesty," said the vizier, "It looks as if the gazelle belongs to the young man. If you wish, I will ask his permission to buy her, or to have him give her to you as a gift."

"Yes, please do," said the king.

At the palace gate they asked permission to enter. The slaves went to their master, the lord of the palace.

"There are two men at the gate. They seem to be royalty, and they want to come in and see you."

"Bring them before me," he said.

17.4   They were allowed to enter the palace, and though he looked left and right, the king could find no sign of the gazelle. When they had sat down, tables covered with leaves of gold and richly laden with food were brought before them. They ate, and then they started to drink. When the drink had started to affect the king, he turned to the young lord of the palace.

"You must honor us, for I need something from you."

"Your Majesty," said the young man, "the palace and all it contains is yours. Whatever you need, consider it done."

"Give me the gazelle," said the king. "Or sell it to me."

"May God protect the king!" exclaimed the young man, "She is not a gazelle. She is my wife."

"That's the strangest thing I've ever heard," said the king.

And here the dawn reached Shahrazād so she ceased to speak.

17.5   *Fihrās the Philosopher spoke:*

The Ninety-Sixth Night   She said, Master, the king was astonished at what he heard. The young man got up and disappeared for a time, then returned with the gazelle trailing behind him.

"By the right of Him who granted you the ability," he said to the gazelle, "would you not return to the form in which God created you?"[118]

He had barely finished speaking when the gazelle shook herself and changed back into a young woman, the most beautiful of God's creation. The king was dumbfounded by her beauty and perfection.

"How about selling her to me?" said the king. "Name any price you wish."

"How could I sell my wife who has given me two sons?" asked the young man. "Her story is one of the most astonishing that anyone has heard."

"Tell me—I would gladly hear it," said the king.

"Very well, Your Majesty," he said, and so he began:

"I am from Damascus. My father had great wealth and fortune   17.6
but only one son. I was taught the Qur'an, grammar, and science
and I became an educated man. The teacher my father had chosen
for me was the most learned, intelligent, and virtuous of men.
When my teacher saw how well I had understood and grasped all
there was to learn, he said, 'I have taught you everything I know,
and I have nothing left to pass on to you except this one spell. It is a
powerful one and I will inscribe it for you. It will protect you against
humans, jinn, and devils.'

"'Yes, sir,' I said. 'Please do so.'

"He inscribed it for me on a leaf of gold, and told me to hang it   17.7
from my right forearm, which I did. Then he died, may God show
him mercy.

"When I came of age I busied myself with horses and the fight
and the raid in the dark of night until I became a valiant horseman.

"'My son,' said my father when he had grown old and grey, 'I
want to marry you to your cousin while I'm still alive.'

"'As you wish,' I told him.

"So he had a great feast prepared for me and my marriage to my
cousin was consummated.

"One day, while I was sitting in the upper story of my palace I
espied an armed horseman, clad in chainmail. He came forward,
asking permission to camp, and I ordered that he be brought food
and drink. He ate what he needed while I kept him company.

"I asked where he came from.

"'I am from Basra,' he replied.

"He stayed with me for ten days and the more he told me about the city of Basra, the more I longed to visit it.

"'I must leave for Basra,' he told me afterwards.

"'I'll be sorry to see you go,' I said.

"So we spent that night talking about Basra, and when the blessed morning came I got him ready for his departure and bade him farewell. When he had left, I could not stop thinking about the city he had described to me. I told my wife about it, and she too fell in love with Basra.

"'Well,' she said, 'why don't you just do it and go to Basra? It must be done, God willing.'

"So I sold all my goods and properties and set out on foot until I reached the city of Basra. I settled in one of its houses and there I stayed for a number of days. One day I was sitting there and heard a knock on the door. I went out to find a handsome youth at the door.

"'Do you recognize me?' asked the youth.

"'No,' I replied.

"'I'm the one you hosted so generously,' he said.

"Then I recognized him! We greeted each other warmly and he said, 'Come with me,' so I went with him to a great palace, where there was a large group of people.

"'This is the man I've been telling you about,' he told them.

"They rose in my honor and welcomed me, gave me the best place to sit, and brought me food. Together we ate and drank until the end of the day, and I returned to where I was staying. I remained with the young man for two whole months.

"Then the young man fell very ill. He summoned the judge and jurists and bequeathed half of his fortune to me. Then he passed away, may God show him mercy."

And here the dawn reached Shahrazād so she ceased to speak.

Fihrās the Philosopher spoke:

She said, Master, "When the young man from Basra died I bought a ship with what he had bequeathed me.

"'Who wants to travel to India?' I proclaimed.

"And so I set out to sea with my wife. We sailed on good winds for a whole month until we had used up all of our fresh water.

"'Is there somewhere here where we can find water?' I asked the ship's captain.

"'God willing we'll come to a large island tomorrow, where there are lots of trees and fruits,' he said. 'But there's a problem: nobody can go ashore because it's inhabited by a jinni demon.'

"'Take us there,' I said.

"The next day, we arrived at that island. I set out alone, sword in one hand, water jug in the other. But as I was about to go, a harsh wind began to blow and a huge figure with the legs of a horse and the face of a lion appeared before me. He let out a great cry, and I fainted. When I came to, he was right by my side. I looked at him and saw he was the jinni demon I had been told about, but he was unable to hurt me, thanks to the blessings of God and of the spell inscribed on the amulet I was wearing. I struck him and he turned to flee. I struck him again and again until he took to the air and flew toward the ship, where he seized my wife and flew off with her, though I did not know this at the time.

"My companions were delighted at my return, but then they told me what had happened to my wife. I was overcome with grief.

"'Do you know,' I asked them, 'if this demon has some secret refuge?'

"'Yes,' one of them said. He goes to an island known as Such-and-Such.'

"I turned to the ship's captain. 'Take us there.'

"So on we went to the island which we discovered was inhabited. We disembarked and stayed for a month with them. I asked about the demon and they told me how dreadfully they suffered from him. They said that he came to them every year and they would put out for him the most beautiful young woman they had. If they failed to put out a beautiful woman, he would let out a cry so loud that it would make pregnant women miscarry. He would ruin their land and burn their trees. They had repeatedly resolved to leave the island because of him, but their king forbade it. And today was the day the demon had come to take the young woman, as he did every year.

"'How do you know what young woman he wants to take away?' I asked.

17.13   "'We know the sign,' they said. 'A wind comes upon us, and all our faces turn sallow, except for one young woman: her face turns red. We bring her to the bath, get her ready and then they take her, with food and drink, to a certain cave.'

"I stayed with them until, just as they had claimed, the wind began to blow. All their faces turned sallow but one: that of the king's own daughter. He ordered that she be made ready and the cushions brought to the cave, along with food and drink.

"So I took my weapons and went with them to the cave. They set up a bed and put the young woman on it, and there they left her. The king bade farewell to his daughter, and they went back.

"When everyone was gone, I entered the cave and hid there for a while. Suddenly the demon was there—he advanced upon the woman, and I took my sword and dealt him a blow while reciting the spell from the amulet I have already told you about. The demon turned and fled before me. I followed him for a while, then went back to the girl who had fainted. I sprinkled water on her face, and soon she came to.

17.14   "'I've been blessed!' she exclaimed. 'Who are you?'

"'I am human like you,' I replied. 'And that demon is my enemy.'

"'Stay,' she told me. 'Eat and drink and stay here with me until morning.'"

And here the dawn reached Shahrazād so she ceased to speak.

Fihrās the Philosopher spoke:

She said, Master, "The young man remained with her until morning, and then he concealed himself.

"When the blessed morning came, the people came to carry the bed away, but they found the girl was still in the cave. They hurried back to the king and told him the story. He and the other notables rode swiftly back to the cave. He went in, and clutched his daughter close.

"'What's happened to you?' he asked. 'Are you alright?'

"She told him all that had happened to her, and told him about the young man.

"Then the young man came to the king and kissed his hands, telling him all about the demon and how he had kidnapped his wife.

"'Yes, right from that ship anchored there in your harbor! That's my ship—I was on my way to kill this demon.'

"'God be praised! I've been blessed!' said the king. 'But I would give up hope for your wife. However, through you, God has rescued this young woman, and you are more deserving of her than anyone. You will have from me the best of rewards!'

"'All I ask from you,' I told him, 'is that you join me in the search for my wife and that you tell me where this demon lives.'

"'The demon lives in a great valley that no human or jinn can reach. It is three days from this island.'

"'Help me with what I have asked and then you may go,' I said.

"So they took me to the rim of an enormous well.

"'This is the entrance,' they said.

"I took a rope and tightened it around my waist.

"'Let me down,' I told them, 'and when I pull on the rope, pull me back up.' We set a deadline of three days hence.

"Down I went into the depths of the well, sword in hand and amulet on my arm. I untied the rope and looked all around the inside of the well, and saw a light coming from an underground passageway.

"I entered the passageway, which opened out onto a wide space. Before me stood a great palace.

17.18 "An old woman was sitting at the door of the palace. In her hand was a key.

"When she saw me she said, 'Are you the Damascene come in search of your wife?'

"'Yes,' I replied, 'how did you know me?'

"'I knew you by the signs your wife described to me,' said the old woman.

"'Is she alive or dead?' I asked.

"'Alive,' she said, 'and the demon hasn't gone near her, thanks to the wounds you gave him. Every day your wife comes and asks me if you've turned up yet and I tell her, "No! How could he possibly get here, to this place?" and she says, "I know him. He would never abandon me even if I were at the very edge of the seventh hell."'

17.19 "While we were talking, a young woman as beautiful as the shining full moon came from the palace.

"'O Damascene,' she said to me, 'we must honor you.'

"'How did you know I'm from Damascus?'

"'From the signs my brother described to me,' she replied.

"'And who is your brother?' I asked.

"'He is the demon you've come looking for,' she replied.

"'Young lady,' I said, 'why are you going to honor me when I am the enemy of your brother and I have come to kill him if I possibly can?'"

And here the dawn reached Shahrazād so she ceased to speak.

17.20
Fihrās the Philosopher spoke:

The Ninety-Ninth Night

She said, Master, "When I spoke these words to the young woman, the demon's sister, she answered, 'I would be delighted if you killed him, because of all the grief he has caused me. He is an unbeliever, and I am a believer.'

"'How do I kill him, then?' I asked.

"'You will not be able to on your own,' she told me. 'I can lead you to him and help you kill him. But we must make a pact between us.'

"'What sort of pact?' I asked.

17.21

"'That you be my husband, and I be your wife,' she answered.

"'If my cousin, my first wife, agrees,' I said, 'that will be fine.'

"While we were talking, my cousin appeared, and when she saw me she threw herself into my arms, greeted and hugged me, and shed copious tears.

"'Quiet now, don't cry,' said the demon's sister. 'I have been wanting to destroy my brother, but you must accept one condition.'

"'And what is that condition?' asked my cousin.

"'That you share your husband with me,' she said. 'Then I will help you kill my demon brother, and I'll give your husband everything in the palace.'

"'That is fine with me,' she replied.

17.22

"When they had agreed, the demon's sister turned to me.

"'You will not be able to enter the palace directly because he is sitting there, and no one can get in. I'm afraid for you—just stay where you are until I get back.'

"So she entered the palace and went to the top of the wall. She lowered a rope and pulled me up to the highest story in the palace. She took me by the hand and led me inside, where there were a hundred girls, daughters of kings, who had been abducted by the demon. The sister then went to a door in the floor that had a golden lock. She opened it and went in. We could see the demon, lying on a golden bed.

"When his sister looked in at him, he rebuked her.

"'Damn you!' he cried. 'I can smell the Damascene on you!'

"'That's just your imagination,' she said. 'Your fear of him is get- 17.23 ting the better of you.'

"Once the demon was asleep, she seized her chance and, putting her hand under the bed, pulled out a sword.

"'Take this!' she said to me.

"I took it and went up to the demon. I gave him a mighty blow across his throat with the sword. He died instantly.

"Then all the jewelry, clothing, and everything else in the palace were brought to me. I went back to the well through the passageway. I shook the rope, and they hauled up all the contents of the palace, as well as the girls who had been in there and the old lady. I came up last.

17.24 "At the sight of this, the king was overjoyed. He sent each girl back to her father, while I stayed with him and married his daughter. I stayed with him until he died, God show him mercy, and then I assumed the kingship for a while, until I grew weary of the island. Somebody else became king, and I went back to my own country with my wives: my cousin, the king's daughter, and the demon's sister, who is this gazelle that you see right now. Then my cousin died, and I grieved for her, and then the king's daughter died, may God show her mercy."

And here the dawn reached Shahrazād so she ceased to speak.

17.25 *Fihrās the Philosopher spoke:*

The Hundredth Night She said, Master, the young man from Damascus went on:

"When my cousin and the king's daughter died, I found my own country oppressive, so I came out to this meadow and built this palace. I stayed here in the good company of the demon's sister. She can change into any kind of creature—sometimes she's a peacock, sometimes a gazelle, as you see her right now. And she has given me two sons. And that is my story."

The king and the vizier were astonished at his story, and when the blessed morning came, they bade farewell to the Damascene, leaving him in his palace, where they would come and visit him every year thereafter, until there came to them that from which there is no fleeing, and praise be to God, Lord of all being.

The Story of the Vizier Ibn Abī l-Qamar and ʿAbd al-Malik ibn Marwān[119]

Shahrazād said: Mighty monarch, courageous king, they say that **18.1** the Commander of the Faithful ʿAbd al-Malik ibn Marwān had a vizier named Ibn Abī l-Qamar. He was intelligent and learned in all the sciences, and ʿAbd al-Malik held him in high regard.

The Umayyad clan grew very jealous of this vizier and they would tell the king that people were speaking ill of Ibn Abī l-Qamar. But the king would have none of it.

Not, at least, until they fabricated a document claiming that the vizier was planning to rebel and that the most upright people of the land had born witness to the plot. The king changed color when he got the document and could not restrain himself.

"When the vizier Ibn Abī l-Qamar rides up tomorrow," he told one of his slaves, "strip him of his robes and give him this message: If I find you anywhere in my realm, I'll kill you and crucify you. If you are innocent, God will spare you; if you have acted unjustly, He will destroy you."

When the blessed morning came, the vizier went out as was his **18.2** custom, but he was met by the slaves who acted in accordance with the king's orders.

"What did I do? What sin or crime have I committed?" the vizier said to himself.

He left the realm and traveled, though he had no idea where he was headed. He wandered, bewildered.

It was winter. He came to a city and entered it in the evening, as hunger and cold had got the better of him, not to mention fear and fatigue. He was on the verge of perishing when he came across an inn for merchants, the sort of place where many eminent people might store their goods and their monies. Confused and not knowing what to do, he said to the innkeeper, "Is there a room where I could spend the night?"

18.3 "By God, no," the innkeeper said. "This is not a place for the poor and homeless to spend the night! Merchants keep their goods and monies here, and I'm not going to be responsible for what you might do."

So the vizier remained at a loss until one of the merchants turned up and said, "Innkeeper, give him a room for the night. I'll be his guarantor."

So the innkeeper led him to a newly built room[120] which the vizier entered only to find that it did not even have a mat. He wanted to sit down but could not because of the cold. He wanted to lean his back against the wall, but he couldn't do that either, because of the cold. As night was drawing in, he was at his wit's end. Everybody had closed their doors. There were some who stayed in their rooms and some who spent the time reciting verses.

" «Surely we belong to God, and to Him we return,»"[121] the vizier said. "What a horrible mess I've got myself into. Maybe I should just take shelter on top of a baker's oven for the night."

18.4 He thought about his situation, and about the good fortune that once was his and how it was all taken away from him, out of spite. And he recited these verses:

> If death were for sale I'd buy it,
>> for life's goodness can't be found.
> You know when I see a tomb,
>> I wish I were in the ground.

Show mercy to the mad lover,
But grant death to his brother.

When he had finished reciting, there was a knock at the door. He was puzzled. He opened it, and there was the man who was his guarantor. He came in with a brass lamp, which he hung on the wall. Then he brought a lit brazier, a nice blanket, some clothes, and a tray with food and water. He took the vizier's cloak and gave him the clothes; he offered him food and drink and the vizier soon regained his strength. All this while, the merchant spoke kindly to him and kept him company.

"O brother," said the merchant, "what is your story? I can tell from your verses that you are pure of heart."

"My brother," said the vizier, "my words are like those of Jacob, eternal peace be his: «I make complaint of my anguish and my sorrow unto God.»"[122]

So the merchant continued to treat him well, but the vizier could not tell him anything of himself because he still feared the wrath of the king.   18.5

The merchant took pity on him.

"I have four daughters," said the merchant, "and I have one thousand dinars of capital. Half is for me and the other half I pledged to use only to please God. I have not found anyone more worthy of it than you. So take it, and may God bless you by it."

"I cannot accept," said the vizier.

"Then perhaps you will accept half of it," answered the merchant.

But the vizier would not allow himself to take it. The merchant continued to press him, until finally he accepted one gold dinar.

When the blessed morning came the vizier turned to the merchant.

"May God bless you and thank you for what you've done for me," he said.

After bidding farewell to the vizier and calling for his blessing, the merchant went back to his room, and the vizier was alone again.

18.6   He thought about his own situation, and while he was doing so one of the Commander of the Faithful's slaves rode up to the door of the hotel, carrying a cloth with some things in it.

"Did a man named Ibn Abī l-Qamar spend last night here?" he asked the innkeeper.

"There was a miserable fellow who stayed in that room there," he replied. "One of the merchants paid his fees out of charity."

The servant made for the room, and when the vizier saw him he was seized with terror.

"Do not fear," said the slave. "You have the good will of my master. He has crucified your enemies and he now knows that you were in the right. Their accusations were false and worthless. Sir, take this horse and put on this garment."

18.7   The vizier praised and thanked God, then stood up and put on the clothes.

He rode with the slave back to the city, and they went past 'Abd al-Malik's gardens and parks.

When the vizier entered, the king stood and honored him and embraced him.

"O vizier," he said, "all the parks and gardens that you have just passed through—I grant them to you as recompense for the mistake I made and for having believed what people claimed."

The emir returned him to his former station and the vizier accepted all he was granted.

18.8   God's plan was this. The merchant who had helped the vizier was traveling one day in a caravan when it was attacked by thieves who forced them to dismount and plundered everything. The merchant had nothing left.

"By God," he said to himself, "I'll go to the city—hopefully I'll find somebody who'll give me a loan, since I have a good reputation among merchants. Perhaps God will be as generous to me as He sees fit."

And here the dawn reached Shahrazād so she ceased to speak.

Fihrās the Philosopher spoke:

She said, Master, when the merchant got to the city, which was Damascus, he passed through the gardens and parks that the king had granted to the vizier. He was at a loss as to what to do or where to go, when all of a sudden the vizier appeared, coming out from a park and heading towards his house. The merchant saw him and, as he drew closer, recognized who it was.

"Isn't that my friend for whom I did such-and-such?" he asked himself. "By God, I must show myself to him and perhaps he'll be generous!"

So the merchant walked where he was sure the vizier could see him, but the vizier did not recognize him because there were so many people around and because the vizier was busy and preoccupied, in an altogether different state from their previous meeting. So too was the merchant, for he was covered in dust.

"I'll introduce myself to him," thought the merchant, "and then maybe he will be merciful to me."

He asked some people who the man was, and they told him that he was the king's vizier. The merchant followed him to his house. Then he took a piece of parchment and wrote on it two lines of verse by which the vizier would recall what he had recited that night at the inn. The two verses were these:

> Tell the vizier, and don't be shy,
> > to remind him of a time gone by:
> You were saying to me in a state of disquiet:
> > if death were for sale I'd buy it!

When he had finished writing the letter, he gave it to the vizier's servant.

"Give this paper to your master," he said.

The servant went to his master and gave him the paper. When he read the verses, he understood their meaning and remembered his own story. He went outside to greet and embrace the merchant.

"By God," he said, "the way you look, you would have had to kill the servant to get in here!"

He brought him inside and held a great banquet for him, and gave to the merchant all that the king had previously granted to him. Then he brought him to the king.

"This is the man I told you about," he said, "and I have granted to him all that you granted to me."

The king installed him in a great residence for the good deed he had done to an unknown man who turned out to be the vizier, and the king became very close to him. He and the vizier remained like brothers until there came to them that from which there is no fleeing, and praise be to God, Lord of all being.

18.12   This story of the *One Hundred and One Nights* was
completed in 1190, through God's kind
assistance and guidance.
Praise be to Almighty God. Praise
be to the Lord of all.

Notes

1   Bābil is a region of Iraq; Khorasan is not a city but a large region encompassing northeastern Iran and parts of what are today Turkmenistan and Afghanistan. The name is slightly misspelled in the Arabic; rather than *khurāsān* we find *khurasān*, and when used as an adjective, we find both *khurasānī* and *khuraṣānī*.

2   *Maḍrabah*: Ṭ includes this in a list of specifically Tunisian words, saying it is "a kind of musical instrument, perhaps a tambourine (*daff*)." However, the attested meaning of "seat" seems more appropriate (Dozy, s.v.).

3   Or : "a Meringa twig."

4   "Flower of the Gardens."

5   *Al-ṭanābur wal-ʿīdān wal-maʿāzif wal-mazāmir wal-shīrān*: A set passage of somewhat rhymed prose listing musical instruments that occurs, with slight variations, several times in the collection. *Ṭanābur* are long-necked lutes; *ʿīdān* are short-necked lutes. *Mazāmir* are wind instruments, usually of the oboe or clarinet family, less likely to be a flute, which I have used here for the rhyme. *Maʿāzif* are usually stringed instruments, but I render it here as "timpani" on the basis of Biberstein Kazimirksy's *Dictionnaire*, which is particularly good for post-classical North African usages. The last term, *al-shīrān*, is defined by Ṭ as a Tunisian word for banners and flags, which sits awkwardly with the musical instruments. It is possible that *al-shīzān* or something like it was intended. For *al-shīz* Dozy gives "baguettes de tambour," adding that *al-shīzān* is either the dual form or some kind of musical instrument. The latter seems more likely. His source

is Miguel Casiri, *Bibliotheca Arabico-Hispana Escurialensis*, where *al-shīzān* is found in a list of items related to singing and music (I 527b–528a). Since *shīrān* occurs in several of the manuscripts, and as the intended sense remains unclear, I have not emended the Arabic text.

6 Sh adds here: "The king said to him: 'That is the reason for your illness, now tell me what it was that cured you?' The youth would not answer, but the king insisted, threatening him with the sword." For the most part Sh is virtually identical with B2. One wonders if this perceptive sentence is a vestige from a more ancient recension or a much later insertion by someone familiar with the *Alf laylah* tradition, where the younger cuckold hesitates to tell the whole story, and the older brother insists (Mahdi, ed. *Alf laylah*, 60–61).

7 Paragraphs 36–40 are taken from T, for reasons explained in the Introduction.

8 This tale is composed of a number of recognizable segments or motifs, of which the first is the young man, recently orphaned, who disobeys some sound advice (see Chauvin, *Bibliographie*, 7:138–39).

9 Another well-known motif is "the palace of women," in which a man is promised enduring pleasure on the condition he can exercise patience and restrain his curiosity. The best-known example of this is the tale of the Third Dervish in the *Thousand and One Nights*. There is a fascinating treatment of this and related motifs by Claude Bremond, in Bencheikh, et al., *Mille et un contes de la nuit*, 83–233, esp. 83–162. He deals with Muḥammad ibn ʿAbdallāh al-Qayrawānī on pp. 153–55. See also Gaudefroy-Demombynes, *Cent et une nuits*, 48–58.

10 The manuscript here has what appears to be *kadhdhār*; Ṭ emends this to *kadhdhāl*, including it in a list of specifically "Tunisian" terms as a kind of clay-like rock. According to Dozy, (*Supplément*, ii, 458, s.v. *k-dh-dh*), *kadhdhān* or *kaddān* are the most common forms for a kind of tufa or pumice stone, frequently used in decoration but also in construction.

11 "Master of the Kingdom, son of Crown of Stars."

12 "Star of Lights," presumably meaning "Brightest of stars" or "Brightest of Lights."

13   "Flame of Illumination, daughter of the Protector of Glory."

14   A similar phrase occurs at §5.4; both are likely corrupt. It is not clear whether the words *al-khaḍūrah* or *al-khaḍrah* are place names (as *al-ḥamād* appears to be) or distorted attributes indicating verdure.

15   "Meadow of Blossoms."

16   "Meadow of Flowers."

17   §§3.6–3.7 are absent from A; I have taken them from T and B2.

18   The same verses are recited in §2.26.

19   Both *bulbul* and *umm al-ḥasan* are nightingales. The *karawān* is more properly a plover or some kind of shore bird, but Biberstein-Kazimirsky gives partridge, which I use for two reasons. First, Kazimirsky's dictionary is generally the closest to the linguistic and cultural world of these MSS, and second, "partridge" seems in any case to be more appropriate to the mood of the description (never "a plover in a pear tree").

20   Q Raʿd 13:41; cf. 13:11.

21   The translation is tentative; the Arabic text is likely corrupt.

22   "Camphor Island" and "The Vizier and his Son" (§6) are tales of exploration and treasure hunting with added morality lessons on the transience of worldly goods and possessions. There are many examples of such tales, but the classic is "The City of Brass" as it appears in the *Thousand and One Nights*. As mentioned in the Introduction, "The City of Brass" appears in only two of the extant manuscripts of *A Hundred and One Nights*. One of these was that used by Gaudefroy-Demombynes, and he included copious notes on the tale and its variants (306–17). See also Pinault, *Story-telling Techniques*, 148–239; Chauvin, *Bibliographie*, 5: 32–35; Fudge, "Signs of Scripture."

23   These lines closely resemble *Murūj al-dhahab* of al-Masʿudi (d. 345/956), *Murūj al-dhahab*, 168–69 (bāb 15), which was in turn likely taken from an earlier travel account. See Ferrand, "Note sur le livre des *Cent et une nuits*."

24   In A, the second passage is spoken uniquely by the chamberlain. This would appear to be a corruption and I have followed the structure of the passage as found in B1 for the most coherent reading. B1 has

Egypt as the "source of wisdom" rather than Ethiopia. Gaudefroy-Demombynes, translator of B1, suggests that the change arises from an "African" editor who would be inclined to see Egypt as the country of wisdom. In the Mas'ūdī passage, India takes this role. Gaudefroy-Demombynes concludes his remarks: "Il est presque inutile de noter que ce récit épisodique cadre mal avec le début du conte tel qu'il est déplacé à la cour de Kesra Anouchirevan" (279 n. 3). Manuscript Ḥ has the following short variant, spoken entirely by the old man: "The kings of this world are four, believers and an unbeliever (*muminūna wa-kāfir*) [sic]. As for the believers, they are Sulaymān ibn Dāwūd and Dhū l-Qarnayn. As for the unbelievers (*kuffār*) they are Nimrod and Nebuchadnezzar (al-Nimrūd wa-Bakht Naṣar [sic]) and it is said also Shaddād ibn 'Ād."

25   Another name for the island of Borneo.

26   At this point the narrative switches from first to third person.

27   Ferrand notes a similarity here with the travel account of Ibn al-Wardī (1290–1349), *Kitāb kharīdat al-'ajā'ib* and an anecdote in the *Abrégé des merveilles*. Ferrand, "Note," 317–18.

28   Occasionally the text reverts briefly to a first-person narration. I have not noted these brief instances in the translation.

29   Here and elsewhere in the collection, one can assume that the lions or humans standing guard over tombs and treasures are automata, operated by mechanical ingenuity and/or magic, though this is usually not specified. On the automata, one may consult Yamanaka, "*Les Mille et une Nuits* et les automates: L'interaction infinie de la science et de la fiction."

30   It is not entirely clear from the text whether the ruse is unexplained or consists simply of the laying of planks across the entryway. The former is more likely.

31   The text of A reads *Ḍāfir*, no doubt reflecting North African pronunciation. I have used the conventional transcription of the name for the translation.

32   In A and B1 he bids farewell to his brother; in the other versions it is his father.

33 The reading is uncertain. The poem appears, with slight variation, only in A and B1.

34 This translation is tentative; the passage is likely corrupt. *Sarīs* is cichorium or chicory, which has blue or lavender flowers.

35 Q Anfāl 8:42.

36 Cf. Q Anʿām 6:96.

37 A reference to the hadith: "Treat women well. They were created from a rib, and the most crooked part of the rib is the upper portion. If you try to straighten it out, it will break, and if you leave it, it remains crooked. So treat them well" (al-Bukhārī, *Ṣaḥīḥ al-Bukhārī*, 4:161).

38 "Mighty Blade, Son of the Slayer."

39 "Sun of the Lights," presumably meaning "Brightest of Lights" or "Sun amid Lights."

40 The Arabic reads, "the King Hārūn al-Rashīd."

41 The "Sea of Darkness" or more literally the plural "darknesses" (*baḥr al-ẓulumāt*) is a name for the Atlantic Ocean (D. M. Dunlop, "Baḥr al-Muḥīṭ" in *EI2*). The name here is slightly different (singular, *baḥr al-ẓulmah*) but must recall the name of the Atlantic. However, since the travelers have departed from Basrah, they would have to be in the Indian Ocean in any case.

42 The Arabic is not entirely clear here.

43 Literally, "look at the valley/*wadi*," a reading attested in other manuscripts. Possibly the indentation of the encircling moat is intended. As far as I am aware, the word *wādī* (here *wād*) is used only for natural formations, and not for something like a man-made moat. At the same time, the text does not specify that the water channel is man-made.

44 This genealogical name is a fabrication, composed of names from Arab tribes and their ancestors, but not in any recognizable fashion. The other manuscripts contain similar variations.

45 ʿAbdallāh "al-Baṭṭāl" or "the Hero," was a Muslim warrior of the early eighth century renowned for his military exploits against the Byzantines. His exploits would later serve as the basis for warrior epics in both Arabic and Turkish (Khalīl Athamina, "al-Baṭṭāl, ʿAbdallāh").

46 "The Bane of Foes."

47 "The Trampler."

48 "He Who Unfurls the Banner."

49 On the Azāriqah, see the glossary, although it is not clear whether the reference in the text is meant to refer to this group.

50 That is, they were unbelievers.

51 "Moon among Flowers."

52 A play on words: *kumayt* refers both to a chestnut horse and to a wine whose color is a mix of black and red.

53 *Bayḍah ʿādiyyah*: "an ʿĀdī helmet"? *Ādiyyah* most likely refers to the ancient kingdom of ʿĀd, but what sort of helmet this is meant to evoke is anybody's guess.

54 The term is used for the caliph, but as Sulaymān's father ʿAbd al-Malik is still alive in the story, he would have had that title, not Sulaymān.

55 This three-month period is known as *ʿiddah*, the three menstrual periods a divorced or widowed woman must wait before remarrying in order to avoid any confusion of paternity.

56 The man's account clearly differs from that told by the first Christian girl in 8.3, in which the girl was sent to a monastery because of her cousin's desires.

57 Whether this is the consummation of the marriage or not depends on which version of the story one chooses to follow: the young man's or that of the Christian girl. When these tales mention sexual intercourse, it almost always includes the taking of virginity and conception. It is slightly unusual (in the world of these stories), then, for this couple to have been married but childless, unless this occasion was the consummation of their marriage.

58 This tale is clearly a relative of "Nuʿm and Niʿmah" from the *Thousand and One Nights*. Gaudefroy-Demombynes compares the two stories; see *Cent et une nuits* 281–82n10 and Chauvin, *Bibliographie*, 6:96–97.

59 Literally, "the splitter of the dry grain"; Q Anʿām 6:95.

60 A *khādim* may be a male or female servant; the grammatical gender here is feminine. In the notes to his French translation, Gaudefroy-Demombynes points out that it should be a female to bring the bridal

trousseau, but a male to drive the mule, and the text appears to have conflated the two (281n5).

61   "Strange Beauty."

62   "White Antelope of the Palaces."

63   A tentative reading; the verses are almost certainly corrupt.

64   Cf. Q Maryam 19:14.

65   The first part of this tale is a rudimentary version of the beginning of "The Three Apples" in *The Thousand and One Nights*. In a now-lost manuscript, the river in question is the Tigris, not the Nile (Chauvin, *Bibliographie*, 6:146), indicating perhaps that the story originated in the East and was later given North African details. The mention of the "Iraqi apple" is probably also a trace of this transition.

66   In "The Tale of the Three Apples" in *Alf laylah*, we do not discover until later that the son had been given the fruit and the husband's suspicions were unfounded. This is a good example of the way in which *Mi'at laylah* tends not take advantage of opportunities to create suspense or to manipulate the reader's expectations.

67   Q Anʿām 6:96.

68   On this tale and its analogues, see Chauvin, *Bibliographie*, 6:171–72 and the references in Gaudefroy-Demombynes, *Cent et une nuits*, 282n7.

69   "Gazelle of the Palaces."

70   The young man, usually the son of a merchant, who squanders his inheritance is a very common motif. For numerous examples from the *Thousand and One Nights*, see Chraïbi, *Mille et une nuits*, 117–23.

71   It is possible that this is a *nisbah* ("a name of relation to a father, mother, tribe, town or district, art or trade, &c" [Lane, s.v.]) relating to the village of Buzār near Nishapour, or that of al-Bazzāz, a district in southern Iraq (Yāqūt, I 408–9). More likely it is a corruption of *bazzāz*, cloth merchant, which is the reading in AKM. Manuscripts B1, B2, and T have *bazzār*, grain merchant, which is also possible.

72   The Arabic verses are followed by a further description of the garden, which I have incorporated into the preceding paragraph to avoid repetition.

73 Q Āl 'Imrān 3:37.

74 As related by Abū Hurayrah, for example, the Prophet said, "I shall accept the invitation even if I were invited to a meal of a sheep's trotters, and I shall accept the gift even if it were an arm or a trotter of a sheep" (al-Bukhārī, *Ṣaḥīḥ al-Bukhārī*, 3: 201).

75 The first section of this tale, in which four people each employ their own special skill to help recover a precious object, is similar to one found in the Seven Viziers/Seven Sages tradition (in the *4 liberatores* tale) as well as in other storytelling traditions. See Chauvin *Bibliographie*, 8:76; also Gaudefroy-Demombynes, *Cent et une nuits*, 287n6.

76 See Chauvin, *Bibliographie*, 8:33–34.

77 "The Mighty Blade."

78 Titles of the individual stories do not appear in any of the manuscripts. Tales that occur in the European tradition of "The Seven Sages" are known by Latin names, and these are given in the following notes where relevant.

79 "At the second hour of the day." The day and the night were each divided in twelve equal periods of time, called *sāʿah*, which has since become a uniform unit of sixty minutes.

80 It may appear at first glance that the prince's violation of the vow of silence, without apparent consequence, is a major weakness. A comparison with the European version, "The Seven Sages," however, is instructive. In the latter rendition, the prince does not utter a word until the permitted time. In a Christian context, this appears to emphasize the virtues of obedience, humility, and restraint, recalling vows of monastic silence. This interest in the silence interferes with the narrative. "The Seven Viziers," on the other hand, respects "the most universal of narrative constraints: when a taboo or prohibition is announced, we generally expect that someone is going to violate it before too long," in the words of Yasmina Foehr-Janssens. The danger arises precisely because of his failure to keep silent, when the woman learns what danger she is in. In the Western version, silence is both the cause of the prince's misfortune and his salvation, which is less

satisfying in terms of narrative logic. One should add that Greek and Spanish versions of the "Seven Sages" frame correspond to *A Hundred and One Nights* version. Foehr-Janssesns, "Oriental Wisdom in Roman Clothes."

81   The Latin title of this story is *leo*; see Chauvin, *Bibliographie*, 8:35.

82   The story title in Latin is *avis*; see Chauvin, *Bibliographie*, 8:35–36. This tale also occurs in *The Thousand and One Nights*, inserted into the story of "King Yunan and the Sage Duban." See *Arabian Nights Encyclopedia*, I:226 and Chauvin, *Bibliographie*, 6:139.

83   Cf. Q Yūsuf 12:28.

84   See Chauvin, *Bibliographie*, 8:36–37.

85   See Chauvin, *Bibliographie*, 8:38.

86   Latin title: *gladius*; see Chauvin, *Bibliographie*, 8:38–39.

87   See Chauvin, *Bibliographie*, 8:39–41.

88   Latin title: *mel*; see Chauvin, *Bibliographie*, 8:41–42.

89   See Chauvin, *Bibliographie*, 8:42.

90   Latin title: *fons*; see Chauvin, *Bibliographie*, 8:43–44.

91   See Chauvin, *Bibliographie*, 8:44.

92   Latin title: *canicula*; see Chauvin, *Bibliographie*, 8:45–46.

93   *Yā maḥalla wālidatī*: The sense of this expression is not clear; perhaps something like "O you who are in the place of/like my mother"?

94   See Chauvin, *Bibliographie*, 8:66.

95   Latin title: *canis*; see Chauvin, *Bibliographie*, 8:66.

96   See Chauvin, *Bibliographie*, 8:57–58.

97   Latin title: *simia*; see Chauvin, *Bibliographie*, 8:67.

98   The Arabic here and in several places below is properly "guard" or "escort" (*ḥaras*), but perhaps *ḥāris* is meant? I have used "thief" throughout in English.

99   See Chauvin, *Bibliographie*, 8:68.

100   Latin title: *nomina*; see Chauvin, *Bibliographie*, 8:51–52.

101   See Chauvin, *Bibliographie*, 8:69.

102   *Wa-hamma bi-hā*. Cf. Q Yūsuf 12:23.

103   *ʿalā ruʾūsihim*: lit. "on their heads," implying that they will be called to account for what they are about to hear.

104 In Arab Islamic civilization, sandalwood was considered to have a quality of "coldness."

105 See Chauvin, *Bibliographie*, 6:7–8. A *thuʿbān* is usually a snake, but may also be a dragon. Dragons, in the Islamic Near East, were in any case largely serpentine, see Sara Kuehn, *The Dragon in Medieval East Christian and Islamic Art* (2011).

106 *Yamūj qāṭina-hu wa-yartajj bi-sākini-hā.* Approximately: "It moves the one who stays there and is convulsed by the one who rests there."

107 "Sun of the Serpents."

108 Q Raʿd 13:2.

109 Presumably because she had earlier attacked and driven them from their homes.

110 As Gaudefroy-Demombynes points out, this tale is composed of a number of very common elements: the younger son who seeks a life-restoring remedy; the wise hermit or shepherd; the beautiful girl asleep; the jealous brother and, in the first part, the benevolent beast and ungrateful human (*Cent et une nuits*, 299n15).

111 "The Ebony Horse" is one of the best-known examples of this kind of story, found in varying versions in the nineteenth-century editions of *Alf laylah wa-laylah*. See Chauvin, *Bibliographie*, 5:221–31.

112 The wearing of wool in Islamic tradition is a mark of asceticism or poverty; here, it is a mark of grief or penitence.

113 *Abkhas khurūj*: literally something like "the most paltry departure." However, in B1 when the prince claims to be the husband her father has chosen for her, she replies, "I was afraid he would kill you because you could not pay the bride price." *Abkhas/bakhs* is associated with unworthy prices (see Q Yūsuf 12:20) and is here doubtless a vestige of the version in B1.

114 See note 111 above.

115 The term here is *kisrāwī*, after Kisrā (Khosrau/Khusrow), the name of a character in Iranian mythology, which has come to mean ruler or king, and in the Arabic context would mean "Persian ruler." It seems to be used here in a derogatory sense, though this is not reflected in

the translation. No doubt Richard Burton would have come up with something more colorful.

116 Q Yūsuf 12:76.

117 There is a significantly different version of this tale in manuscript T; otherwise it occurs only in A.

118 *Bi-ḥaqq alladhī wahaba la-ki l-istiṭāʿah ilā mā rajaʿti ilā ṣūratiki khalaqaki Llāh ʿalayhā*: The precise meaning of the phrase is unclear, and it may well be corrupt.

119 This tale occurs only in A. The ruse of sending a secret message in prose or verse is a common motif in Arabic literature.

120 *Bayt jadīda musaṭṭaḥ* [*sic*]: this must mean recently built, but whether *musaṭṭaḥ* here means with a floor or a roof is not clear.

121 Q Baqarah 2:156.

122 Q Yūsuf 12:86. The vizier compares his situation to that of Jacob, who knows what his sons do not, as he says in the remainder of the Qurʾanic verse: «. . . for I know, from God, something that you do not know.»

Appendix

The alternative version of §§1.36–39, as found in A

The king remained like this for some time, but eventually he felt the need for a wife. However, he would only stay one night with her and then would have her killed in the morning. Eventually he had gone through all the daughters of the aristocracy as well as those of his viziers and men of state.

Now the Chief Vizier had two daughters: the older one was Shahrazād, the younger was Dīnārzād.

"Marry me to your daughter," the king told the vizier.

"She is your servant," he replied. "And her sister too. I'll send them both to you tonight."

When night fell, the vizier sent his elder daughter Shahrazād to the king's palace. The king slept with her that night and then, upon rising, was going to have her put to death.

"Your Majesty," said Shahrazād, "if you let me live another night I will tell you a story the likes of which you have never heard before!"

"You know some stories, then?" inquired the king.

"Yes, I do," replied Shahrazād.

So that night they stayed together, and then he left, sealing the door with his seal and leaving her inside, while he went about the business of ruling and judging.

The First Night

The following night, the king returned and, as was his custom, broke the seal on the door and slept with the girl.

Then, at the appointed time, Dīnārzād called out, "O sister, O Shahrazād! Please will you tell his majesty the king one of your excellent stories?"

"Very well," replied Shahrazād.

Glossary

'Abd al-Malik ibn Marwān   (§§7, 8, 18) Umayyad caliph, ruled 72–86/692–705 (though his rule was held by some to have begun in 65/685).

Amalekites   (§§3, 4, 5, 7) an ancient people named in the Bible and in some Islamic histories. In the latter case, the Amalekites are sometimes said to have ruled Mecca in a pre-Abrahamic period. More generally, in Arabic writings such as the *101 Nights*, the Amalekites represent one of a number of previous great civilizations.

Azāriqah   (§7.18) a branch of the Khārijites, a group of early Muslims who opposed both the pro-Alid and the proto-Sunni factions in Islam's formative years. The Khārijites were especially known for uncompromising and radical positions, particularly with regard to judging who was an unbeliever. Certain of the more moderate Khārijite sects, mainly the Ibāḍiyyah, survive in parts of North Africa. The Azāriqah were among the more radical subgroups.

Barmakids   (§6) a prominent family of viziers and administrators in the early Abbasid period. Their power and influence came to an abrupt and shocking end when the Caliph Hārūn al-Rashīd (s.v.) confiscated their wealth and had the leading members of the family executed or imprisoned. The reasons for the caliph's decision remain obscure, but the incident gave rise to a number of salacious or sensational explanations.

Dhū l-qarnayn   (§6) "The Two-horned," a Qur'anic figure (Q Kahf 18:82–98). Later Islamic tradition identifies him as Alexander the Great, although the reason why Alexander would have had horns has never been satisfactorily explained.

dīnār   unit of currency, usually a gold coin worth approximately twenty dirhams.

dirham   unit of currency, usually a silver coin; most commonly said to be one twentieth of a dīnār.

emīr   (Ar. *amīr*)   literally, "one who holds or possesses command." Originally a commander of a province retaining broad military and/or administrative powers, it has come to indicate more generally a commander, prince, or king, as is the case in *A Hundred and One Nights*. A caliphal title was *Amīr al-mu'minīn* ("Commander of the Faithful"), which also appears in the collection.

Fars   (§§4, 11, 16) province in what is now southwestern Iran.

Hārūn al-Rashīd   (§§6, 13) Abbasid caliph (r. 170–93/786–809). There is a popular perception that his reign constituted the high point of Abbasid political power and cultural achievement, a reputation due in part to his portrayal in the *Thousand and One Nights*.

Iblīs   (§5) the Devil.

Khusraw Anūshīrwān   (§4) a pre-Islamic Sasanian king of Persia (r. AD 531–79).

al-Ma'mūn   (§12) Abbasid caliph (r. 198–218/813–33).

Maslamah ibn ʿAbd al-Malik   (§§7, 8) (d. 121/738) son of the caliph ʿAbd al-Malik and renowned Umayyad general and governor, remembered especially for leading a siege of Constantinople in 98–99/716–18.

Muḍar   (§7) an important North Arabian tribe. Along with the tribe of Rabīʿah, a name used to indicate great number, as in the phrase "as numerous as Rabīʿah and Muḍar," found in a number of hadith reports.

al-Muʿtaṣim   (§9) al-Muʿtaṣim bi-llāh, Abbasid caliph (r. 218–27/833–42).

raṭl   unit of measure of mass. There is considerable regional variation in the measure of a *raṭl* (or *riṭl*). It could even vary according to the product being measured (e.g., meat, grain, etc.). Definitions varied between 250 grams and 2 kilograms, with most tending to the lower end of the spectrum, around 250 to 500 grams.

Sahl ibn Hārūn   (§13) poet and administrator of Persian origin, companion of Caliph Hārūn al-Rashīd.

Sulaymān ibn ʿAbd al-Malik   (§7) Umayyad caliph (r. 96–99/715–17).

wadi   Arabic word for valley or dry riverbed.

al-Walīd ibn ʿAbd al-Malik   Umayyad caliph, (r. 86–96/705–15).

Bibliography

Editions

Mi'at laylah wa-laylah. Edited by Maḥmūd Ṭarshūnah. Tunis and Libya: al-Dār al-Arabiyyah lil-Kitāb, 1979. Second edition, Cologne: Manshūrāt al-Jamal, 2005.

Translations

Les Cent et une nuits. Translated by Maurice Gaudefroy-Demombynes. Paris: Sindbad/Actes Sud, 1982. First edition, 1911.

Cento e uma Noites: Histórias Árabes da Tunísia. Translated by Mamade Mustafa Jarouche. 2nd ed. São Paulo: Martins Fontes, 2005.

Hyakuichiya Monogatari: Mōhitotsu no Arabian Naito [*"The Hundred and One Nights": Another "Arabian Nights"*]. Translated by Akiko Sumi. Tokyo: Kawade Shobō Shinsha, 2011.

101 Nacht. Translated by Claudia Ott. Zurich: Manesse, 2012.

Other Works

Abbott, Nabia. "A Ninth-Century Fragment of the Thousand Nights: New Light on the Early History of the *Arabian Nights*." *Journal of Near Eastern Studies* 8, no. 3 (1949): 129–61.

Arabian Nights: Tales of 1001 Nights. Translated by Malcolm C. Lyons with Ursula Lyons. 3 vols. London: Penguin Classics, 2008.

Ariosto, Ludovico. *Orlando Furioso.* Milan: BUR Rizzoli, 2012.

Athamina, Khalil. "al-Baṭṭāl, ʿAbdallāh." *Encyclopaedia of Islam 3*, edited by Kate Fleet, Gudrun Krämer, Denis Matringe, John Nawas, and Everett Rowson. Brill Online, 2015.

Basset, René. "*Les Cent Nuits* et le *Kitab ech chelha*." *Revue des traditions populaires* 6, no. 8 (1891): 449–65.

Bellino, Francesca. "Stylistic and Linguistic Features of the Theme of the Duel in the *Ġazwat raʾs al-ġūl*." In *Moyen arabe et variétés mixtes de l'arabe à travers l'histoire. Actes du Premier Colloque International (Louvain-la-Neuve, 10–14 mai 2004)*. Edited by Jérôme Lentin and Jacques Grand'Henry, 39–61. Leuven: Peeters, 2008.

Bencheikh, Jamel Eddine, Claude Bremond, and André Miquel. *Mille et un contes de la nuit*. Paris: Gallimard, 1991.

Biberstein Kazimirsky, A. de. *Dictionnaire arabe-français*. 2 vols. Paris: Maisonneuve, 1860. Reprint, Beirut: Librarie du Liban, n.d.

al-Bukhārī. *Ṣaḥīḥ al-Bukhārī*. Cairo: Dār maṭābiʿ al-shaʿb, n.d.

Casiri, Miguel. *Bibliotheca Arabico-Hispana Escurialensis*. 2 vols. Madrid: Antonio Perez de Soto, 1760.

Chauvin, Victor. *Bibliographie des ouvrages arabes ou relatifs aux arabes*. 10 vols. Liège: Imprimerie H. Vaillant-Carmanne, 1892–1907.

Chraïbi, Aboubakr. *Les Mille et une nuits: Histoire du texte et classification des contes*. Paris: L'Harmattan, 2008.

Clinton, Jerome W. "Madness and Cure in the *1001 Nights*." *Studia Islamica* 61 (1985): 107–125.

Cosquin, Emmanuel. "Le prologue-cadre des Mille et une nuits, légendes perses et le livre d'Esther." *Revue Biblique* 6 (1909): 7–49. Also in Cosquin, *Études folkloriques*. Paris: Edouard Champion, 1922, 7–49.

Dozy, R. *Supplément aux dictionnaires arabes*. 2 vols. Leiden: E. J. Brill, 1881. Reprint, Beirut: Librarie du Liban, n.d.

Dunlop, D. M. "Baḥr al-muḥīṭ." In Vol. 1 of *Encyclopaedia of Islam*, second edition, edited by H. A. R. Gibb, et al. Reprint, Leiden: E. J. Brill, 1986.

EI2 = *Encyclopaedia of Islam*. 2nd ed. Edited by P. Bearman, Th. Bianquis, C. E. Bosworth, E. von Donzol, and W. P. Heinrichs. Leiden: E. J. Brill, 1960–2009.

Ferrand, Gabriel. "Un note sur le livre des 101 Nuits." *Journal Asiatique* 17 (1911): 309–18.

Foehr-Janssens, Yasmina. "The Seven Sages: Oriental Wisdom in Roman Clothes." Paper presented at the conference *Les Sept Sages et les Sept Viziers: Vers une histoire comparée des textes*, University of Geneva, November 6, 2014.

Fudge, Bruce. "More Translators of the Thousand and One Nights." *Journal of the American Oriental Society* 136, no. 1 (2016): 135–46.

———. "Signs of Scripture in the 'City of Brass.'" *Journal of Qur'ānic Studies* 8, no. 1 (2006): 88–118.

Garcin, Jean-Claude. *Pour une lecture historique des* Mille et une nuits. Paris: Sindbad/Actes Sud, 2013.

Gavillet Matar, Marguerite, ed. and trans. *La Geste du Zīr Sālim, d'après un manuscrit syrien*. 2 vols. Damascus: Institut français du Proche-Orient, 2005.

Ḥājjī Khalīfah. *Kashf al-ẓunūn ʿan asāmī l-kutub wal-funūn*. 2 vols. Edited by Şerefettin Yaltaka and Kılısı Rifaat Bilge. Istanbul: Maarif Matbaası, 1941–43.

Harrell, Richard S. *A Short Reference Grammar of Moroccan Arabic*. Georgetown: Georgetown University Press, 2004.

Heinrichs, Wolfhart. "Modes of Existence of the Poetry in the Arabian Nights." In *The Heritage of Arabo-Islamic Learning*. Edited by Maurice A. Pomerantz and Aram A. Shahin, 528–38. Leiden: Brill, 2016.

Ḥikāyāt al-ʿajībah wal-akhbār al-gharībah, al-. Edited by Hans Wehr. Wiesbaden: Steiner, 1956.

Houdas, O. *Chrestomathie maghrébine*. Paris: Ernest Leroux, 1891.

———. "Essai sur l'écriture maghrébine." *Nouveaux mélanges orientaux*, n.s., 19 (1886): 85–112.

Irwin, Robert. *The Arabian Nights: A Companion*. London: Allen Lane, 1994.

Kilito, Abdelfattah. *Les arabes et l'art du récit. Une étrange familiarité*. Paris: Sindbad-Actes Sud, 2009.

Kuehn, Sara. *The Dragon in Medieval East Christian and Islamic Art*. Leiden: E. J. Brill, 2011.

Lane, Edward W. *An Arabic-English Lexicon*. London and Edinburgh: Williams and Norgate, 1863. Reprint, Cambridge: The Islamic Texts Society, 1984.

Lentin, Jérôme. "La langue des manuscrits de Galland et la typologie du moyen arabe." In *Les Mille et une nuits en partage*. Edited by Aboubakr Chraïbi, 434–55. Paris: Sindbad/Actes Sud, 2004.

———. "Middle Arabic." In *Encyclopedia of Arabic Language and Linguistics*, edited by Kees Versteegh, 3:215–24. Leiden: Brill, 2006.

———. "Unité et diversité du moyen arabe au machreq et au maghreb: Quelques données d'après des textes d'époque tardive (16ème–9ème siècles)." In *Moyen arabe et variétés mixtes de l'arabe à travers l'histoire. Actes du Premier Colloque International (Louvain-la-Neuve, 10–14 mai 2004)*. Edited by Jérôme Lentin and Jacques Grand'Henry, 305–19. Leuven: Peeters, 2008.

———. "Variétés d'arabe dans des manuscrits syriens du Roman de Baybars et histoire du texte." In *Lectures du roman de Baybars*, edited by Jean-Claude Garcin, 91–111. Marseille: Éditions Parenthèses/MMSH, 2003.

MacDonald, D. B. "The Earlier History of the Arabian Nights." *Journal of the Royal Asiatic Society* 3 (1924): 355–57.

Mahdi, Muhsin, ed. *Kitāb Alf laylah wa-laylah min uṣūlih al-ʿarabiyyah l-ūlā*. 3 vols. Leiden: E. J. Brill, 1984–1994.

Marzolph, Ulrich. "The *Arabian Nights* in Comparative Folk Narrative Research." In *The Arabian Nights and Orientalism: Perspectives from East and West*, edited by Yuriko Yamanaka and Tetsuo Nishio, 3–24. London: I. B. Tauris, 2006.

Marzolph, Ulrich, and Aboubakr Chraïbi. "*The Hundred and One Nights*: A Recently Discovered Old Manuscript." *Zeitschrift der Deutschen Morgenländischen Gesellschaft* 162, no. 2 (2012): 299–316.

Marzolph, Ulrich and Richard van Leeuwen, eds. *The Arabian Nights Encyclopedia*. 2 vols. Santa Barbara: ABC-CLIO, 2004.

al-Masʿūdī. *Murūj al-dhahab wa-maʿādin al-jawhar*. 7 vols. Edited by Charles Pellat. Beirut: Publications de l'Université Libanaise, 1965–74.

Perry. B. E. "The Origins of the Book of Sindbad." *Fabula* 3, 1/2 (1959): 1–94.

Pinault, David. *Story-telling Techniques in the Arabian Nights*. Leiden: Brill, 1992.

Tales of the Marvelous and News of the Strange. Translated by Malcolm C. Lyons, with an Introduction by Robert Irwin. London: Penguin, 2014.

al-Tawḥīdī, Abū Ḥayyan. *Al-Imtā' wa-l-mu'ānasah*. Edited by Aḥmad Amīn and Aḥmad al-Zayn. 3 vols. Cairo: Lajnat al-Ta'līf, 1939–53.

Versteegh, Kees. *The Arabic Language*. Edinburgh: Edinburgh University Press, 1997.

Yamanaka, Yuriko. "Les Mille et une Nuits et les automates: L'interaction infinie de la science et de la fiction." *In Les Mille et Une Nuits en Partage*, edited by Aboubakr Chraïbi, 39–52. Paris: Sindbad/Actes Sud, 2004.

Further Reading

Apart from brief mentions in the *Arabian Nights Encyclopedia* (eds. Marzolph and van Leeuwen) and Robert Irwin's *The Arabian Nights: A Companion*, there is almost nothing in English on *A Hundred and One Nights*. There are two exceptions. First, the article by Marzolph and Chraïbi, "*The Hundred and One Nights*: A Recently Discovered Old Manuscript" contains a good introduction to the work and an important discussion of the Agha Khan manuscript (although the second half of the article is in French). The monograph of David Pinault, *Story-telling Techniques in the Arabian Nights*, especially in the chapter on "The City of Brass," describes well how there exist vast numbers of unedited manuscripts, including those of *A Hundred and One Nights*, containing these types of stories and the difficulty in determining how the variants may relate to each other.

Readers of other languages are slightly better served, although the bibliography remains very short. The most important sources would be the introduction to Ṭarshūnah's Arabic edition and the extensive notes to Gaudefroy-Demombynes French translation. The latter is particularly important because it shows so well how *A Hundred and One Nights* bridge what we might call "classical Arabic literature" and other storytelling collections, European or Asian.

However, readers of *A Hundred and One Nights* will presumably be interested in other examples of this semi-popular narrative literature. The following list includes secondary sources treating various aspects of the *Thousand and One Nights*, the collection known as *Al-Ḥikāyāt al-ʿajībah*, and the Arabic popular epics. One will note that there are relatively few monographs on these topics and hence many of the works below are collected volumes, all of which contain a number of excellent and worth-while articles.

Chraïbi, Aboubakr, ed. *Les Mille et une nuits en partage.* Paris: Sindbad/ Actes Sud, 2004.

Garcin, Jean-Claude, ed. *Lectures du Roman de Baybars.* Marseille: Éditions Parenthèse, 2003.

Gaudefroy-Demombynes, Maurice. *Les Cent et une nuits.* Paris: Sindbad/ Actes Sud, 1982. First edition, 1911.

Grotzfeld, Heinz and Sophia Grotzfeld. *Der Erzählungen aus "Tausendundeiner Nacht."* Darmstadt: Wissenschaftliche Buchgesellschaft. Second revised edition, Dortmund: Verlag für Orientkunde, 2012.

Heath, Peter. *The Thirsty Sword: Sīrat 'Antar and the Arabic Popular Epic.* Salt Lake City: University of Utah Press, 1996.

Irwin, Robert. *The Arabian Nights: A Companion.* London: Allen Lane, 1994.

Kennedy, Philip F. and Marina Warner, eds. *Scheherazade's Children: Global Encounters with the Arabian Nights.* New York: New York University Press, 2013.

Marzolph, Ulrich, ed. *The Arabian Nights Reader.* Detroit: Wayne State University Press, 2006.

———, ed. *The Arabian Nights in Transnational Perspective.* Detroit: Wayne State University Press, 2007.

Mottahedeh, Roy P. "'Ajā'ib in The Thousand and One Nights." In *The Thousand and One Nights in Arabic Literature and Society,* edited by Richard G. Hovannisian and Georges Sabagh, 29–39. Cambridge: Cambridge University Press, 1997.

Ouyang, Wen-Chin and Geert Jan van Gelder, eds. *New Perspectives on Arabian Nights: Ideological Variations and Narrative Horizons.* London and New York: Routlege, 2005.

INDICES

The function of these indices is to demonstrate the repetition of formal elements in the collection. A "motif" is an event, an element in the plot or story. Stock phrases or expressions are lexical combinations that reoccur in more than one story.

The entries do not conform to those of any other classification system and there is no pretention to exhaustiveness (many of the details of palatial splendor, for instance, are not included).

The numbers refer to the paragraphs.

MOTIF INDEX

Highwaymen attack caravan 2.16, 10.9, 18.8

Hooking of stirrups in battle 5.23, 7.14, 7.37

Island 4.9, 4.13, 6.1, 6.2, 6.12, 13.5, 17.12

King discovers intruder in harem 9.16, 15.24

Lion 3.20, 4.15, 5.22, 7.10, 11.2, 11.3

Lost hero 3.15, 8.1, 8.7, 18.2

Muḥammad ibn ʿAbdallāh (as proper name) 2, 6.1, (9.4: ʿAbdallāh ibn Muḥammad)

Poetic inscription 3.17–3.18, 4.20–4.21, 6.14, 15.19, 15.20, (6.17—no poetry)

Recognition 2.33, 3.25, 7.16, 7.22, 7.33, 7.38, 8.11, 9.14, 10.6, 10.10, 17.18, 17.19, 18.8, 18.11

Recounting to king what happened in palace 11, 13.18–13.19

Search for most beautiful person 1, 3.2, 7.2–7.3, 11.1–11.2

Shepherd 3.20, 5.21

Sneaking into palace 9.11, 12.3, 13.10, 15.20, 16.7, 16.32, 17.22

Tied to a tree and discovered by passers-by 2.22–2.23, 15.24–15.25

Trapdoor, secret entrance 1.19, 2.27, 4.15, 4.17, 6.12, 17.17

Virginity 5.19, 15.22, 16.56

Index of Stock Phrases/Expressions

Birds in garden or forest 3.15, 5.4, 15.17

Cloud of dust on horizon 3.31, 4.1, 5.8, 7.13, 15.6

Dark and distant sea 4.9, 4.12, 4.15, 4.22, 6.7, 6.21.

Defied description 4.4, 4.9, 4.17, 5.7

Drooping lips and glowing eyes 1.19, 7.13

Feeding the people from the city and the countryside 1.25, 7.2, 16.56

Fragrant musk 2.30, 3.4, 5.4, 7.9, 15.17

Fresh breeze blew and the fabrics fluttered.: 1.7, 2.24

Full moon at night or a gazelle in flight 4.14, 7.11, 9.1, 12.4, 16.24

God is Wise and All-knowing of the unknown 1.2 , 2.1

Great calamity and big disaster 5.7, 7.12, 7.29

Hanging sword(s) (and bows laid down/and spear stuck in ground), 5.5, 5.10, 7.11, 15.12

Head resting on thigh 5.9, 11.4, 13.6

Horse and the fight and the raid in the black of night 3.1, 5.18, 7.1

Human or jinn? 2.32, 11.5, 12.5, 16.20, 16.24

Invincible and solitary 3.9, 5.7, 7.12

I've been blessed! 6.4, 17.14

Likes of which had not been seen before 2.34, 7.2, 16.7

Market of the Perfumers 1.5, 9.9

Master of the Unknown does as He wills 9.6, 15.25

Mighty mountain and swollen sea 5.14, 7.14

Mounted girl behind him 2.16, 2.18, 2.20, 16.32, 16.37, see 2.22.

About the NYU Abu Dhabi Institute

The Library of Arabic Literature is supported by a grant from the NYU Abu Dhabi Institute, a major hub of intellectual and creative activity and advanced research. The Institute hosts academic conferences, workshops, lectures, film series, performances, and other public programs directed both to audiences within the UAE and to the  worldwide academic and research community. It is a center of the scholarly community for Abu Dhabi, bringing together faculty and researchers from institutions of higher learning throughout the region.

NYU Abu Dhabi, through the NYU Abu Dhabi Institute, is a world-class center of cutting-edge research, scholarship, and cultural activity. The Institute creates singular opportunities for leading researchers from across the arts, humanities, social sciences, sciences, engineering, and the professions to carry out creative scholarship and conduct research on issues of major disciplinary, multidisciplinary, and global significance.

About the Translator

Bruce Fudge is Professor of Arabic at the University of Geneva. After studying history at Queen's University and Islamic studies at McGill University, he learned Arabic at the American University in Cairo and received his doctorate from Harvard University in 2003. He is the author of *Qurʾānic Hermeneutics: al-Ṭabrisī and the Craft of Commentary* (2011) and a number of articles on medieval and modern Arabic literature and Qurʾanic exegesis. Among his research and teaching interests are the life of Sayyid Quṭb, Arabic fictional narrative, and the history of Orientalism.

The Library of Arabic Literature

For more details on individual titles, visit www.libraryofarabicliterature.org.

Classical Arabic Literature: A Library of Arabic Literature Anthology
 Selected and translated by Geert Jan van Gelder

A Treasury of Virtues: Sayings, Sermons and Teachings of ʿAlī, by al-Qāḍī
 al-Quḍāʿī with the *One Hundred Proverbs* attributed to al-Jāḥiẓ
 Edited and translated by Tahera Qutbuddin

The Epistle on Legal Theory, by al-Shāfiʿī
 Edited and translated by Joseph E. Lowry

Leg over Leg, by Aḥmad Fāris al-Shidyāq
 Edited and translated by Humphrey Davies

Virtues of the Imām Aḥmad ibn Ḥanbal, by Ibn al-Jawzī
 Edited and translated by Michael Cooperson

The Epistle of Forgiveness, by Abū l-ʿAlāʾ al-Maʿarrī
 Edited and translated by Geert Jan van Gelder and Gregor Schoeler

The Principles of Sufism, by ʿĀʾishah al-Bāʿūniyyah
 Edited and translated by Th. Emil Homerin

The Expeditions: An Early Biography of Muḥammad, by Maʿmar ibn Rāshid
 Edited and translated by Sean W. Anthony

Two Arabic Travel Books
 Accounts of China and India, by Abū Zayd al-Sīrāfī
 Edited and translated by Tim Mackintosh-Smith

Mission to the Volga, by Aḥmad ibn Faḍlān
Edited and translated by James Montgomery

Disagreements of the Jurists: A Manual of Islamic Legal Theory, by
al-Qāḍī al-Nuʿmān
Edited and translated by Devin J. Stewart

Consorts of the Caliphs: Women and the Court of Baghdad, by Ibn al-Sāʿī
Edited by Shawkat M. Toorawa and translated by the Editors of the
Library of Arabic Literature

What ʿĪsā ibn Hishām Told Us, by Muḥammad al-Muwayliḥī
Edited and translated by Roger Allen

The Life and Times of Abū Tammām, by Abū Bakr Muḥammad ibn
Yaḥyā al-Ṣūlī
Edited and translated by Beatrice Gruendler

The Sword of Ambition: Bureaucratic Rivalry in Medieval Egypt, by
ʿUthmān ibn Ibrāhīm al-Nābulusī
Edited and translated by Luke Yarbrough

Brains Confounded by the Ode of Abū Shādūf Expounded, by
Yūsuf al-Shirbīnī
Edited and translated by Humphrey Davies

Light in the Heavens: Sayings of the Prophet Muḥammad, by
al-Qāḍī al-Quḍāʿī
Edited and translated by Tahera Qutbuddin

Risible Rhymes, by Muḥammad ibn Maḥfūẓ al-Sanhūrī
Edited and translated by Humphrey Davies

A Hundred and One Nights
Edited and translated by Bruce Fudge

The Excellence of the Arabs, by Ibn Qutaybah
Edited by James E. Montgomery and Peter Webb
Translated by Sarah Bowen Savant and Peter Webb

226 |

Scents and Flavors: A Syrian Cookbook
    Edited and translated by Charles Perry

Arabian Satire: Poetry from 18th-Century Najd, by Ḥmēdān al-Shwēʿir
    Edited and translated by Marcel Kurpershoek

ENGLISH-ONLY PAPERBACKS

Leg over Leg: Volumes One and Two, by Aḥmad Fāris al-Shidyāq

Leg over Leg: Volumes Three and Four, by Aḥmad Fāris al-Shidyāq

The Expeditions: An Early Biography of Muḥammad, by Maʿmar ibn Rāshid

The Epistle on Legal Theory: A Translation of al-Shāfiʿī's Risālah, by al-Shāfiʿī

The Epistle of Forgiveness, by Abū l-ʿAlāʾ al-Maʿarrī

The Principles of Sufism, by ʿĀʾishah al-Bāʿūniyyah

A Treasury of Virtues: Sayings, Sermons and Teachings of ʿAlī, by al-Qāḍī al-Quḍāʿī with *The One Hundred Proverbs,* attributed to al-Jāḥiẓ

The Life of Ibn Ḥanbal, by Ibn al-Jawzī

Mission to the Volga, by Ibn Faḍlān

Accounts of China and India, by Abū Zayd al-Sīrāfī

Consorts of the Caliphs: Women and the Court of Baghdad, by Ibn al-Sāʿī

A Hundred and One Nights

Disagreements of the Jurists: A Manual of Islamic Legal Theory, by al-Qāḍī al-Nuʿmān